THE GREEKS OF ODESSA
Diaspora Leadership in Late Imperial Russia

John Athanasios Mazis

EAST EUROPEAN MONOGRAPHS, BOULDER
DISTRIBUTED BY COLUMBIA UNIVERSITY PRESS, NEW YORK
2004

EAST EUROPEAN MONOGRAPHS, NO. DCXLVII

ISBN: 0-88033-545-9

Library of Congress Control Number: 2004108570

Printed in the United States of America

To Holly

Always And Forever

Table of Contents

Preface

The study of the life and times of the Greeks of Imperial Russia in general, and those of Odessa in particular, has been the subject of a number of important scholarly works by Russian scholars such as Grigorii Arsh and Grigorii Piatigorskii, Greek scholars such as Constantine Papoulides, I. K. Hassiotes, and V. Kardasis and in this country, Patricia Herlihy, Stephen Batalden, Theophilus Prousis, and Gregory Bruess. The Greeks of Imperial Russia belong to that subcategory of minorities favored by the state. Unlike the Jews and the Poles (among others) who were discriminated against, the Greeks, and the German colonists of South Russia, to name just two examples, were privileged. The Russian state provided land and loans, along with a degree of autonomy, and thus attracted a large number of Greeks to its domain. It is of interest that while tsarist Russia was not normally a haven for most minority groups some, like the Greeks, found fame and fortune there.

The Greek Benevolent Association of Odessa (*Grecheskoe blagotvoritel'noe obshchestvo*) was an organization that epitomized the enterprising spirit of the Greek community of Odessa. It also was decisive in guiding the activities of the Greeks of that city for the last half century of Imperial Russia. While the existence of this organization is known to historians, there has not been a detailed account of its creation and activities. It has been generally known that the Greek Benevolent Association of Odessa, henceforth GBAO, took care of Odessa's Greek church, participated in the operation of a school teaching the Greek language and if and when the opportunity presented itself helped some widows and orphans. Given the fact that the Greeks are by nature political creatures, it was hard for me to imagine a civic group organized by Greeks which would be entirely devoid of political dimensions. This last assumption of mine ran contrary to what most secondary sources on the Greeks of Odessa in late nineteenth century recorded. As it turned out the GBAO was indeed active in Greek education and charitable activities but, as I had suspected, it had a political agenda from its inception.

A number of excellent studies dealing with the Greeks of Russia and/or Odessa chose to focus on the large picture. Some of these works were biographies of Greeks who built a reputation and a career in Russia. Other works examined the Greeks of Russia in general terms, noting their cultural and economic activities in their host country. In some cases the authors noted that there existed a number of civic groups among the Greeks but did not elaborate on the subject. Similarly, the GBAO has been mentioned in such a manner and often identified with the Greek community of Odessa as a whole. The above mentioned studies painted a useful but general picture of the Greeks of Russia. After reading such works, one acquires an overall impression of the Greeks in Russia, but the details of their various activities would be sketchy at best. My work seeks to redress the balance; while I do put the GBAO in the broader context of Russian society as well as that of the Greeks in the country. I decided that a closer look at the day to day activities of the GBAO might shed some light at the Greek community as a whole. Since the GBAO was a philanthropic organization, it came into contact with those Greeks who had failed to prosper in their host country. This group of have-nots is precisely the segment of the Greek diaspora in Russia which has not been closely examined. I believe that the number of poor Greeks in Odessa, their needs, and the reasons for their poverty are of importance for those who seek to study the phenomenon of the Greek diaspora. Another aspect of the GBAO's operation was the creation and/or support of such community institutions as the church, schools and a nursing home. Behind every decision to start any of the above institutions stood the need of the Greeks of Odessa to take care of their own. As was the case with support for the poor, the creation of a nursing home was an attempt to take care of people with limited means, in this case the elderly. In the case of supporting Greek education, the GBAO assumed the leading role of a Greek community which saw its numbers dwindling as more of its younger members became assimilated into the dominant culture of the host country. A closer look into the educational endeavors of the GBAO reveals that part of the impetus for a Greek education was a response to political pressure from the host country which attempted to assimilate its minority population. The study of the relationship between the GBAO and the Russian authorities helps to explain how the Greeks of Odessa combated the danger which the so called "Russification Policy" posed to their survival as a distinct people within the empire. Finally, a closer look at the finances of the GBAO might explain the organization's power and longevity, as well as give an idea of the resources of Odessa's Greek community as a whole. This approach, hopefully, will provide the evidence for the significance of the organization as well as provide concrete examples of the benevolent activities of the wealthy Greeks in that city.

From the early 1870s to the early 1920s the GBAO offered almost cradle to grave care to Odessa's poor Greeks. Hundreds of people each year received assistance for food, shelter, medicine, clothes, heating fuel, and even cash to take care of other needs. The GBAO ran two of Odessa's best schools, the Commercial School for Boys, which it inherited, and the School for Girls which it created. Those two schools educated generations of young Greeks but more important, as far as the GBAO was concerned, they provided Greek education thus becoming responsible for preserving the Greek language to the third and fourth generation of Odessa's Greeks. Finally, the Nursing Home for the Elderly took care of those unfortunate Greeks who were too poor, or did not have any family, to look after their needs. As the record of the GBAO reveals, the organization operated with two main guidelines in mind: consideration for the needy, and responsibility towards the association's resources. The nineteenth-century middle class has often been portrayed as being conservative but at least in the case of the Greeks of Odessa the opposite was true. Even though the leaders of the GBAO were wealthy middle aged men, the organization that they created was progressive in nature. The GBAO offered a first class education to both men and women, while its philanthropic activities did not exclude those who found themselves in need of assistance due to some personal failing (such as being jailed). Such forward thinking would be considered progressive today, but it was even more so when the GBAO was instituted in the 1870s. As a result the record of the activities of the GBAO is one of financial stability, success in its endeavors, and a legacy that must have pleased all those who worked hard creating and running it.

While I was impressed by the GBAO as a strictly philanthropic organization, I was even more impressed by its political side. Although the tsarist regime discouraged political involvement by its citizens, and the GBAO charter was strictly that of a philanthropic organization, the

Greeks of Odessa, nevertheless, were highly politicized. In the beginning, most of the political involvement was geared towards helping Greece in its irredentist attempts, that is to say, its efforts to reclaim parts of the Ottoman Empire inhabited largely by Greeks. During various Greco-Turkish wars the GBAO offered humanitarian aid to Greek refugees but also helped financially the families of those Greeks from Odessa who joined the Greek army. In later years, the GBAO contributed generously to the Greek government for various causes. Then, towards the end of Russia's Imperial era, the GBAO became overtly political by assuming a leadership role among Russia's Greeks and attempting, albeit belatedly, to organize in a political pressure group which would lobby the Russian government. The leaders of the GBAO were firmly on the liberal side of the political spectrum vis-à-vis the body politic in both Russia and Greece. The October Revolution brought an end not only to Greek political activity but also spelled the end of the GBAO as an organization.

While the GBAO was clearly an organization of the Greek diaspora it was also, by virtue of its location as well as the laws under which it operated, a Russian philanthropic association. As such it belongs to the wider phenomenon of Russian civic groups which came to existence as a result of the Great Reforms of the 1860s. The GBAO belongs among the few of thousands of such entities which enjoyed appreciable resources, thus enabling it to sponsor successfully many of its projects. In comparing the membership of the GBAO with that of other Russian civic groups, it becomes clear that the claim that the former was an organization with little appeal among Odessa's Greeks is inaccurate. According to the organization's charter, all adult Greeks who could pay the 3 rubles per year dues were automatically accepted. That alone contradicts the charge that the GBAO was an elite organization. The membership of the GBAO was over 300, a number which compares favorably with other Russian organizations of the kind. Seen from all possible angles the GBAO was a success story among Russian philanthropic groups. By focusing on the day to day activities of the GBAO one can form a picture of the Greek community of Odessa as a whole: the leaders of the community and their relevant economic and social power; the poor and their needs; the educational endeavors of the Greek community; relations with the Russian government; and finally the political involvement of the Greeks as individuals and as a community. In short, this book is a case study of private charity and diaspora leadership in late Imperial Russia.

In the course of researching and writing this book I have become indebted to a number of institutions and individuals. My research trips to Greece and Ukraine were made possible by grants from the History Department of the University of Minnesota, the Basil Laourdas Fellowship in Greek-Slavic Relations from the Modern Greek Studies Program of the University of Minnesota, and the Greek Ministry of Culture. My research in Athens was made easier by the help and cooperation of the staff of the Archives of the Historical Section of the Ministry of Foreign Affairs (particularly its director Photini Constantopoulou), the Gennadius Library at the American School of Classical Studies, the Library of Parliament (Vouli), and the Greek National Library. I would also like to thank B. Kondes, the director of the Institute for Balkan Studies in Thessaloniki, Greece. My work in Odessa was helped by the staff of the Foundation for Hellenic Culture (especially its director Sofronis Paradissopoulos), the Odessa Region State Archives (especially the head of Records Information and Foreign Relations Department Lilia Beloousova), and the Maxim Gorkii Public Library of Odessa (in particular its director Olga Botushanskaia). I would also like to thank the Wilson Library at the University of Minnesota and its staff for the support while I was compiling my bibliography of secondary sources.

Over the years I have been the beneficiary of support and advice from a number of individuals, foremost among them my academic advisor Professor Theofanis G. Stavrou a great mentor and a role model also Soterios Stavrou, a true friend and a sounding board for my ideas and problems. Constantine Papoulides has encouraged and helped me in my work while Adele Lindenmeyr helped me to better understand the role and scope of charitable associations in Imperial Russia.

Finally, I owe a debt of gratitude to my family: my parents, Athanasios and Artemisia Mazis, my wife Holly, who for many years now has been a rock of emotional support without which I know I could not have finished such a long term-project; and my daughters Misia and Zoe, who many a day had to tiptoe around the house because Dad was working on his "very important project."

I
The Historical Background

Greeks have been present on the Black Sea coast for thousands of years. They have been living in southern Russia before the Slavs (early Rus') were even residents of what became the domain of the Russian Empire. In some respects, the Greeks can be considered as native peoples of the area. It is well documented that ancient Greek city-states colonized the Black Sea littoral before classical times.[1] While those early colonies were mainly isolated "islands" amidst people, mainly Scythians, whom the Greeks thought as barbarians, in time the Greek colonies became a part of the world which surrounded them.[2] Initially the colonies were trading centers whose role was to acquire and send to the growing Greek urban centers the wheat which was abundant in the Black Sea area. The well-known myth of Jason and the Golden Fleece represents Greece's quest for wheat, its staple food. Unlike the typical diaspora, which usually involves people emigrating due to war, political uncertainty or economic necessity, the ancient Greek diaspora of the Black Sea belongs to the so called "trade diaspora." In such cases, emigration is planned by individuals with money who know how and where to encourage emigration, economic opportunity is the main attraction.[3] Although the Greek colonists rarely penetrated the interior of the land in which they lived, the native people became increasingly dependent on the colonies for manufactured goods unavailable in their country (a relationship reminiscent of that between eighteenth-century Europeans in India and Africa and the native peoples of the interior of those areas). As a result of the exchanges that took place, many a Scythian chief acquired a taste for luxury goods as well as a veneer of Greek culture.[4]

After the demise of classical Greece, the Greek Black Sea colonies continued to perform their role with the Romans, Byzantines and Ottoman Turks who controlled in turn the eastern Mediterranean basin.[5] In the process, the Greek colonies lost their independence and even their Greek character as more and more non-Greeks resided in their cities.

This metamorphosis occurred more during the last of the above three eras. The Romans did not physically occupy the North shore of the Black Sea, while the Byzantines who did were thoroughly Hellenized. The final change which occurred to the descendants of the early Greek colonists was the loss of their distinctive culture and their absorption by the dominant culture of their Turkish/Tartar overlords. That transformation was the natural outcome of the takeover of the area by the Mongols (Tartars) in the thirteen century AD. The Tartars were tolerant of other cultures and allowed the Greeks to continue living and operating in the area. Still, with the passage of time the Greeks who remained started living and dressing like the Tartars. Eventually they lost their linguistic identity as well, although they remained Orthodox Christians and aware, albeit tenuously, of their Greek roots.[6]

While the Greek colonists had mainly commercial and personal contact with the people of southern Russia, cultural and political contacts began to develop on an official level as well. When the Rus' took control of the lands which later became Russia, the Byzantine Empire with Constantinople as its center was at the peak of its power. The Rus' had frequent contact with Byzantium as traders, mercenaries, and occasional raiders of Byzantine lands. At the time the Byzantine Empire was too strong, and the Rus' too weak for the raids to be anything more than occasional nuisance. In any case, the contact between the two people was enough for the Rus' to be impressed by Byzantine splendor, wealth, and its social and political system. That became even more so in the tenth century AD when Grand Prince Vladimir of Kiev (the strongest of the Rus' principalities) was looking for ways to reform his state. Vladimir sought to introduce a monotheistic religion, both as a means of providing a unifying force for his people and as an outward sign that his country was advanced.[7] The prince examined Judaism, Christianity and Islam and chose Christianity.[8] As is known, at the time of Vladimir's rule, two versions of Christianity were available: Roman Catholicism and Eastern Orthodoxy. Both attempted to lure Vladimir but finally the prince chose the Constantinople-based Eastern Orthodoxy. It appears that Vladimir made his choice more for political than religious reasons. The Catholic Church enjoyed wide independence from lay authorities and often became the center of opposition against a prince. In contrast, Eastern Orthodoxy had a tradition of working closely with the state, promoting its aims and the Orthodox Patriarch enjoyed second place to the head of state. This was exactly the kind of "symphonia" or interdependence that Vladimir was looking to establish in his country. He might also have calculated the benefits of sharing a common religion with the most powerful state of the time.[9] An alternative theory has Vladimir converting to Orthodoxy in order to marry the Byzantine Princess Anna, sister of Emperor Basil II. By some accounts Vladimir had helped Basil militarily with the understanding that one of the emperor's sisters would marry the prince. Basil refused to honor his commitment unless Vladimir, and his people, were converted to Orthodoxy.[10] In any event, Vladimir (who was later proclaimed a saint) converted to Orthodoxy (AD 989) and forced his subject to do the same.

With Kiev's (and in time the rest of Russia's) conversion to Orthodoxy, there was a wholesale introduction of Greek culture and letters to Russia. Vladimir had to import Orthodox priests to teach the new religion,[11] architects and painters to construct churches,[12] scholars and teachers to instruct the new converts.[13] Since Orthodoxy was dominated by Greek culture (hence often referred to as Greek Orthodox Church rather than Eastern), Kiev's conversion meant that the Russians came into closer contact with the Greek world.[14] In time, enough Russian priests were trained to minister to their people, and the scriptures were translated into Russian (Church Slavonic), but the hold of Greek culture remained. In fact educated Russians, most of them churchmen, had to learn Greek while the church hierarchy had to have the approval of the Patriarch of Constantinople in matters of faith. Over the years, Russian rulers had come to accept the fact that the Byzantine Emperor and the Patriarch of Constantinople had the right to interfere in the affairs of Russia's Orthodox Church.[15] As late as 1452 (the eve of the Fall of Constantinople) the Grand Prince of Moscow recognized that the Emperor of Byzantium had certain prerogatives which transcended the borders of his domains.[16] Often when the Russian Church faced dogmatic challenges, both internal and external, it turned to Constantinople for advice and it was not uncommon for a Greek cleric and/or scholar to be dispatched as a troubleshooter.[17] Also, the head of the Russian Orthodox Church was not only approved by the Patriarch but at times was a Greek cleric imported for the job.[18] Since the Patriarch of Constantinople operated in accordance with the emperor's wishes, the Russian lands were treated, at least in ecclesiastical matters, as an extension of the Byzantine Empire. While Greek letters and culture was becoming a paradigm for the Russian elite, the fortunes of the Byzantine Empire were about to undergo a dramatic change.

Byzantium was declining for centuries and the final blow came in 1453 when the Ottoman Turks conquered Constantinople and made the city the capital of what ultimately came to be known as the Ottoman Empire. The fact that the Turks, who were considered non-Christian barbarians, were able to conquer the Christian capital, Constantinople, made the calamity even more astonishing. In Russia the news of Constantinople's fall had far-reaching repercussions. In some respects Tuesday 29 May 1453 (the day that Constantinople fell to the Turks) marked the beginning of Russia's coming of age. The Russian Grand Prince became the only free Orthodox ruler in the world.[19] Overnight Russia found a mission which justified its existence as a state, and its authority to expand. Orthodox people all over the East were looking for reasons to explain how Constantinople, to them God's chosen city, was allowed to perish. The only acceptable theory was that the lay and ecclesiastical authorities of the Byzantine Empire had turned away from the true faith. This was proven by the fact that the Orthodox Church had come to an agreement with the Catholic Church to accept the Pope's supreme authority. Since Constantinople betrayed its mission, God punished the people by allowing Muslim Turks to destroy the city. On the other hand, Moscow had retained its Orthodox purity by rejecting the authority of the Pope. Isidor, the Greek Metropolitan of Moscow, went to the Council of Florence (1441) and signed the agreement for Church reunification, and was rewarded with the red cap of a cardinal for his obedience. However Russian public opinion was so outraged that on his returned he was charged with heresy. He was allowed to escape to the West and was eventually replaced.[20] The feeling, among Russian clerics and lay leaders, that the Emperor and the Patriarch of Constantinople were leading Orthodoxy down the wrong path (by recognizing the Pope's supremacy) was so strong that in their minds the fall of Constantinople occurred not in 1453 when the Turks conquered the city but in 1441 when the Orthodox Church submitted to the Catholics.[21] From the time that Russia rejected church unification (1448), the Russian Orthodox Church became *de facto* independent from Constantinople.[22] Russian church and state authorities advanced the "Third Rome" theory, according to which both the original Rome and Constantinople (the Second Rome) had displeased God and thus lost all of their moral authority among Christians. Now it was time for Moscow to assume the mantle of Christian leadership and become the "Third Rome" which was destined to fulfill God's work.[23] Thus the leaders of Moscow assumed added importance in world affairs: They became God's instruments and their actions received divine justification.[24]

Russia's new-found mission was symptomatic of the changing relationship between Greeks and Russians. In time the Russian Church became autocephalous, that is completely independent from the Patriarch of Constantinople.[25] In practice, the Russian Church was independent even before 1453 but as a matter of respect the Patriarch of Constantinople was always consulted in major decisions and the head of the Russian Church, the Metropolitan of Moscow, deferred to the Patriarch's wishes. Now, since the Patriarch was for all practical purposes captive to the Turks, the Russian Church decided to declare its complete independence. Thus the Metropolitan of Moscow assumed the title of the Patriarch and was accepted as equal to the other Orthodox Patriarchs (those of Constantinople, Jerusalem, Alexandria and Antioch). Ecclesiastical independence was the prelude to intellectual independence as well. While Greek churchmen and scholars were still welcomed in Russia, they were not accepted automatically as intellectually and spiritually superior. Besides ecclesiastic and spiritual leadership in the Orthodox world, Russia assumed political leadership as well. As the Ottoman Empire conquered East-Central Europe and the Near East, millions of Orthodox people (many of them Slavs like the Russians) came under Turkish control. The Grand Prince of Moscow (who assumed the title of Tsar of Russia in the late sixteenth century) became the only Orthodox leader who could protect and eventually free his co-religionists from the Turkish yoke. Thus by the 1500s the relationship between Greeks and Russians had changed dramatically. The former began to look to the latter for material help and for leadership. This new level of relation is demonstrated by the fact that the Russian Tsar was often petitioned by the Patriarch of Constantinople for money, but also by the fact that a number of other church prelates, while still under the jurisdiction of the Patriarch of Constantinople, wrote to the tsar directly asking for support.[26] At the same time, even though the Russian state and Church were achieving pre-eminence among Orthodox people, Constantinople and the other old-established Churches retained some of their aura. Even though Moscow could, and did, become an autocephalous church, in important matters it asked and received the blessing of Constantinople.[27] The relationship between the patriarchate of Constantinople, which was dominated by Greeks, and its Russian offshoot was a complex one. The Russians came to resent the arrogance, as they perceived it, which Greek clerics exhibited towards Moscow. At the same time, the official leadership of the Russian Church accepted the fact that their liturgy had deviated from the norm and needed to return to its Greek roots.[28] In times of religious crises the Russian leadership turned to Greek church leaders for support. Such a crisis occurred in the 1660s, when the Russian Tsar was in the process of removing Nikon (architect of the reforms which attempted to purge the Russian church from certain practices deemed western and un-orthodox) from the office of Russian Patriarch. Although the tsar could, and did, act unilaterally, he looked to religious leaders outside of Russia for advice, support and approval.[29] While Russia was assuming the role of the "big brother" to the orthodox people under Ottoman domination its support for the Greeks and the other peoples of the Balkans was chiefly symbolic. The Ottoman Empire was too strong to be challenged openly, while the Russian Tsars could not even reform their own country's antiquated political and economic system. Under such conditions, challenging a major power such as Turkey, was out of the question. All that began to change at the beginning of the eighteenth century when Peter Alekseevich Romanov (later Emperor Peter I or the Great) became Russian Tsar (1689–1725).

II

Among Peter the Great's many plans was one which called for Russia to become a regional maritime power. Peter needed access to a southern warm water port in the Black Sea coast. To achieve that end Russia would have to fight Turkey and their vassals the Crimean Tartars. In 1710 Peter, at the head of his army, invaded the Danubian Principalities (present day Romania). This was the first time since 1453 that an Orthodox army posed a threat to the Ottoman Empire. By that time the Greeks of the Ottoman Empire had become important to the administration of that state and many of them were prominent in the Ottoman ministry of foreign affairs, the bureaucracy of the Turkish Navy, as well as in commerce.[30] It became customary for Greek interpreters (dragomans) to be attached to all foreign missions to Constantinople as well as Ottoman delegations abroad. From the late seventeenth century, the head of the Ottoman Empire's Foreign Service (Grand Dragoman of the Porte) was also a Greek. Over the years, many influential Greeks had moved to the Danubian Principalities either as merchants seeking fortune or as administrators in the Ottoman bureaucracy. Indeed, after Peter's Danubian adventure, described below, the rulers (*hospodars*) of both Walachia and Moldavia were Greeks appointed by the Turks.

Peter believed that once his army invaded lands inhabited by Orthodox people, the latter would welcome him and help defeat the Turks. In order for his plan to succeed, Peter counted on influential Greeks to support Russia overtly and covertly. It is not clear what the local orthodox people had to gain from helping Russia. Besides the obvious sympathy with which they were viewing their co-religionists to the north, the people of the Balkans were implicitly promised freedom from the Turks (although that did not necessarily mean independence but rather possible inclusion in the Russian Empire). Since 1453, the people of the Balkans had looked to Russia for moral support and among the Greeks there were many legends and prophesies regarding the "Blond Race" of the North which would help its fellow Orthodox and free them from the Turks.[31] Unfortunately for Peter, he failed to realize that the Near Eastern Orthodox people were not ready for a major revolt and that the elite was too sophisticated to act on impulses based on prophesies. Thus the Balkan elites, Greek in character if not always in blood, refused to endanger their privileged positions in the Ottoman state apparatus, in favor of a romantic adventure. As a result, the popular revolt which Peter expected to aid his campaign did not materialize and the Russian army was quickly defeated. Peter had to bribe his way out of a military disaster.[32]

That Balkan adventure had a sobering effect on Russian foreign policy. Peter blamed his failure on the unworthiness of the Balkan peoples. He particularly blamed the Greek elite for duplicity and unwillingness to put aside their own material comfort for the common good. Although officially Russia continued to declare its solidarity with the Orthodox people under Ottoman rule, in private Peter and his successors turned their attention to other projects. For sixty years Russia stayed away from the Balkans. It was only when Catherine II or Great came to the throne that Russia appeared once more, in a major way, on the Balkan scene.

Catherine the Great (1762–1796) had similar diplomatic goals as Peter. She wanted to take over large areas from the Ottoman Empire and eventually even push the Turks away from Europe, not to say the Bosporus. In order to achieve her goals, Catherine needed the cooperation of the Orthodox people of the Ottoman Empire as well as the tacit support of some of the European powers. The First Russo-Turkish War (1768–1774) was Catherine's first attempt to dismember the Ottoman Empire. As was the case with Peter, the Russian army planned to capture parts of the Danubian Principalities and defeat Turkey's vassal, the Crimean Tartars. In an effort to relieve some of the pressure which Turkey put on her army, Catherine attempted to create mischief in the Mediterranean aiming at diverting Turkish attention. To that end Catherine sent her fleet in the Mediterranean while at the same time she attempted to find allies among the Italian states.[33] At about the same time Catherine formulated a plan for action which ultimately became known as the "Greek Project."[34] According to that plan Catherine was going to resurrect the old Byzantine Empire independent from Russia but with a Russian prince as the emperor. It has never been ascertained how serious Catherine was about the "Greek Project." She did name one of her grandsons Constantine (a name common to eleven Byzantine emperors and according to legend the name of the one who was to recapture Constantinople from the Turks) and gave him a Greek nursemaid to teach him the language.[35] However, at times it seemed that Catherine's favorite Potemkin was much more interested in liberating Greece or recreating the Byzantine Empire. There were rumors that in the 1780s Potemkin, who knew that his future was far from secure once Catherine was out of the picture, was planning to make himself king of Greece.[36] As is the case with other aspects of Catherine's policies, one is not sure if she was serious or just paid lip service to an idea which sounded good and noble. By claiming to recreate a long lost empire, of which Russia was a spiritual heir, she gave her struggle against Turkey a noble justification. At the same time, her promises of freedom from Turkey was a gesture of support to the Orthodox people of the Ottoman Empire, whom Catherine cultivated as allies. Whatever the case might have been, Russia now became truly embroiled in Balkan affairs. While a Greek revolt might or might not have been in Catherine's initial plans, some Greeks of the diaspora who served Russia were involved in the early stages of Russia's Mediterranean venture. Russia's representative in Venice was

Marchese Pano Maruzzi of the well known phanariot family (Russia's first ever representative to Venice sent by Peter the Great in 1711 was also a Greek, Demetrios Bozis).[37] The appearance of a Russian fleet in the Mediterranean encouraged those who, like the Greeks, viewed Russia as their potential savior from Turkish occupation.[38] A number of Greeks in Russian service were sent to prepare their countrymen for action. Antonio Psaros, Angelos Adamopulos, Panajotti Alessiano and above all Giorgio Papasoli were particularly active on behalf of Russia.[39] Finally, Alexis Orlov (brother of Catherine's favorite Grigorii) was sent to Greece with instructions to lead a revolution which would distract the Ottoman Empire and force her to keep troops in Greece, away from the northern theater of operations. In 1770 Orlov visited Greece and succeeded in enticing the Greeks to a massive revolt. A major incentive for many young Greeks to join Russia's cause was Catherine's recruitment of men for her regular armed forces, with all the financial and other advantages which such positions implied.[40] Since 1453 there had been numerous Greek revolts against the Turks but this was the biggest to date, and remained so until the 1821–1829 Greek War of Independence. The Greeks expected Russia to help with large numbers of troops. Orlov's plans however were to commit as few Russian troops as possible and let the Greeks carry the heavier load.[41] The Russian navy did play an important role and Orlov's victory over the Turkish fleet in the vicinity of Chesme earned him the title of *Chesmeskii*.[42] However, the war in the Balkans was going to be decided on land not on water. The Russian victory at sea was useless without land forces to occupy the area. Without concrete support from Russia, the revolt died down and the Turks were able to defeat the few rebels who continued to resist. Once the revolt was completely extinguished Turkey allowed large numbers of Albanian paramilitary formations to invade southern Greece (Morea) which had been the hotbed of the revolt, and pillage it. The destruction of Morea by the Albanians was so systematic that in time even the Turks themselves were alarmed. In 1779 Turkish forces appeared on the scene and with help from the Greeks turned against the Albanians and forced them to submit.[43] Adding insult to injury, once Catherine had accomplished her war aims (by conquering the Crimea), she ended the war and signed a treaty with Turkey. The whole affair embittered the Greeks and the so called *Ορλωφικά* (the Orlov affair) became a turning point in Greek-Russian relations.

After centuries of expecting Russia to help liberate them, the Greeks came to the conclusion that they had to fight for their own freedom without hopes for external help. The negative impact which the Orlov affair had on Greek-Russian relations became evident during the Second Russo-Turkish War (1788–1792). At that time Russia attempted to prompt another major Greek revolt but the result was failure. The one notable exemption was the activities of some Greeks led by one of their compatriots in Russian service Lambros Katsonis.[44] The life of this individual is a good illustration of the opportunities which a Greek could find in Russia, but also the possibility of using Russia and the Greeks of the diaspora to free Greece from Turkish oppression. Katsonis was born in 1752 in the Greek town of Livadia (Λεβαδειά). In 1770, he joined Count Orlov's fleet and fought against the Turks. After the end of the war Katsonis emigrated to Russia where he married and continued to serve in Greek military units of the Russian army.[45] His military record attracted the attention of his superiors and in 1784 he was promoted to the rank of captain and awarded 1,000 rubles by the Empress Catherine for his actions during the war with Persia.[46] When the second Russo-Turkish War started (1788), Katsonis, by then a major, was commissioned by Potemkin to go to the Mediterranean and with help from his Greek compatriots to create problems for the Turks.[47] Katsonis went to Trieste, then part of the Austrian Empire, and with money from that city's wealthy Greeks he bought and armed a U.S. built ship which he named "Minerva of the North" (Αθηνά της Άρκτου) in honor of Catherine the Great.[48] In the next four years Katsonis raided Turkish ships and coastal towns, as well as ships of other countries friendly to Turkey. By 1792 Katsonis' force had grown to about 18 ships of various sizes (all under Russian flag), most of them being captured from the enemy but manned by Greeks. Important as the actions of Katsonis were, the Greek public at large, remembering the way Russia deserted them in 1774, refused to revolt. Katsonis found himself in a difficult position in 1792 when Russia ended the war against Turkey with the signing of the Treaty of Jassy. Unlike other Greeks in Russian service who had "hang a foreign tassel to their sword" Katsonis (recently promoted colonel and created a knight by Russia) was his own man. He refused to stop fighting commenting that "The Empress might have signed a peace treaty but Katsonis did not."[49] Soon after the above comment Katsonis was forced to quit due to lack of money and logistical support. He was branded a common pirate and an outlaw.[50] Lambros Katsonis made his way to Russia slowly as he was afraid of official sanctions for having disobeyed the first order to stop fighting. He arrived in St. Petersburg in 1796 and petitioned the authorities for compensation and rewards for those Greeks who had followed him and were now suffering as a result. At that time Catherine, who might have been disinclined to help, died and her son and successor Paul favored Katsonis.[51] Lambros Katsonis received from the emperor 470,000 rubles most of which he distributed among his followers.[52] With the remaining of the money Katsonis, who retired from active army service, bought extensive properties in the Crimea. He renamed the nearby town Levadia, like his birthplace in Greece, and died there in 1804.[53]

While the Orlov affair was a disaster it did have some positive results. One of the articles of the 1774 Treaty of Kutchuk-Kainardji (which brought an end to the First Russo-Turkish War) allowed the Greek merchant marine, already numerous, to sail under Russian flag and thus have many of the privileges accorded to the ships of a powerful nation. This allowed Greeks to buy inexpensive grain from the newly conquered lands of the Crimean Tartars and sell it in western Europe for substantial profits. As a result the Greeks became the owners of an extensive merchant fleet (at the time armed in order to defend itself against pirates) which became useful during the Greek War of Independence. At the same time, thousands of Greeks (crews of the above mentioned ships, merchants, etc.) came into close contact with Russia and its people. As a result, the ancient close relations between the Russian and Greek peoples, which had been limited due to the Ottoman control of Constantinople and Greece, were reestablished. Also, according to Articles 7 and 14 of the same treaty, Russia was recognized as the protector of the Orthodox Church inside the Ottoman Empire and by extension to all orthodox people as well.[54] From that time on, Russia used Articles 7 and 14 of the Treaty of Kutchuk-Kainardji as the legal justification to call itself the "Protector of Orthodox People" in the Ottoman Empire, and intervene in the internal affairs of Turkey.

III

Modern Greek emigration to Russia in a significant way started at the time of Peter the Great. Up to that time emigration had taken the form of colonization (as in ancient times) or (in the case of the middle ages) it was a small scale affair in which a Greek scholar or notable came to Russia. In both cases the immigrants did not have much contact with the wider Russian public. The one notable exemption to the above was the Greek community of Nezhin. The Greek commercial community of that city was numerous and influential enough to receive special attention from Moscow. In 1657 the Greeks were given some privileges by the local authorities but in 1696 those privileges were codified by the central administration and the Greeks were allowed to create their *Greek Commercial Brotherhood of Nezhin*. Peter the Great confirmed those privileges in 1710. By the time of Catherine the Great (1762–1796) while the Greeks of Nezhin were declining in importance in comparison with the newer Greek communities on the coast of the Black Sea, their political power increased as they were allowed their own autonomous governing body with judicial power over its members.[55] Besides the above notable exemption, the early colonists created their own cities which remained for centuries outside the mainstream of Russian life. By the time they were forced to integrate, they had lost most of their unique characteristics. In the case of individuals emigrating again, their contact with the average Russian was minimal. Being educated scholars and clerics, those Greeks were part of the elite. Their lives in Russia were confined to the Kremlin or the bishop's palace. In contrast, the new immigrants were more numerous and destined from the start to intermingle with Russian society.

Around 1700, Peter the Great realized that in order to modernize his state and his army he needed educated people skilled in arts and crafts in which his own people were ignorant. For instance, Peter needed skilled shipbuilders to create a Russian Navy, and men educated in the science of modern warfare. Since few, if any, Russians possessed such skills (and the foreigners already living in Russia were not enough) Peter instructed some of the noblemen in his immediate circle, who happen to be in the West at the time, to entice foreigners with promises of high wages, bonuses and positions in the Russian state apparatus. Among the large number of foreign craftsmen who took up the Russian offer were a number of Greeks.[56] This first group of Greek immigrants did not achieve fame and fortune in their new home. Although they contributed in creating Russia's first navy, none achieved high rank in the state bureaucracy. Most of them remained anonymous to the historian, a small footnote to Russian history.[57]

A second category of early Greek settlers in Russia consisted of those who were included in the expanding empire by virtue of the fact that their places of residence were conquered by Russia. In this category belong thousands of Greeks (descendants of the ancient colonists) living among the Crimean Tartars. These Greeks belong to the new emigration wave, since their move was massive and by virtue of their professions (mainly farmers and traders) came into contact with Russian society. At the same time the fact that they were already living in the area, and that they had lost most of their national characteristics, puts them in a separate class from the core Greek emigration.[58] A number of those Greeks were lured away from Crimea to the area of Mariupol were they prospered as farmers. Over the years they became Russian-speakers but retained a sense (however vague) of their national origins.[59]

The bulk of the Greek immigrants which concerns this study were either refugees of war, or others who came from Greece proper during the second half of the eighteenth and the beginning of the nineteenth century. They came to Russia to seek shelter, or because they were enticed by Russian authorities due to the benefits which their knowledge of agriculture, trade, etc. could give their new homeland. Catherine the Great, whose reign was characterized, among other things, by rapid expansion, realized that the vast and fertile southern plains, which the Russian army had been conquering gradually since 1739, had tremendous potential. If enough people were to populate the new territory (appropriately named New Russia) farming, animal husbandry and trade could help the rest of the country's economy. Catherine gave large grants of land to some of her nobles but it became evident soon that the institution of serfdom, already condemned by many proponents of the Enlightenment, was unsuited to New Russia's frontier society and economy. Serf owners were reluctant to invest the money and energy needed to develop the agriculture of the new areas.[60] It became clear that what was needed was the energy and ingenuity of free farmers, a species virtually unknown in pre-emancipation Russia.[61] Catherine and her advisers decided to entice foreign agriculturists from Europe. Russia promised free land, no taxation for thirty years, exemption from many onerous duties (such as conscription to the army) and loans with low or no interest to all farmers who would agree to emigrate to New Russia. If the new immigrants preferred they could retain foreign citizenship without repercussions from Russia. Thousands of farmers from North and West Europe took up the offer. Many Protestant Mennonites from the German states came to New Russia and became successful beyond any expectation.[62]

While Russia had sent emissaries to Europe to advertise the opportunities in New Russia, Greece, being part of the Ottoman Empire, was not part of that campaign. However the outcome of the Orlov affair was the catalyst in Greek emigration. As it has been noted, as soon as the revolt in Greece ended Turkey dispatched Albanian paramilitary bands which destroyed communities and killed and raped indiscriminately. It took decades for Morea to recover from the physical devastation. Besides the dislocation caused by the war and the plunder that accompanied it, the Turks rewarded the Albanian troops with grants of land in the area. As a result, thousands of Greeks, mainly from Morea and the islands, became refugees. Over 30,000 Greek refugees arrived at the nearby domain of the Venetian Republic but due to political pressures they had to leave and either returned to Greece, and an uncertain future, or looked for help elsewhere.[63] Many of them resigned to the fact that they could not return to their homes again. Catherine, while not admitting any responsibility for the calamity of the Greeks, she did feel obligated to accommodate those co-religionists, many of whom had fought in Russian-organized military units. Even though as a result of the Orlov affair many Russian officers who served in Greece were critical of the Greeks, several of them urged Catherine to help their co-religionists.[64] Actually, the Russian government had allowed Greeks to establish themselves in the South as early as 1770, while the Greek revolt was just starting. Distribution of free land to the Greeks was hailed at the time, by the St. Petersburg published *Gazzetta universale* as "…a prediction of the reestablishment of the Greek empire in Eastern Europe…."[65] Such a statement from a Russian publication reveal that the "Greek Project" had captured the public's imagination, just as Catherine must have hoped it would. Since Russia needed more settlers for the South, Catherine was able to kill the proverbial two birds with one stone. As an added bonus, the Greeks being Orthodox could offset the emigration of Protestants while at the same time being fighters they could be co-opted to develop as well as defend the new territory (the Mennonites being proponents of non-violence were unsuitable for defense). Also unlike the Mennonites, who lived either in farms or small communities of their own, the Greeks were settled among the local population. Most of those Greeks were settled on seaside cities, a number of them in the Crimean towns of Symferopol, Sevastopol, Balaklava, Kerch and Yeni-kule (the last one is situated across the mouth of the Sea of Azov from Crimea but is close enough to be counted as part of the peninsula). Others inhabited the nearby newly built towns of Kherson, Taganrog, Nikolaev and Odessa.[66] Before long, Russia's southern province became the new home and the destination of choice for most Greek immigrants, a situation which lasted for a hundred years until the United States became the new "promised land."

While Greek emigration to Russia did not end after the 1790s, the 1770–1790s era represents the high water mark of Greek emigration. The Greeks who came to Russia in the nineteenth century can be divided into two categories. Those who came individually lured by the promise of easy riches, and those who came by the thousands as refugees from the Russo-Turkish wars of 1828–1829, 1853–1856 and 1877–1878.[67] A somewhat smaller number of refugees reached Russia as a result of the Greek-Turkish war of 1897 while about 135,000 more Pontic Greeks crossed the frontier from Turkey to Russia during the First World War.[68] The impact of those relative newcomers to the more established colonists of earlier eras should not be underestimated. As it has been pointed out by some scholars, the newcomers were able to prosper in their adopted land and, as the earlier immigrants moved out of business enterprises to owning land, bonds, etc., they came to dominate trade and shipping between the Black Sea and Europe.[69] Also, as will be pointed later in this work, those newcomers, being recent refugees, were more intensely nationalistic, and as they took control of various Greek institutions in Russia they attempted to retain their national identity and counter the effects of the host country's "Russification" policy. One should keep in mind that by the end of the 1820s the various Greek communities in Russia were already well established. By the middle and late nineteenth century, when the newcomers appeared on the scene, a way of life, a pattern of economic activity of the Greeks of Russia was already in place. The Russian government, helpful as it was to the Greek refugees, did not extend to them the generous tax and land concessions which were instrumental for the establishment of earlier Greek communities. Going back to the theory of diasporas as defined by Cohen, the Greek emigration of the eighteenth century is closer to its classical counterpart. In ancient times colonization was planned and financed by the country of origin in order to fulfill some need such as overpopulation, trade, etc. In the eighteenth century model, while the immigrants were for the most part refugees of war (thus closer to the modern type of diaspora) the planning and financing of the enterprise was undertaken by the country of *destination* in order to fulfill some need such as underpopulation of an area and the need for merchants and cultivators. In contrast, the Greeks who went to Russia in the nineteenth and twentieth centuries were either individuals who moved without benefit of state planning or masses of refugees fleeing war. While the Greek refugees of the nineteenth century built villages in the Caucasus area, percentage wise they were never as important as their earlier counterparts in the creation of cities such as Odessa, Nikolaev, Taganrog and Mariupol. For those reasons one can claim that the late eighteenth-early nineteenth centuries was the "Golden Era" of Greek emigration to Russia.

II
Odessa: Profile of a City

Trade was the primary reason for Odessa's existence. Russia's southward expansion was motivated by the need to secure its southern flank from Turkish/Tartar attacks and the desire to establish a warm water port which would allow the empire to trade year-round with the West. As early as the time of Peter the Great, Russia attempted to transform the port of Azov to a permanent Russian urban harbor. However, a reversal of fortune forced the Russians to return Azov to Turkey. Still, the end of the eighteenth century, Russia had prevailed and the area known as New Russia (Novorosiia) became the empire's new frontier. Although small and mid-size towns were already established, by and large they were inadequate for the mercantile needs of the empire.[1] On orders from Catherine II, the port-city of Kherson was founded but its harbor was not deep enough to accommodate large ships. In 1789, a Russian force under the command of Admiral de Ribas attacked and captured the small fort of Khadzhibei.[2] It was this Turkish village that was destined to become Odessa, the capital of New Russia, the empire's fourth most populous city and, after St. Petersburg, its second port of export.[3] The fact that de Ribas was a sailor must have been Odessa's good fortune. The admiral had the knowledge and experience to realize that the harbor of the newly acquired town was good for Catherine's purposes.[4] From the beginning, Odessa became the beneficiary of fortuitous circumstances: the governors-general of New Russia, who were directly responsible for the city's progress, were either able men or had excellent connections in St. Petersburg, which translated in better treatment for Odessa. De Ribas convinced Governor-general Prince Platon Zubov (at the time Catherine's favorite) to promote the new site as worthy of royal favor. This was easily accomplished and Catherine allocated the money to built the new city. Like St. Petersburg, the empire's capital, Odessa did not grow by accident but was a planned city from its start. There was an ancient Greek colony in the general vicinity called Odessos (Οδησσός) and the new city was named after the old one.

Catherine herself changed the name to Odessa which in Russian is a female noun.[5]

The chief purpose of having a good harbor in the South of Russia was to export the agricultural products of the area. The main agricultural products of South Russia were cereals, especially wheat. The two types of flour that one could mill from the different varieties of wheat were hard and soft. It seems that Western European markets favored the soft type while South Europe used hard flour for the manufacturing of pasta.[6] As more people were encouraged to cultivate the land, the amount of cereals and other agricultural products increased and the traffic to points West became a major undertaking. Although transportation routes inside the empire were primitive, there was still enough volume available to be transported through Odessa's harbor. Along with agriculture, animal husbandry was an appreciable source of wealth for the area. Initially, cows constituted the largest part of animal exports, being on demand mainly for their leather and tallow. Gradually, with the active support of the Russian government, merino sheep were introduced and the Odessa area became a center of wool production.[7] Additionally, thousands of small farmers produced vegetables and fruits, especially watermelons, to make the area a major producer. Finally, with the encouragement of the state wine producing became a major industry as well.[8] The economic development of Odessa can be divided into two periods. The first one, from 1795–1856, witnessed rapid growth with emphasis on the export of agricultural products. This first period is characterized by the involvement of the government due mainly to the patronage of the various governors-general of New Russia. It is interesting to note that while the early period was often punctuated by wars (the Napoleonic War up to 1815, then the Russo-Turkish War in the late 1820s and the Crimean War 1854–1856) which are usually bad times for international trade, Odessa managed to thrive.

A few years later the US consul in Odessa reported that business was booming. In the year 1833 goods worth over fifteen million rubles were imported through Odessa while exports worth 25,646,803 left the harbor. For the year 1835 the numbers were 17,223,651 for imports and 23,537,158 for exports.[9]

TABLE 1
Odessa's Imports and Exports, 1795–1802 [10]
(In Silver Rubles)

YEAR	IMPORTS	EXPORTS	TOTALS
1795	43,065	24,824	67,889
1796	92,559	79,422	171,981
1797	129,492	79,091	208,583
1798	117,888	90,977	208,865
1799	303,822	111,258	415,080
1800	264,651	287,540	552,191
1801	501,820	519,906	1,021,726
1802	719,982	1,534,114	2,254,096

TABLE 2
Odessa's Imports and exports, 1802–1813 [11]

YEAR	IMPORTATION	EXPORTATION	DUTY
1802	772,047	1,525,671	
1804	1,223,027	2,339,509	155,037
1805	2,156,298	3,399,291	203,605
1806	1,845,125	822,927	209,757
1807	490,330	336,022	76,319
1808	1,901,766	1,975,013	256,706
1809	2,259,004	1,776,290	231,424
1810	2,736,874	3,146,994	445,216
1811	7,040,080	7,747,544	829,241
1812	2,313,521	5,855,045	386,918
1813	3,169,895	8,861,956	683,607

The second period of Odessa's development, 1856–1914, was not as prosperous due chiefly to the changing or shifting patterns of international trade. Argentina and especially the United States of America became major wheat exporters. In the case of the US its wheat was cheaper to grow, could be transported faster and cheaper, and was of better quality than its Russian counterpart. Mechanization and new methods of cultivation were the main reasons for America's rise to supremacy in the field. As was the case in many other areas, Russia was lagging behind. Although railroads replaced carts as the means of transportation from the hinterland to Odessa, transportation costs were still higher than those of its American competitor; the same can be said for the cost of production. Then there was the low quality of Russian wheat. This problem can be attributed to old methods of cultivation but also to the fact that speculators were cheating the buyers and in the process gave a bad name to Odessa merchants in general.[12] Indeed, as a result of economic decline many established Odessa merchants moved to other cities or transferred their fortunes to other fields. By the end of the nineteenth century, new men had taken over Odessa's export trade.[13] While most of the new merchants were dealing in good faith, others succumbed to the temptation of quick profits thus damaging the reputation of all Odessa merchants. A favorite method of cheating the western buyer was to misrepresent the quality of the merchandise sold. A merchant from Odessa might send a sample of excellent quality wheat for the buyer to examine. Once the unsuspecting buyer had paid for a shipment of wheat of a quality similar to that of the sample he had received, he was send wheat of lesser quality often adulterated with foreign objects.

The Russian government was also responsible for Odessa's economic decline as an export harbor. In the first period of the city's history, the state generously subsidized the construction of the city and its various port facilities. In the second period, state investment declined appreciably. Although the central government was responsible for the construction of railroads, the maintenance of the city infrastructure was entrusted to the city government and local revenues. As a result, the port of Odessa fell behind and although it continued to be important it was never again "first class." Also, the nearby port of Nikolaev became the recipient of state support and gradually became a rival to Odessa. However, although Odessa experienced a relative decline that does not mean that the city itself became impoverished. Odessa's growth kept up with the rest of the empire and to the end of the Imperial era the city remained Russia's second largest port of export.[14] As late as 1911–1913 the combined value of imports and exports from the port of Odessa was 103 million silver rubles per year.[15] While Odessa was never as great a center of industry as some North Russian cities, as the nineteenth century came to its close more factories appeared which employed thousands of workers. As was the case in all large Russian cities, labor unrest became a common occurrence disrupting the city's economic life and thus contributing to its overall decline.[16]

II

As a result of the prosperity that trade brought to Odessa, as well as the state's early favorable policies, the city became a showpiece of civilization and elegance in the fringes of Russia's steppe. As it has been noted earlier, New Russia became the beneficiary of the high caliber of governors-general who were sent to govern the frontier territory. Early on people like Potemkin and Zubov yielded great power by virtue of their personal relationship with the Empress Catherine II.[17] During the brief reign of Paul, the South was ignored but his successor, Alexander I, in 1803 appointed a Frenchman, the Duc de Richelieu, as Odessa's governor and from 1805 governor-general of New Russia as well. Seldom has a person been as well suited for the job he was given. As his name suggests, Richelieu (1766–1822) was a relative of the cardinal who ruled France in the name of the king during the seventeenth century.[18] The young nobleman was forced out of France during the time of the French Revolution and found employment in Russia. Richelieu spent many years in the South, first under Potemkin and then his successors. During his term in office (1803–1814), South Russia in general and Odessa in particular grew rapidly.[19] The city of Odessa, which had a population of 2,349 in 1795 grew to 51,988 by 1829.[20] During the second period of Odessa's development, its population continued to multiply.

TABLE 3
Population of Odessa, 1861–1914 [21]

Year	Population	Year	Population	Year	Population
1861	115,567	1875	188,700	1891	310,438
1862	117,540	1876	194,500	1892	340,526
1863	118,412	1877	200,400	1897	403,815
1864	120,708	1878	206,500	1899	410,000
1865	116,917	1879	212,800	1900	450,000[22]
1866	120,163	1880	219,300	1905	511,000
1867	127,775	1881	226,000	1906	461,000
1868	133,000	1882	233,000	1908	450,000
1869	139,462	1883	244,609	1910	520,000
1872	145,463	1887	271,000	1911	620,143
1873	193,513	1889	301,039	1914	630,000[23]
1874	188,700	1890	313,687		

The Duc de Richelieu enjoyed the complete confidence of Alexander I and thus any requests from the governor-general were treated favorably by St. Petersburg. Richelieu contributed to the area's development by lobbying the central government for more money to improve the infrastructure and by encouraging and promoting private initiative. He also encouraged the emigration of European farmers to South Russia and was instrumental in their early success. But his most important work was the architectural transformation of Odessa. It was Richelieu who secured from the government the funds needed to make Odessa's harbor world class. Besides work on the harbor itself (including building a mole), there was also the building of supporting structures such as warehouses, customhouse, etc. Richelieu made the beautification of Odessa his personal mission. It was through his patronage that public buildings and squares were build in the latest architectural styles.[24]

Richelieu's modest life style, his genuine love for Odessa, and his administrative skills made him extremely popular with the common people. In fact the citizens of Odessa named a city street after him and they commissioned a statue of their beloved governor. Richelieu is not the only one honored in this manner. Various individuals and groups, who have contributed to Odessa's history are commemorated with street names and/or statues. The main commercial street of Odessa is to this day named after de Ribas while another major street, and a public beach, are named in honor of Governor Langeron.[25] Grigorii Maraslis, Odessa's first mayor, and a major figure of the city's Greek community, was honored a year after his death (1907) with the naming of a street in his honor.[26] Besides the already mentioned statue of Richelieu there is one of Governor Vorontsov. The cosmopolitan character of Odessa is reflected in such street names as "Albanian," "Jewish," "Armenian," "French" and "Greek" (there is also a "Greek Square").

It was Odessa's misfortune that in 1814 the restored royal house of France lured Richelieu back where he served as his country's prime minister performing superbly once more. While Odessa lost an able governor, his work continued because Alexander chose as his successor one of Richelieu's closest collaborators and fellow Frenchman the Count de Langeron.[27] Langeron's term (1815–1822) was a continuation of the Richelieu regime.[28] Especially in financial matters the two Frenchmen had identical views. Richelieu was a free trader and as early as 1808 he had allow merchants to store their wares in municipal warehouses free of charge for twelve months. Soon after that, he petitioned St. Petersburg to declare Odessa a free port thus stimulating import-exports and decreasing the profitability of contraband.[29] Langeron continued pressing for free port status and in 1817 he succeeded.[30] Although devoted to his work in Russia as his predecessor and friend had been, Langeron was never as popular as Richelieu. His manner was more detached and although he lived in Russia for thirty years (and in the end died there), Langeron did not learn to speak the language.[31] Langeron was replaced as governor-general by Count (later Prince) Michael Vorontsov. Vorontsov has the distinction of being the longest serving governor-general (1822–1856) of New Russia. At times he served concurrently as governor-general of New Russia, viceroy of Bessarabia and as the Emperor's Lieutenant in the Caucasus.[32] Unlike his two immediate predecessors, Vorontsov was an ethnic Russian and like the first governor-general, Potemkin, he was also a great personage in court circles. Vorontsov came from a prominent aristocratic family, was educated in England, and was a free trader by conviction and an entrepreneur by temperament. All those qualities combined for the benefit of New Russia and Odessa. Unlike Richelieu who lived in frugal circumstances (not by need but by choice), Vorontsov lived and entertained in grand style. Also, his connections in court and abroad were used for the advancement and development of Odessa and the region. Finally, Vorontsov's entrepreneurial undertakings were of benefit to the agriculture and industry of the region.[33] After Vorontsov, Count Stroganov (1856–1863) and General Kotsebu (1863–1874) became the last governors-general of new Russia.

The monumental administrative changes that occurred in Russia in the 1860s had a direct effect on the future of Odessa and New Russia. The office of governor-general was abolished and its powers were diffused among other military and political office holders. From that time on, the occupants of the various offices which administered New Russia were bureaucrats and army generals rather than well connected courtiers, grand seigneurs of the Potemkin, Richelieu and Vorontsov style. The old style governors viewed the well-being of the land and the people of New Russia as their responsibility and assumed a paternalistic, almost proprietary interest in their office. In contrast, the new careerists saw their office as a temporary one on the way to advancement and thus were less inclined to identify with the particular needs of the area. Whereas the names and work of early governors are well known, that of the later ones remain relatively obscure underscoring their modest impact on the development of the area.

Port cities are usually cosmopolitan places and Odessa was not an exemption to that general rule. Indeed, one could argue that the city was cosmopolitan from its inception. Originally it was a Tartar/Turkish fort which was taken over by a force led by de Ribas, a Spanish-Irish born in Naples and serving in Russia. Soon after Odessa was built, a number of refugees from the Balkans (Greeks, Bulgarians and Albanians) gave the city its early population boost.[34] As it has been already stated, the early nineteenth century was dominated by the administration of two Frenchmen Richelieu and Langeron. Even Russian governors like Stroganov and especially Vorontsov were cosmopolitan in outlook and might have been more comfortable in the drawing rooms of London and Paris than in the Russian frontier. Besides the multitude of foreigners who came to Odessa looking to make a fortune from trade (and that includes people from all over Europe and even America) New Russia itself was far from being homogeneous in its population. Besides the Tartars who were already there, New Russia received many ethnic Russians, Ukrainians and Poles. Also, since much of Western New Russia was within the pale of Jewish settlement, a large number of Jews was permanently settled in the area. The pale of settlement was the area in which the Russian authorities limited Jewish life and commercial activities. Depending on the times, enforcement of the law could be more or less strict. Odessa was from the start included in the pale thus making it one of the few urban areas where Jews could legally live and work.

Since Odessa became the administrative and financial capital of New Russia, and soon also its largest city, it was natural that it received a large number of the foreigners who inhabited the province. Many of those foreigners were successful merchants who became a dominant force in commerce.[35] Although the city was (and still is to this day) Russian in its character, people of many nationalities found it a hospitable place. During Odessa's early history one would hear Greek and Italian, along with Russian, spoken in the market. By the middle of the nineteenth century Russians came to dominate but Jews and Germans entered the picture as major players in commerce. At the same time, Polish, Ukrainian and Russian landowners from the interior made Odessa their destination to sell their crops and spend their money in more sophisticated environment that their rural estates could offer. As late as 1897, years after the early boom times were over, the majority of Odessa's inhabitants (56.4%) were not born in the city.[36] Although Odessa was cosmopolitan, it was not a "melting pot," the various ethnic groups interacted in the market place but outside it there was little contact. A multitude of churches and synagogues, clubs and associations catered to the needs of sub-groups isolating them from each other.[37]

What gave Odessa its charm and beauty, evident even to this day, was a number of buildings and boulevards which gave the city an appearance more Italian than Russian. To be sure, some Europeans visiting the city during the early period of its existence commented negatively about its appearance. The limestone used to build most of the city's public buildings deteriorated fairly quickly producing an unpleasant picture of the buildings themselves.[38] But what made the worst impression to the visitor from the West was the condition of Odessa's streets. They were dusty in the summer and muddy in the fall and spring and quite unsuitable for a modern metropolis.[39] One positive element of Odessa's town planning was that its streets were running parallel and met at right angles thus allowing for future growth in an orderly fashion.[40] The credit for that planning should go to the Dutch engineer Franz de Voland who designed Odessa's harbor and its early streets.[41] By 1827 the major complains about city streets were addressed and those who had previously commented negatively had to admit that major improvements were made, mainly by building better new roads, macadamizing some of them.[42] As the city grew prosperous, wealthy merchants built imposing beautiful homes and places of business.[43] But the main credit for the city's appearance has to go to its extensive public building. From the beginning, city officials commissioned professional architects and city planners to lay the streets and squares of Odessa. For example, de Ribas used the Dutch architect de Voland while Richelieu used the Russian A. I. Mel'nikov. The latter was responsible for some of the most beautiful public buildings in the center of the city. These architects or civil engineers, as well as others, such as Thomas de Thomon, had worked for the beautification of St. Petersburg, which explains why Odessa and St. Petersburg share a certain similarity of architectural style.[44] Richelieu had planted trees and gardens in Odessa. At his own expense, he imported and planted white acacia trees throughout the city. Citizens whose houses happened to have trees in front of them were fined if they failed to water the them regularly. Citizens who were given city plots for building were obliged to plant trees. Richelieu, again out of his private income, started planting gardens in the city.[45] He is also credited with forming an architectural committee which was charged with reviewing plans for new private buildings and assuring that the facades of these buildings were of the classical/neoclassical style and did not clash with the rest of the city's architecture.[46] The fact that the Imperial government stopped spending money for Odessa's building from about 1825 was a blessing in disguise.[47] Odessa might have lost the funds but on the plus side it did not have to conform to the stylistic tastes of the emperors. Thus, while in the rest of the empire public buildings were being built according to neogothic styles, Odessa continued to grow according to its own tastes. Count Vorontsov, who had already built in Crimea his famous palace *Alupka* added to the city's architecture by building his city palace on a cliff overlooking the sea. A crescent belvedere with twenty Doric columns gave the structure an ancient Greek or Roman character and made it a landmark visible from both land and sea.[48] It was designed and constructed by the Italian architect Boffo and was situated on the North end of Odessa's famous Nikolaevskii (now Primorskii) Boulevard. On the other end of the boulevard, a large white classical building housed the stock exchange (designed by another St. Petersburg architect Giacomo Quarenghi)[49] which became later (and up to this day) the city hall. Behind the city hall there were constructed, over the years, a number of public buildings (mainly to house various departments of the administration) together with Odessa's public library (the first local public library in the empire) and the museum of antiquities.[50] It should be noted that besides generous government grants, Odessa was the recipient of large private donations from civic minded residents.[51] In the last quarter of the nineteenth century, there was a great number of public building focusing mainly on the construction of institutions of public charity (state hospitals, homes for the elderly, etc.) but also gardens and markets. One of the architectural gems built at the time was the Opera House which is still in use today.[52] Odessa's love for the theater and musical performances was so great as to prompt some to characterize it as "...the musical city of the empire."[53] As a result of continues, extensive construction, the city budget was usually running a deficit but that did not seem to have negative effects on the city.[54]

TABLE 4
Odessa Municipal Budgets 1878–1892

YEAR	REVENUES	EXPEND-ITURES	SURPLUS	DEFICIT
1878	1925444	1918954	6490	
1879	2021705	2024435		2730
1880	1904466	1926483		22017
1881	1953049	1941036	12004	
1882	1958848	1910707	48141	
1883	2177482	2023591	153891	
1884	2239847	2093972	245875	
1885	2559056	2932744		373688
1886	2904758	2898106	6652	
1887	3161635	3307570		145935
1888	3625337	3513096	112241	
1889	3745370	3855829		110459
1890	3531665	3434879	96786	
1891	3426689	3668454		241765
1892	3294985	3804768		509783

Most of Odessa's major public building occurred before 1900. By the turn of the century, a visitor would have encountered a beautiful city reminiscent of its Mediterranean counterparts. A number of foreign visitors commented admiringly about the beauty of the city while a famous writer from the New World, Mark Twain, noted that Odessa reminded him more of an American city.[55] Looking at the city from an incoming ship the early twentieth century traveler would have first noticed the lighthouse and the lengthy mole which protected the harbor. At about the same time one would have seen the white colonnade of Vorontsov's palace on top of the hill appearing as if it was suspended between sea and sky. The visitor would have landed at the foot of the "Grand Staircase."[56] Constructed between 1837 and 1842, the staircase has 192 stairs divided by ten landings; it is 142 meters long and is constructed in such a way as to appear even longer. A person looking from the top of the staircase down sees only the landings while one looking up sees only steps.[57] In 1905 the crew of the Russian battleship *Potemkin* which was anchored in Odessa harbor mutinied. The story of that affair was made into a movie by the famous soviet film director Sergei Eisenstein. Since that time, the staircase is universally known as the "Potemkin Steps."[58] On the top of the steps, the visitor would have stood at the foot of the famous monument to the Duc de Richelieu. The sculpture of the duc, covered by a classical toga points to the sea; behind the sculpture, two neoclassical crescent-shaped buildings cradle the monument like two outstretched arms. Taking the road straight ahead between the two buildings, one could reach the center of the town.[59] An affluent visitor most likely would have turned left on the Primorskii Boulevard and gone to the "London" one of Odessa's eleven first class hotels.[60] Then, as now, the best hotel in the city it, is situated about half way between the city hall and Vorontsov's palace. One side of the street is dominated by neoclassical buildings enjoying a spectacular view of the sea. The boulevard itself served mainly as a promenade and was planted with shady trees and colorful flowers. A number of hotels, restaurants and teahouses catered to the discriminating customer. On the corner of de Ribas and Catherine streets, across from Cathedral Square, one would have found the department store/hotel "Passage" a beautiful building, then as now the hub of activity.[61] One characteristic architectural style of Odessa was the large houses set off from the street. One went through an arched open tunnel to enter a tilled inner courtyard.[62] Often those courtyards were interconnected creating a maze of privacy a few yards from the noise of the city. Even the harshest foreign critics of the early nineteenth century would have had to agree that Odessa had been transformed in to a beautiful, modern metropolis.

It should not be assumed, however, that Odessa managed to escape the social problems which burdened other urban centers. Behind the facade of prosperity there was a high poverty rate. Many people who came to Odessa either from abroad or the interior of the country were unable to fulfill their dreams of fame and fortune. Away from the city's fashionable center and wealthy neighborhoods there was a different world of small homes without plumbing and with high mortality and crime rates. The two worlds of Odessa existed side by side but with little contact with each other.[63] It was this Odessa, full of opportunities but also problems, which offered haven to many emigrating Greeks during the nineteenth century.

III
The Greeks of Odessa

The Greek nation is composed by individuals who, after the fall of Constantinople, did not stop being Orthodox Christians, speak the language of their forefathers and remain under the spiritual and lay jurisdiction of their church....

Letter of John Capodistrias to W. Harton, British Undersecretary of State for War and Colonies
October 27, 1827

The period of time between the end of the eighteenth and the beginning of the nineteenth century was in many respects the "Golden Age" of Greek emigration to Russia. As a result of wars and revolutions, an unusually high number of Greek refugees was entering the empire. Most of the refugees were peasants, others were educated individuals who could be utilized by the government of their adopted country. Since most Greeks in nineteenth-century Russia gained fame as merchants, one might assume that trade was the only sphere in which the Greek immigrants were involved. This, however, was not the case. Throughout the Imperial era Greek immigrants and their descendants were involved in Russia's public life as bureaucrats, officers in the armed forces, and educators.

As early as the 1770s Catherine the Great recognized the potential of the Greeks and for that reason she created a special educational institution the *Institut du corps des Cadets Grecs*. Apparently the reputation of that institution was so good that it attracted the sons of Russian nobles as well.[1] This particular institution was unique because it did not require its students to be members of the nobility, as other schools of the kind did, but accepted 200 boys a year between the ages of 12-16, provided they had "honest" parents. After studying (among other subjects) geography, history, mathematics and a number of foreign languages, the young men were eligible for entry into the military academies and thus could achieve noble status.[2] The existence of such an institution, geared towards educating Russia's Greeks, is testament to the relative high number of Greeks in the empire but also to the fact that the Russian authorities recognized early on the potential of that minority not only as farmers and merchants but possible material for the military and the state bureaucracy. The *corps des Cadets Grecs* did not survive in the nineteenth century but a number of its students achieved the rank of admiral or general.[3] The fact that the school was closed was not due to decrease in the number of students or change of Russian policy. It appears that this institution, among others, became a victim of the hatred that Emperor Paul exhibited toward most of his mother's pet projects. The 195 students studying in the *corps* at the time of its disbandment were transferred to the army and navy academies.[4] During the late eighteenth century, a pair of Greek churchmen came to Russia and left their mark in church administration and letters. Eugenios Voulgaris (1716–1806) was a Greek Orthodox priest who had gained some fame as a philosopher. Catherine the Great invited him to Russia where he became Archbishop of Kherson and member of the Russian Academy of Sciences.[5] Voulgaris' friend and student, Nikiforos Theotokis (1731–1800), followed his mentor to Russia and had a similar career as Archbishop of Astrakhan and Stavropol.[6] Other prominent Greeks of the time were the Melissinos brothers, both army officers who are credited with founding the Moscow Masonic Lodge.[7]

In the nineteenth century a new wave of educated Greeks found their way to the Russian Empire. A number of Greek aristocratic families from the Danubian Principalities (present day Romania) fearing retribution from the Turks, due to political antagonism, escaped to Russia. In most cases, the children of those political refugees made careers in the Russian army and bureaucracy. Thus the four Ypsilantis brothers, became officers in the exclusive guards regiments together with their kinsmen Princes Soutsos, Ghika and Cantacouzenos.[8] Other Greeks found employment in Russia's diplomatic service, indeed for some time the Asiatic Department of the Russian Ministry of Foreign Affairs was staffed by a number of Greeks, such as Prince Stourdza (scion of a Hellenized Rumanian family), S. Destounis and his son Gavriil, also K. Rodofinikis (who was the head of the department from 1819–1837).[9] A number of Greeks served Russian interests abroad as diplomats, such as

Count Mocenigo, G. Katakazi, S. Destounis and K. Basili.[10] The Basili family provided three generations of diplomats for Russia. Konstantin Basili (1809–1884) graduated from Odessa's Richelieu Lycee and served as Russia's Consul General in Syria and Palestine (1839–1853). He was a schoolmate and friend of the writer Nikolai Gogol with whom he corresponded for many years afterwards. After attending the Paris Peace Conference in 1856, Basili retired from the diplomatic service to devote his time to writing. His son Alexander (?–1902) was also a diplomat who became undersecretary of state for foreign affairs. Finally, Nicolas de Basili (1883–1963) was also a diplomat attached to the tsar's headquarters during the First World War. It was Nicolas, at the tsar's request, who drafted the emperor's abdication declaration in 1917. After Nicolas de Basili's death, his papers were donate to the Hoover Institute where they form part of that institution's Russian collection.[11] Also, for many years the Greek general J. Gorgolis was chief of police in St. Petersburg.[12] The best known Greek in Russian service (and the best known Greek in Europe at the time) was John Capodistrias (1776–1830).

Born on the Venetian-held Greek island of Corfu to an aristocratic family, Count Capodistrias studied medicine in Italy. During the Napoleonic Wars Russia took control of Corfu and the rest of the Ionian islands (1801–1807). At that time Capodistrias served as minister of education in the Russian protectorate of the Ionian Republic and later he went to Russia where he served with distinction in that country's foreign service eventually becoming Russia's Foreign Minister.[13] For a period of time following the end of the Napoleonic Wars Capodistrias enjoyed the confidence of Emperor Alexander I. Capodistrias was considered a political enemy of the reactionary Austrian Foreign Minister Prince Metternich. In time, Alexander came to agree with Metternich's plan of a Europe dominated by the Great Powers of the day with no consideration and accommodation of the national inspirations of various peoples. Capodistrias who (although not a liberal) was in favor of coming to an understanding with those who wanted to change the status quo, forced out of office. After retiring from Russian service Capodistrias lived in Switzerland until he was invited to become Greece's first president, a difficult job which he executed admirably for three years until he was assassinated in 1830. Capodistrias' life and career in Russia has come to epitomize the opportunities which a Greek could have in that country.

The life and career of Greeks in Russia is beyond the scope of this work but the above examples serve to illustrate the overall favorable conditions which Russia offered to Greeks at the time. Even though Greeks were emigrating to other parts of the world, Russia remained the destination of choice for most Greek immigrants. Even later in the nineteenth century, when Greek emigration to Russia decreased and that to other countries (notably the United States) increased, Russia was the one place where Greeks could still make a career in government service. Thus in the middle and late nineteenth century, a number of Greeks who lived in Russia became university professors, while others became officers in the armed forces.[14] A number of Greeks were even appointed or elected to political office. The overwhelming majority of those politicians were active in municipal affairs. Thus early in Odessa's history the Greek merchant Demetrios S. Inglezes was appointed City Leader.[15] Later on the wealthy Greek Grigorii Grigorevich Maraslis became Odessa's first elected mayor (it should be noted that like the rest of Russia's cities Odessa had a very limited electorate) and kept the office for twenty years between the 1870s and the 1890s.[16] In some cases politicians with Russian-sounding names were of Greek descent. Odessa's last mayor before the October Revolution was a certain Moiseev who had a Greek mother.[17] Odessa was not the only city which had had a Greek mayor. According to S. Kiouze-Pezas, Greek Consul-General in Taganrog in the early twentieth century, that city had had a number of Greek mayors over the years.[18] Indeed like Odessa, Taganrog was also a city where the Greeks enjoyed great financial advantages and social prestige. In an interesting historical footnote the famous Russian writer Anton Chekhov had close connections with Taganrog's Greek community. The writer's brothers and father worked in the trading house of the Vallianos Brothers. Chekhov's father spoke some Greek and had been given the opportunity to study in Athens, an offer which he declined.[19] In the 1880s, a certain Ivan Tolli, son of Greeks from Odessa, became mayor of Kiev.[20] Finally, after the 1905 October Manifesto and the establishment of the Russian Duma, Pandelis V. Synadinos, the Greek mayor of Kishinev, was elected to that body.[21]

As it has been noted earlier, during the nineteenth century more Greek immigrants chose Russia as their place of destination than any other country in the world. In this century the United States of America supplanted Russia as the destination of choice among Greeks. Due to that phenomenon, a certain degree of comparison between the lot of Greeks in those two countries might be in order. According to Cohen, modern diasporas share certain common characteristics.[22]

1) Dispersal from an original homeland, often traumatically, to two or more foreign regions;
2) alternatively, the expansion from a homeland in search of work, in pursuit of trade or to further colonial ambitions;
3) a collective memory and myth about the homeland, including its location and history;
4) an idealization of the ancestral home and to protect and/or create it;
5) Development of a "return" movement;
6) strong ethnic consciousness over long period of time based on a sense of distinctiveness;
7) A troubled relationship with the host societies;
8) a sense of empathy and solidarity with co-ethnic members in other countries;
9) The possibility of a distinctive creative, enriching life in host countries with a tolerance for pluralism.

In general, the Greeks who emigrated to both Russia and later to the US were motivated mainly by economic factors, although the need to leave due to war was not that rare. Both Greek communities conform to Cohen's paradigm, points 1-6 and 8. Point 5, development of a return movement, was never (in the experience of the Greeks of Russia and the US) a mass movement, as was the case with the Jewish diaspora before the creation of Israel. It was rather an individual goal of many, if not most, of Greek immigrants. In both instances, the Greeks prospered in their adoptive land (that is Cohen's point 9, although Imperial Russia did not have a reputation of "tolerance for pluralism"). In their land of origin both Russia and the United States had the reputation of the land of opportunity. Finally, the Greeks of Russia and its counterpart in the United States created their own community institutions and associations. A closer look at the conditions of the Greek immigrants in the two countries reveal some important differences as well.

During the height of Greek emigration to Russia that country was governed by an autocratic, at times oppressive regime, while the United

States was from its inception governed by democratic principles. Thus one would expect Russia's Greeks to face certain difficulties in contrast to those choosing the United States as their adopted country. In reality quite often the opposite was true. Whereas the Greeks in America were a minority amidst an alien culture, those of Russia were, by virtue of their Orthodox faith and long friendly Greek-Russian relations, foreigners but not aliens. Also, while Russia made it official policy to attract Greek immigrants to settle, the United States perceived the influx of non-Protestant minorities as a threat to the Anglo-Saxon dominant culture of the country and through immigration restrictions attempted to limit the number of Greeks (among others) who were allowed in the country.[23] To a great extent the attitudes of the citizens of the host countries towards the Greeks mirrored that of their governments. While some Russians might have felt resentment at those foreigners who prospered in their country, the Greeks were, generally speaking, left unmolested. This is remarkable given the fact that periodically Russian mobs turned against another merchant minority, the Jews, with tragic results. In all the pogroms which occurred in South Russia every ten years or so between the 1850s and 1905 there is only one instance in which the mob turned against the Greeks. That occurred in Kiev in 1905 but the damage was minimal as the Greeks fought back forcing their attackers to move to easier targets.[24] On the other hand, violence against Greek immigrants in the United States was, if not common, not unheard off either. In the most notorious case an armed mob attacked Greek businesses and individuals in South Omaha, Nebraska while other such incidents occurred in Idaho, Kansas, and Chicago. In some instances the local authorities looked the other way and even blamed the victims for provoking the attacks.[25] In an ironic way the Greeks who settled in autocratic Russia were less anxious for their personal safety and property than their compatriots who lived in a free and democratic country. Whereas the Greek community of early twentieth century United States faced the problem outlined by Cohen as point 7—"A troubled relationship with the host societies"—that of Russia was welcomed on the official level and left unmolested by Russian society as a whole.

As it has been noted earlier Russia's Greeks were involved in many aspects of Russian life and in many different parts of the empire. As the reader may have noticed, the world of Greek immigrants in Russia was a man's world. Greek women were usually confined to the domestic sphere. However, a number of women, almost exclusively from the wealthy and aristocratic classes, became involved in charity and donated money to Greek communities throughout Russia. For a period of time during the late nineteenth century Kalliroe Paren (1861–1940) was director and teacher at the Girls' school in Odessa. Paren was one of the early Greek feminist and from 1887 publisher of the newspaper "*Η Εφημερίς των Κυριών*" (Ladies' Journal) which was the earliest Greek publication with a feminist message.[26] However most of Greek activity in Russia (as well as the largest number of immigrants) was concentrated on the South and Odessa was the Russian urban center with the largest concentration of Greeks. When Russian troops took control of Khatzhibei (1789), there were already some Greeks living in the fort.[27] Soon the original Greek inhabitants were reinforced with settlers from the fringes of the Russian Empire as well as refugees from Greece.[28] The Russian government made Greek settling in and around Odessa an attractive proposition by offering free land, money and other incentives.[29] Some of the earliest Greek settlers were men, and their families, who served in a Greek paramilitary unit in Russian service. Indeed, the commander of that unit was for awhile *ex officio* leader of that early Greek community. The first commander, Colonel Kesoglou, became the middleman between the Greek settlers and the Russian government. Kesoglou was given a tract of land inside Odessa's city limits as well as money to build houses. It was Kesoglou's responsibility to settle Greeks in those houses, collect rents and make sure that the buildings were kept in good order. Kesoglou's decisions had the power of law and there was no right of appeal to a higher authority. The system generated abuses and by some accounts Kesoglou's regime was far from ideal. He favored some settlers over others, was quick to evict settlers who could not pay their rent and did not always release to the community all the money entrusted to him by the Russian government.[30] According to the Marxist historian John Kordatos four fifths of the early Greek settlers died within a few years of their arrival. Although it is reasonable to assume that deaths through disease and hardship in a semi-civilized area did occur, Kordatos' numbers are suspect.[31]

In examining the phenomenon of Greek emigration to Russia, sooner or later one has to deal with the question of numbers. There is no clear way to establish the number of Greeks who lived in Russia in general and Odessa in particular. For many years the Russian government itself had no knowledge of the exact numbers of immigrants. It is known, however, that in 1794 there was a Greek elementary school in Odessa which had an enrollment of 72 pupils. Soon there was a need to establish another such school and that was done in 1800 when a second elementary school was created with a student body of 70.[32] Thus one can assume that by the beginning of the nineteenth century the Greek community of Odessa grew appreciably. In 1816, the Russian government counted 11,500 Greeks in the city, a number that some historians believe to represent the high water mark of Odessa's Greek population.[33] After that time, there are no reliable statistics of the Greek population in Odessa until the government census of 1897 (considered by most historians as reliable although there is never an explanation as to why this particular census was better than the rest). During that census the inhabitants of Odessa were classified according to their native language.[34]

TABLE 5
The Ten Largest Groups by Native Language in Odessa, 1897

Language	Males	Females	Total	% of Total
Russian	104,173	89,081	193,254	50.78
Yiddish	61,156	62,530	123,686	32.50
Ukrainian	13,224	8,302	21,526	5.66
Polish	11,174	5,864	17,038	4.48
German	5,253	4,680	9,933	2.61
Greek	3,166	1,847	5,013	1.32
Tatar	970	459	1,429	0.38
Armenian	929	470	1,399	0.37
French	423	701	1,124	0.30
Belorussian	799	296	1,095	0.29

The same census gives the number of Greeks in the whole of the empire as 62,470, a number so low as to call into question the accuracy of the whole undertaking.[35]

According to the above numbers, the Greek-speaking population of Odessa was rather small. It is also interesting to note that the male to female ratio was overwhelmingly in favor of males. This is true for most of the other sub-categories of Odessa residents (with the exemption of Yiddish and French speakers), although the Greek ratio seems to be unusually unbalanced. The above fact has been interpreted to mean that the Greek community of Odessa contained an unusually high number of young males who were transients looking for work.[36] Such analysis does not take into account other possibilities which might point to different findings. It is quite possible that a large number of Greek men were married to women of Slavic descent or Russian-speaking Greek women.[37] On the subject of the Greek population in Russia, Greek sources tend to give higher numbers. This is due to the fact that whereas Russian sources use language as the characteristic of ethnicity, Greek sources claim that a large number of Russian-speakers were in fact Greeks. To give one example of the inability of language to define ethnicity, during that same 1897 census five people who declared Greek as their mother tongue were in fact Jews.[38] The Greek Consul-General in Odessa reported to the Greek Ministry of Foreign Affairs that in 1911 there were 550,000 Greeks in the empire, 10,000 of them were living in Odessa of whom 7,000 were Greek citizens.[39] According to the *Union of Greek Refugees from Russia*, there were 600,000 Greeks in the empire just before the outbreak of the First World War. Most of those Greeks (2/3) were living in rural areas and were mostly Russian-speakers. Of the 200,000 city dwellers 30,000 lived in Odessa.[40] Other Greek sources report the number of Greeks in pre-Revolutionary Russia as being from as low as 207,536[41] to as high as 800,000 and in some cases even higher.[42] Clearly some of the above numbers are unreliable and the result of speculation. Soviet era statistics, while not pertinent to the number of Greeks in earlier years, might help in forming an educated opinion. According to the 1959 Soviet census there were 309,000 Greeks in the Soviet Union.[43] As late as 1989 Soviet census data recorded 357,957 Greeks living in the whole of the Soviet Union and about 125,000 of them spoke the Greek language.[44] For Ukraine alone the numbers in 1989 were 98,600 and 18,000 respectively.[45] Finally, according to Greek government calculations, between the years 1919–1926 about 260,000 Greeks left Russia for Greece.[46]

All the numbers have done little to clarify the picture of Greek emigration to Russia. At times it seems that various writers used whichever number suited their point of view with little regard of how small or large this number was compared with the rest of available data. If one compares the relative high numbers given by Greek sources, as well as the low number given by official Imperial authorities, with those given by the Soviet regime one has to conclude that the truth mast be somewhere between the two extremes. Considering that about 200,000 Greeks left the country after the revolution, and that some tens of thousands entered the Soviet Union as political refugees in the late 1940s (at the end of the Greek Civil War), the 309,000 reported by Soviet authorities in 1959 appears close to the truth. Thus, it is not unreasonable to suggest that the Greeks of Russia before 1917 numbered close to 500,000 with the vast majority of them being Russian-speakers. A similar unscientific calculation should conclude that the Greek population of Odessa (both Russian-speaking and Greek-speaking) was over 15,000. These numbers were relatively small (considering that the population of the empire and of Odessa at the time were 126,411,736 and 630,000 respectively).[47] Thus K. Papoulides was correct when he noted that: "The number of Greeks in Odessa was always small. We should reject the conventional wisdom that existed, or still exists, that Odessa was a Greek city."[48]

II

Since Odessa was the main center of New Russia's import/export trade, it was only natural that as a result it attracted men who already were, or wanted to be, merchants. The country's natural resources, coupled with the government's generous support to the early settlers (as well as its liberal expenditures in municipal improvements) were instrumental in helping those who had the capital and the know-how to prosper in business. The above reasons were helpful to all foreigners who emigrated to Russia. On top of that, the Greek immigrants had the advantage of common religion, and long friendly association, with the host country which made them a special minority among the many new minorities which entered the empire at the same time. This closer relationship however, does not explain the reason why Greek merchant houses came to dominate Europe's eastern trade. (In 1850 300 out of the 400 members of Britain's Eastern Commodity Exchange, which was called "The Baltic Center" and was by far the most important in Europe, were Greeks.)[49] Indeed, by emphasizing all the advantages that the Greeks found in Russia, historians neglect to look closer and attempt to find what were the special qualities which made the Greeks as successful as they were.

Some of the Greek merchants who made Odessa their base where past masters in the trade business. They had a long history of engaging in trade, first in their country of birth and later in the European markets. Starting with little capital, they were able, through hard work, luck, and ingenuity to amass immense fortunes.[50] Thus, when people like Ralli, Rodokanaki, Scaramangas and others, went to Russia they had knowledge, capital to invest and connections to utilize. Next to experience and capital, the Greeks brought with them family connections which were the secret of their success. Before telegraph and telephone, automobiles and airplanes, international merchant houses were dependent on the individual managers of each of their offices. One needed people of great trust to put in charge of far away operations. The Greek merchants were clannish by nature and trusted only family members or people who came from the same home district to fill positions of importance. Thus the Ralli brothers had a family member (either by blood or marriage) in charge of each of its offices. One brother was in London, another in Odessa, a third in Calcutta and the last in New York. An Argenti (related to the Ralli family by marriage) was in charge in Marseilles while a Rodokanaki-Ralli looked after the firm's interests in Leghorn.[51] A brief look at some individuals in London's Greek commercial community illustrates the clannish nature of their lives and trucks their movements. Of the four Mavrocordatos men (from the untitled branch of the princely family) Emmanuel (1830–1909) was born in Constantinople, spent many years in London and died there. His wife was a Ralli. His brother James (1834–1900) was also born in Constantinople, lived in London and died in Athens. His wife was a Skylitzi, another well-known merchant family. Their sister was married to a relative, Michael Mavrocordatos (1817–1892) who was born on the island of Chios (the family's land of origin) and spent his life in Italy where he died. He was made a noble of the Grand Duchy of Tuscany. Another relative, also Michael (1843–1920) was born in Leghorn and died in London. There were three Rodokanaki.

Theodoros was born in Chios in 1797 and died in Odessa in 1882, he was a leading member of Odessa's Greek community and the first president of the Greek Benevolent Association. Petros was born in Leghorn in 1831 and died in England in 1899 while Michael was born in Chios in 1821, grew in Marseilles, married a member of the Petrokokkinos merchant family and died in London in 1901. From the two Petrokokkinos in London, Alexander (1814–1900) was born in Chios, married a member of the Sevastopoulos merchant family in Trieste and died in London. His kinsman Eustratios (1822–1897) was born in Trieste and died in London. His two brothers were active in the family business in Liverpool and Calcutta. The Ralli family was active in London as well. There were ten active members of that family in London's Greek community. Alexandra Ralli (1841–1903) was the wife of Peter and daughter of John Ralli. She was born in Odessa, spent some time in Marseilles and died in London. Despina Ralli was active in London but she and her husband Anthony, were established in New York City. Alexander (1852–1927) was born in Odessa and died in London. His wife was also a Ralli. Anthony Ralli, not the husband of Despina, was born in Chios in 1812 and died in London in 1882. George was born in Liverpool in 1858 and died in Vichy in 1910. Eustartios was born in Chios in 1800 and died in London in 1884 but spent most of his life in Paris and Manchester. Theodore Ralli (London 1849–1906) spent many years in New York. Kostis (Liverpool 1860–1910) was married to a Ralli while Pantias (Chios 1793- London 1865) was married to a Skaramangas. Stephen Ralli (1829–1902) spent most of his life in France. This short list illustrates the mobility of the Greek commercial elite, its members being active in three continents, six countries and over ten cities. It also shows the intermarriage between those families, an ingredient important to their success.[52] It is interesting to note that all of the families mentioned above came from the Greek island of Chios pointing again to the fact that family connections and area of origin were of paramount importance. The importance of family connections and place of origin in the grain trade is illustrated by an episode in the life of George Soures (1853–1919). Soures was a popular Greek satirical poet who was nominated for the Nobel Prize of Literature in 1906. His mother was from the island of Chios and was related to someone with business interests in Azov and Taganrog. As soon as Soures finished high school he was sent to Taganrog to work with his kinsman. Soures was not a good businessman and his stay in Russia was brief (July-September 1870). In later years he wrote a poem titled *Εγώ-Είς Ρωσίαν* (Me in Russia) in which he described in a humorous way his trials and tribulations in that country.[53] The Greek merchants were not only practitioners of networking. Their business practices, particularly those connected with the grain trade, were some of the early ancestors of today's marketing and quality control techniques.

The way the Greeks transacted their business was basically as follows: A ship full of wheat started its long voyage from Odessa to any one of the western ports, usually London. While the ship was slowly making its way West, a small sample of its cargo was sent ahead with a fast courier. Once the courier reached his destination, the local representative of the Greek firm, most often a relative or compatriot, sold the whole cargo on the basis of the quality of the small sample. This was possible only if the traders in the West trusted the integrity and business practices of the Greek firm.[54] This way of doing business was profitable because it allowed the Greeks to sell their merchandise ahead of their competitors but also because it saved on transportation expenses. Since the ship was still on route a quick messenger could divert it to the new port where its cargo had been sold. As a result, the Greeks controlled the commercial routes to and from Russia.[55]

The fact that the Greek merchants of Odessa were enriching themselves became evident as early as 1812. In that year Napoleon invaded Russia and in many areas of the empire there were volunteer collections of money to support the Russian war effort against Bonaparte. The city of Odessa contributed 280,546 rubles for that cause. Governor-general Richelieu gave 40,000 rubles from his personal fortune. The nobles of Odessa gave 28,316 rubles while the rest of the city's Russian citizens gave 94,000 rubles. The non-Greek foreigners who lived in Odessa gave 18,230 rubles. The Greeks contributed 100,000 rubles.[56] A few years later it was reported that seven of the ten richest Odessa merchants were Greeks while in 1851 Fedor Rodokanaki was Odessa's wealthiest merchant with annual turnover of 2,000,000 rubles.[57]

After the Crimean War (1853–1856), the Greek trading houses retreated and were eventually replaced by German and Jewish merchants. This gradual loss of prestige has often been portrayed as the beginning of Greek decline in Odessa's (and South Russia's) economic life.[58] This conclusion is incorrect because it is based on the premise that if a Greek firm closed its doors the owner was impoverished or was forced to retire.[59] It simply was another chapter in Greek-Jewish commercial competition. The competition intensified during the second half of the nineteenth century, as these two ethnic groups continue to be the middlemen for Russia's trade.[60] If the Greeks declined as grain merchants in Russia, they directed their activities to other countries, where they became engaged in other money making enterprises, and changed their life-style. Regarding the claim that Jewish competition drove the Greeks out of trade it should be noted that the Greeks themselves were fiercely competing with each other. Indeed, by the middle of the nineteenth century, those Greek merchants from the islands (mainly Chios) were pushed to the margins by newcomers, Greeks from Asia Minor.[61] That competition did not stop but it continued into the twentieth century with such vigor as to be commented about in a negative manner by an official of the Greek Ministry of Foreign Affairs.[62] In any case, many Greeks opted to move their enterprises and capital outside Russia. Many had had long business association with other European countries and it was easy for them to transfer their capital there. Others looked into new areas of the world. Thus the firm of Ralli Brothers Ltd. opened offices in Calcutta and Bombay, Alexandria, and New York. Finally, there were those who either decided to retire in Greece or took advantage of favorable opportunities and sent their capital to the country of their birth.[63]

The late nineteenth and early twentieth centuries witnessed the diversification of Greek economic activities throughout Russia. To be sure, many Greeks remained involved in the grain trade, and although not as important as before, were still prospering.[64] According to K. Papoulides who compiled a partial list of Greek economic activity in South Russia,[65] 36 Greek trading houses of the first order were still active in the region in 1897.[66] Of them only *seven* were involved in the grain trade while four more became bread merchants.[67] Most of the firms were doing business in a number of commodities simultaneously, mainly fruits, sugar, and tobacco. Others were import-export firms. Many of those firms were doing brisk import business with a great variety of products many of which came from the Far East and Africa. Some Greek products were also popular, especially the Metaxa and Cambas alcoholic beverages.[68] Other firms were into paper import/export, and iron trade. Besides trade, Greeks were also involved in manufacturing. Papoulides records forty-one Greek manufacturers in Russia. Many dealt with industries such as flour milling and tobacco processing, but others were involved in the iron industry, brick making, meat and other food processing, soft and alcoholic drink production and cosmetics manufacturing and trade.[69] Other Greeks were involved in banking and insurance while still others were into mining.[70] A look at the Greek newspapers published in Odessa is an interesting exercise as the advertisements reveal more information about Greek commercial activities. It seems that many Greeks were involved with what would be called today "hospitality industry." Restaurants, coffee and tea shops but above all else grocery stores and hotels. One has the impression that in Odessa's commercial and fashionable neighborhoods every corner was occupied by a Greek grocery store or hotel. The hotels had their own tea rooms and restaurants and usually advertised the fact that the establishment was clean and respectable and that the management was Greek. The Greek-language newspapers of Odessa is an untapped source of general information of the city as a whole and particularly its Greek community. The newspaper *Κόσμος* (The World), which was established in 1906, was published three times a week and was the most "complete" of them all inasmuch as it had local, national and international news, business reports, advertisements, etc. In 1909 Petros Konstantinides, the editor of "The World" obtained permission to publish a Russian-language paper called "Russian World" (*Russkii Mir*). The other three Greek-language papers of Odessa were the weeklies *Φώς* (The Light), *Αναγέννηση* (Renaissance) and *Ελληνικός Αστήρ* (Greek Star). *Renaissance* was a Venizelist paper (that means that it supported the liberal pro-western Greek statesman Eleftherios K. Venizelos who was feuding with the Greek King Konstantine I over Greece's position vis-à-vis the two warring factions during the First World War) and as such attracted some of the prominent community leaders during the period between the February and October Revolutions. There was also a Greek royalist paper named "The Sun"(*Ήλιος*) which was published for a while. The existence of these newspapers in Odessa is testament to the vitality of the Greek community in that city. For many years, the biggest and best department store in Odessa was that of the Petrokokkinos family.[71] During the period of time under consideration Greek financial activities were diversified and a large number of Greeks depended on returns from bonds, stocks, government securities and rents from city properties.[72] In this case, as in many others, G. G. Maraslis can be viewed as a prime example. His father, G. I. Maraslis was a rich merchant but the son did not follow in his father's footsteps. Since he had no need to work, G. G. Maraslis sold the family business and devoted his life to municipal service, service to the Greek community and patronage of the arts. Activities which resulted in his ennoblement by the Russian Tsar. Out of his personal funds Maraslis built schools, and other public buildings in Russia, Greece and Bulgaria (before emigrating to Russia the Maraslis family was part of the Greek diaspora which lived in what later became Bulgaria). He even donated 58 volumes of Greek books to the United States Library of Congress.[73] Maraslis' fortune was invested in stocks and bonds as well as properties in Odessa. In 1873 Maraslis owned over a dozen pieces of choice real estate in Odessa valued at 300,000 rubles which constituted 0.7% of the value of all private buildings in the city.[74] At the time of his death in 1907, Maraslis' net worth was reported to be 2,000,000 silver rubles in liquid assets and 10,000,000 in real estate, a fortune equivalent to over $100,000,000 in today's rates.[75] If place of residence attests to a person's financial position, then the Greeks of Odessa were comfortable indeed. In 1892 46.8% of Odessa's Greeks lived in the city's two best neighborhoods, no other ethnic group had such a high percentage of affluent members.[76]

The late nineteenth and early twentieth centuries comprise what has become known as the "Third Circle" of Greek economic activity in the Black Sea littoral. This period of time is characterized, among other things, by a dramatic increase in Greek ship ownership.[77] Greeks have been ship owners of note for many centuries and had dominated the trading routes of eastern Mediterranean.[78] Odessa had been for many years a popular port of call for Greek ships and part of the capital of Greek merchants from Odessa was always tied in ownership of cargo ships. According to the reports of the Greek merchant John Ralli, United States Consul in Odessa, traffic in the city's harbor by ships under Greek flag increased steadily. In 1836 Greek ship traffic in Odessa harbor was in fifth place, behind that of Russia, Britain, Austria and Sardinia. By 1844 it had reached fourth place and in 1848 171 Greek ships entered Odessa harbor as opposed to 274 British and 189 Sardinian.[79] In 1890 Greek shipping in Odessa had fallen back to fourth place but was holding steady.[80] By 1911 Greek shipping was the biggest in Russian waters while in the port of Odessa it was second only to the British.[81] In reality, Greek shipping throughout this period was even higher than recorded because many Greek ships were sailing under foreign flags, mainly

Russian and Turkish.[82] As a result of the volume of Greek maritime traffic in South Russia, the well-known insurance group Lloyd's of London gave preferential insurance rates to Greek ship owners.[83]

The last reason which might explain, in part, why Greeks retreated from Odessa's commercial activities is change in their life-style. While trade was a profession which promised ample financial rewards, it did not confer to its practitioner social standing. In most European countries of the time those who were involved in trade were viewed as socially inferior. In many cases people who had made a fortune in trade were expected to retire and through land acquisition, and marriage of their offspring to the nobility, enter the upper class.[84] This is what happened, to a large extent, with the Greek merchants of Russia. In K. Papoulides' catalogue of Greek economic activities in Russia there are fifty-four individuals and families recorded as landowners.[85] These individuals owned approximately a total of 390,000 acres. A number of these landowners had estates of 1,000-2,000 acres but estates of 20,000-30,000 acres were equally common. While some of the landowners were the descendants of aristocrats (mainly former princes, *hospodars*, of Walachia and Moldavia) most were people who had made money in trade. Thus the names of Princes Mourouzi and Cantacouzenos appear next to those of Ralli and Maraslis as owners of extensive estates. A number of Greeks married into the Russian or European nobility thus defusing even more the distinction between the groups.[86] During the late nineteenth and early twentieth centuries a number of Greeks, scions of old merchant families, were ennobled by the tsar either for service to the state, like G. G. Maraslis, or as a sign of special favor. It has been already noted that two members of the banking family of Mavrocordatos were ennobled, one becoming a prince, but they were not the only ones. Most of them like Peter Ralli and Pericles Rodokanaki became non-titled nobles of the Russian Empire.[87] A number of them, however, received titles either from the tsar or some other European monarch. In this case, like many others, the Ralli family had more than its fair share. Besides those family members who became non-titled nobles of the Russian Empire, one Ralli became a Baron of the Austrian Empire, a Rodokanaki-Ralli became a Count of the Kingdom of Italy, while the head of the English branch of the family became a Baronet of the United Kingdom.[88]

In the 1860s and 1870s the Greeks of Odessa, both merchants as well as nobles, were looking for ways to make their mark in their community.[89] That activism, prompted by self-serving motives as well as genuine attempt to address a need, were instrumental in the creation of the Greek community's crown achievement, the Greek Benevolent Association of Odessa (*Grecheskoe blagotvoritelno obshestvo*).

IV
The Greek Benevolent Association of Odessa

Imperial Russia, being governed by an absolutist and at times repressive regime, was not a fertile ground for the creation and operation of civic groups. The idea of non-government sponsored and controlled corporate entities was rejected by the regime which believed that sooner or later such "clubs" would come under the influence of anti-government forces.[1] Such corporations as were allowed to exist were ostensibly non-political in nature. Well known international associations such as the Masons existed and attracted many powerful individuals as members but even they were restricted by the government and it was not uncommon for police informants to infiltrate their ranks. Since Russia had problems with many of its minorities, it was deemed dangerous to allow civic groups based on ethnicity to exist as those could easily become hotbeds of opposition to the regime. During the reign of Nicholas I (1825–1855), new restrictions were placed on what might be viewed as civic groups. Since the reign of Nicholas started with the suppression of a revolt organized by an illegal group connected with the Masons and other secret organizations, the new emperor was particularly concerned with the activities of Russia's civic groups in general. The existence of legal groups with political goals or ethnic background as their main characteristics was not allowed. The regime was suspicious of volunteer organizations because the idea of any type of citizens' initiative was considered dangerous. Thus the only legal civic groups allowed in Imperial Russia, that is prior to the Great Reforms of the 1860s, were charity organizations provided that they stayed non-political and continued to be the recipients of official favor.[2]

From the time Russia became a Christian country, tenth century, and up to the reign of Peter the Great, organized charity was by law the realm of the Russian Orthodox Church. In 1718 and 1721 Peter the Great's legislation made the municipal governments and local landowners, in urban and rural areas, responsible for the local poor. As was the case with many other Petrine reforms Catherine the Great continue the trend to "secularize" organized charity by creating special administrative bodies (1775) responsible for the wellbeing of the poorest citizens.[3] In the spirit of the Western European Enlightenment, of which Catherine was an admirer but not always a practitioner, private philanthropic associations were allowed.[4] The Imperial Philanthropic Society which was created in 1816 might have been Russia's first civic charitable association. The influence of the government in the Society was so strong as to make it a state entity in all but name.[5] In any case, the Imperial Philanthropic Society introduced the concept of private initiative into the country, especially since it did not confine its activities to the capital but opened a number of provincial chapters.[6] As it has been noted earlier, Nicholas I limited the number of such civic groups and relaxation of that state vigilance was not achieved until after the tsar's death in 1855 and the relative openness of the society that accompanied the "reform" efforts of the early sixties. As a result, whereas in 1855 there were only about 40 private benevolent associations in Russia the number ballooned to 348 by 1880.[7] To be sure, the government kept tight control of such entities but the general relaxation by the state allowed even minority groups to establish their own associations. Most of the time, though not always, the minority organizations were forced by the state to use the Russian language in their official transactions.[8]

The Greek Benevolent Association of Odessa (GBAO) was neither the only nor the first Greek civic group formed by the Greek immigrants in that city. Indeed, Greek corporate groups existed in Odessa (in one form or another) almost from the founding of the city.[9] As it has been already noted, in the late 1790s the Greek battalion of Odessa, a military unit composed mainly by recent refugees from Morea and the Aegean Islands, assumed functions which went outside the traditional military sphere. The commanders of that unit, first Colonel Kesoglou and then his successors, acted as the leaders of the Greek community as a whole and were recognized as such by the Russian government. Strictly speaking, this early corporate entity was not a civic one. It had been imposed from above and its members, being soldiers, did not have a say on the day to day business of that body. That early arrangement was a convenient way which the Russian government devised to deal with the new refugees. Instead of having to deal with numerous individuals, the Russian government delegated authority to one person who acted as the intermediary, thus simplifying things. The government did not have to go through the expense of appointing bureaucrats to deal with the new immigrants. Additionally, by keeping the above arrangement along military lines, the government was able to exercise strict control. The intermediary was not only a government official charged with the supervision of the immigrants' affairs, but also their commanding officer. During the early years of the nineteenth century, as most Greeks in Odessa were civilians, the battalion's civic importance declined and it soon became a military unit alone. What that early imperfect "club" did was to introduce the idea of the collective in the Greeks of Odessa as well as making the Russian government amenable to the idea of Greek corporatism.

The second Greek organization to be formed in Odessa was more typical of civic groups. In 1808, the growing Greek community of Odessa decided to built its own church. Thus the Greek Orthodox Church of the Holy Trinity was built and it became the focal point of Greek life in the city.[10] In order to finance the building of the church, the Greek merchants, starting in 1804, contributed 15 kopecks for each ton of wheat passing through their businesses.[11] Over the years, the church was enlarged and redesigned and according to some accounts was the most beautiful church in the city.[12] The Church of the Holy Trinity survives to this day and is located on Pushkin Street. It is indeed a beautiful building but whether or not it was the most beautiful church in nineteenth-century Odessa one can not ascertain. The Russian Orthodox Cathedral of the Transfiguration, located on the street with the same name in Cathedral Square, was also a beautiful structure but unfortunately it was totally destroyed in the 1930s during Stalin's persecution of religion. Thus, ironically, today Odessa's Cathedral Square has no cathedral. In 1864, in order to take care of the needs of the Greek Orthodox Church of Odessa, the Greek community instituted a board of trustees which acted as the custodian, the Brotherhood of the Holy Trinity (Η εν Οδησσώ Ελληνική Αδελφότης της Αγίας Τριάδος).[13] The rank and file membership to that association was open to "Every Greek Orthodox and every pious philhellene...."[14] The board controlled the church's property and took care of all its expenses. While that church board was a true civic organization, it was also far from an open body as its members were selected rather than elected. The majority of the Greeks of Odessa played no role in the administration of their church's affairs. The elitist structure of that early Greek organization is manifested in the fact that at some point there was serious thought of creating another Greek Orthodox parish which would totally exclude the lower classes from its flock.[15] The board of trustees of the Greek Orthodox Church of the Holy Trinity remained in existence until 1917 but beginning in the late 1870s, it became an appendix of the GBAO which assumed responsibility and control.

Another Greek organization in Odessa was the most famous of them all. In 1814 three Greek immigrants created a secret society whose goal was the violent overthrow of Ottoman rule in Greece. This was the famous Φιλική Εταιρία (Friendly Society) which indeed ultimately succeeded in its goals.[16] The Friendly Society was not, strictly speaking, an Odessa organization since it accepted Greeks from all parts of the world and soon after its creation it moved from Odessa as its founding members and other leaders dispersed in order to proselytize others to the cause. Nevertheless it was created and had a presence in Odessa. The Friendly Society was organized on quasi-Masonic lines, with various degrees, officers, and initiation ceremonies. In many respects, it was similar to other such illegal organizations which existed in Russia at the time. There is speculation that by 1820 the Greek Friendly Society was in contact with the members of the conspiratorial Southern Society which was responsible for the Decembrist Revolt of 1825. The Friendly Society itself dissolved voluntarily in 1821 once its goal of starting a revolt against the Turks materialized. By then the Russian authorities had discovered the Society and from that time on all attempts by the Greeks of Odessa to organize were viewed with suspicion. Indeed, shortly after the breakout of the Greek revolt (February 1821), the Greeks of Odessa created an organization whose goal was strictly philanthropic, namely the assistance of the thousands of Greeks who were suffering as a result of the revolt. This organization was named The Greek Philanthropic Society of Odessa (Γρεκική Φιλανθρωπική Εταιρία), and it was short-lived.[17] Created in August of 1821, it was dissolved in December of the same year due to the pressure of the Russian authorities which could not believe that any Greek organization was without political aims.[18] It appears that the suspicions of the Russian government were not without merit; almost all the members of the dissolved Friendly Society who were still in Odessa became members of the new organization. Grigorii Maraslis, father of the more famous Grigorii Grigorevich Maraslis, who had allowed one of his properties to be used for the secret meetings of the Friendly Society (the same building which now houses the Odessa branch of the Foundation for Hellenic Culture) was also a generous contributor to the Philanthropic Society. The Russian police put the members of that organization under surveillance and in time the organization died. It should be noted though that by December of 1821 Russian authorities, organizations and individuals, were busy helping the victims of the Greek revolt and in that respect the function of the Philanthropic Society was being fulfilled by others. Not everyone accepts the above as the true course of events. According to K. Avgitides the Greek Philanthropic Society was primarily a revolutionary organization just like the one it had replaced. Avgitides believes that during the Greek revolt the West was openly hostile to Greek aspirations while Russia was covertly supporting them. As soon as the Greek revolt occurred, the West through newspaper articles attacked the Greeks and the Friendly Society. Russia had to go along with the rest of Europe but privately continue to help the Greeks. Allowing the Friendly Society to wither away was one way to pacify western demands. Avgitides even claims that the Philanthropic Society was the equivalent of a Greek provisional government. As proof of his claim he notes that the revolutionary authorities of two Greek islands (Hydra and Psara) sent letters to the Philanthropic Society informing it of their activities. Avgitides also claims that the Philanthropic Society continued to operate until 1851, that is thirty years more than most historians believe that it existed.[19] Avgitides is the only historian who claims that the Philanthropic Society was a revolutionary organization and that it lasted for thirty years. The fact that a number of individuals active in the Friendly Society were also active in the Philanthropic Society points to the close connection between the two organizations. It is hard to believe that as soon as the Greek revolt occurred the Friendly Society dissolved voluntarily, for no apparent reason, and that it disappeared without a trace. Those two facts strengthen the claim that the Philanthropic Society was supporting the Greek revolt actively. That does not mean however that it was a provisional government. The fact that the authorities of two Greek islands sent letters to Odessa does not prove that they asked for guidance or that they recognized the Philanthropic Society as Greece's governing body. Indeed during the early years of the Greek revolt there were a number of bodies in Greece proper which claimed to be Greece's government (the Peloponnesian Senate and the Athenian Arios Pagos come to mind as such governing bodies) but had little universal support. Avgitides' blind spot is his insistence that the Russian government fostered the Greek revolt while the rest of Europe was uniformly against it. In order to strengthen his point, he builds the Philanthropic Society into something that never was and in the process he casts doubts on the accuracy of the rest of his work. Although one might accept as fact that the Philanthropic Society had a revolutionary goal, the claims that it was such a powerful institution and that it lasted for thirty years may be viewed as exaggerations, to say the least.

Between the founding and dissolution of the Friendly Society (1814–1821) yet another Greek civic organization had come into existence. If there was an organization which was the spiritual ancestor of the GBAO that was the Board of Trustees of the Greek Commercial School (also known as Greek Boys' School). This school was founded in 1817 as a training facility for young men of modest or no means who could become clerks in the various trading houses of Odessa. It is interesting to note that the creation of such a school was promoted by the secret organization Friendly Society and the governor of New Russia Count Langeron.[20] Like the GBAO, the Boys'' School had a written charter which outlined the scope of the organization. Also like the GBAO the Boys' School had considerable property, both real estate and cash, to manage. Finally, both organizations provided for elected officers, and a system of checks and balances. It should be noted, however, that unlike the GBAO, the Boys' School was clearly an elitist organization. There were many limitation placed upon the members of the school board. National origin alone was not enough. The members had to be either the founders of the school or their direct male descendants. Others had to be living or own property within the boundaries of the original free port of Odessa (which meant that they were either owners of commercial property, and thus well-off financially, or lived in the upper class districts of the city). Finally, all members had to be graduates of institutions of higher learning either Russian or foreign. Clearly the members of the governing body of the Boys' School wanted to keep the majority of the Greeks of Odessa spectators, rather than actors, in matters of community affairs. As a result the number of Greek individuals involved in the affairs of the school was about 140 out of the thousands of Odessa's Greeks.[21] From the beginning, the Greek Commercial School attracted many non-Greek students: between 1833–1867 out of about

2,400 students 940 were non-Greeks representing eleven different nationalities from the numerous Russians (676 students) to one Jewish boy. That variety of nationalities among the student body continued to the end of the Imperial era.[22] The Boys' School of Odessa was a financial success not only because it received money from rich benefactors, but also because most of its students paid tuition (in the early twentieth century the school's finances were so secure that most of the students, being poor, were enrolled free of charge). Since the Boys' School was the only Greek institution of higher education in South Russia for over fifty years, it became the beneficiary of most private donations. Four Greek-owned insurance companies in Odessa contributed 30%, 20%, 5%, and 7% respectively of their net income to the school while a fifth insurance company gave 10,034 rubles between the years 1833–1835. Another source of income for the school was the rent from two buildings it owned in Odessa. Finally, all Greek sea captains were obliged to pay to the school coffers 10 rubles every time they came to Odessa. The fact that companies and sea captains agreed to pay voluntarily (even though some kind of peer pressure might have also been applied) is a testament to Greek diaspora's civic spirit especially in matters of faith and/or education.[23] In 1893, a year by no means atypical, the school enjoyed an income of 55,901 rubles from its real estate holdings alone. As a result, by the end of the Imperial era the schools' property amounted to 300,000 British golden pounds.[24] The Boys' School operated until 1917 but in the 1870s the GBAO took over its management and used its considerable cash reserves to finance its own educational projects.

The above mentioned organizations (the Greek Battalion of Odessa, the Brotherhood of the Holy Trinity, the Friendly Society, the Greek Philanthropic Society, and the Board of Trustees of the Greek Commercial School), were not the only ones that existed besides the GBAO. They are other which have left a record of their activities. In the early 1800s a number of Greek owned insurance companies earmarked 10% of their annual net income for philanthropic and educational activities for the benefit of Odessa's Greek community.[25] That amount was above and beyond what individual merchants were already contributing. From the time that the Philanthropic Society dissolved itself (1821) until the GBAO was instituted (1871) there were a number of loosely organized bodies which provided philanthropic services. These organizations are largely unknown although references of their existence appear in credible sources. An entity named, like its predecessor Greek Philanthropic Society was created in 1865 but its activities were rather sketchy.[26] Even after the establishment of the GBAO, it was not the only organization of its kind. There are references of several Greek philanthropic bodies working in Odessa although there is no sufficient information about them.[27] One writer claims that around 1900 there were three other Greek philanthropic organizations besides the GBAO, namely Αναγέννησις (Renaissance), Ήλιος (The Sun) and Φώς (The Light). This however might be a case of mistaken identity. In the early twentieth century there were three Greek language newspapers in Odessa with the above names. It would be too much of a coincidence if both the philanthropic organizations, and the newspapers (which were publications of general interest and by no means the journals of associations, clubs, etc.) were sharing the same names.[28]

Although beyond the scope of this work, a few other organizations should be mentioned in order to complete the picture. During the early 1900s there existed one or more social clubs for the Greeks of Odessa. They had no civic responsibilities and they were mostly venues for socializing.[29] At the same time, the Greek students of Odessa's university created their own organization named Ένωσις (The Union). This was a radical organization, as students' unions tend to be, and although not officially suppressed it was viewed with a mixture of contempt and hostility by some of the older members of Odessa's Greek community.[30] In 1917, between the February and October Revolutions, the various Greek organizations in Russia created an umbrella organization in order to respond to the monumental events sweeping the country. All of the Greek philanthropic organizations (all south Russian cities with sizable Greek minorities had their own civic group) were represented and the GBAO was the driving force.[31] The Greek organizations of Russia met on June 29 1917 in Taganrog and they agreed on the following seven objectives:

1) the union of all the Greek associations in Russia;
2) safeguard the independence of the Greek Orthodox Church from its Russian counterpart;
3) achieve the recognition by the Russian authorities of the Greek schools as ethnic schools and allow them to teach Greek language, history, etc.;

4) establish a Greek bank and other institutions which would help the community;
5) publish a Russian-language Greek newspaper;
6) focus on the problems of rural Russia; and
7) define and coordinate the political position of Russia's Greek community so that it could achieve its other goals.[32]

Objectives 2 and 3 deal with traditional institutions which the Greeks of Russia had come to view as national and independent from the host state. The Greeks of Russia were allowed to have churches and schools that were supervised by the state but were Greek in nature. The Greeks wanted to ensure that the new regime would continue to allow such independent entities to exist. Objectives 5 and 6 dealt with the vast majority of ethnic Greeks who were Russian speakers and lived in rural areas. A Russian-language Greek newspaper would have achieve two goals. Reach (potentially) hundreds of thousands of Greeks who spoke only Russian and make the Greek case known to the Russian public in general. By focusing on the rural question, the Greeks of Russia were again having two targets, to protect the interests of the thousands of Russian-speaking Greeks (who were mainly rural dwellers) and also protect the interests of the leaders of the Greek community many of whom were large land owners. At the time of the above meeting the Greeks of Russia were walking a tight rope. On the one hand they wanted to organize themselves on a pan-Russian level and thus take advantage of the liberal policies of the new government which was willing, unlike its tsarist predecessor, to accommodate the various minorities (the attempts by the tsarist government to Russify the Greek element were eased by the new government).[33] On the other hand, the Greeks did not want to get involved in Russia's political affairs and run the risk of being identified with a party that might lose the political battle. As if the point was not clear enough, the same Greek newspaper which reported the meeting and its outcome, editorialized, in the same issue and on the same page, that the Greeks should promote their cause but at the same time stay out of Russia's internal political affairs. In any case the October Revolution changed the country's political and social conditions and that pan-Russian body of Greeks did not play any role in the country's future.

Looking at the various Greek corporate entities which existed in Odessa throughout the Imperial era, one forms the impression that the Greek residents of that city were active in civic affairs. This is not only the opinion of some historians, many of the Greeks of Odessa themselves echoed this assessment. Some historians believe that the various Greek civic groups of Odessa were the product of the activities of a few individuals while the rest of the Greek community had little if any input in those organizations.[34] This view is reinforced by various reports which appeared in the Greek language newspapers of Odessa at the turn of the twentieth century. According to those reports, it was quite common for meetings of the Greek community of Odessa to be postponed due to the small number of individuals present. However, in at least one case a meeting was rescheduled for the following week at which time 175 individuals, out of a total membership of 523, were present.[35] The fact that most of the meetings which were postponed were scheduled on weekdays, when business were open, might account for the low turnout; after all, the membership of the GBAO was dominated by men of business. Letters to the editor in the some papers concluded that the Greek community of Odessa was not as involved in the affairs of its associations as it should have been. An anonymous letter to the editor claimed that with the notable exemption of the Friendly Society all other Greek associations were barely organized. Even such Greek institutions as the Rodokanaki School for Girls, among others, was built by donations from few wealthy donors not the product of community involvement.[36] In the case of some of the Greek organizations, it might be said that their charters did not encourage mass participation.[37] In contrast, as we shall examine later, the GBAO was an open organization with dues so low as to be open to all but the poorest Greeks. Yet it was the GBAO which time and again failed to attract enough members to its various meetings. There are two possible explanations for that phenomenon. According to the GBAO charter, members met in a scheduled general meeting once a year (before the 1st of February) at which time they approved the previous year's actions and passed the proposed budget for the new year. The meetings which the papers noted as being canceled due to low attendance were all extraordinary meetings and more often than not the reasons for their convening were not particularly pressing. When the reason for calling an extraordinary meeting was controversial then attendance was not a problem. In one case, when traditionalists and reformers within the GBAO were vying for power, the meeting of April 7, 1913 attracted 250 members.[38] Additionally, low rate of participation in GBAO might have been the result of that organization's success. From the start the GBAO was a well endowed organization which had no reason to demand more involvement by its rank and file. By the start of the twentieth century, the GBAO was so wealthy as to be totally independent of financial contributions from the members.[39] As a result, the average member of the GBAO had no reason to get involved in the day to day operations of the organization.[40] As in many civic associations, a few activists were intimately involved and these people were reelected to the GBAO offices time after time. Thus it can be argued that the Greeks of Odessa were not involved in the activities of their own civic association not because they could not, but because they chose not to due to the fact that the GBAO was running on "automatic pilot."

II

As it has been pointed above, the Greek community of Odessa was organized in some kind of corporate body throughout its existence. Since several such organizations were in operation in the 1870s, one has to wonder what was the impetus for the creation of yet another civic body. This is especially true since the Greek community was not openly split between rival groups, a condition which tends to foster the creation of splinter groups. As will be discussed below, the GBAO was created by the *de facto* leaders of Odessa's Greek community. The reason for the creation of that new organization was rooted in the rising needs within the Greek community but also due to social and political pressures both from outside forces and from within the Greek community itself.

When one looks at the great success achieved by the Greek merchants of Odessa, and the ensuing prosperity of the Greek community as a whole, one should not forget that all Greeks of that city were not wealthy. For every wealthy Greek merchant there were dozens of clerks, day laborers, small farmers who lived in much more modest circumstances. After the end of the Crimean War (1856), when Odessa experienced a relative decline as a financial center, many of those Greeks lost their jobs or experienced a decline in their standards of living. At the same time, the reputation of Odessa as the "Promised Land" among Greeks who lived in other areas continue to exist. Thus year after year a large number of Greeks came to Odessa seeking their fortune. Most of them were unsuccessful and had to return to their places of origin while others stayed back either because they made a modest living or because they had no money for the trip home. A large number of those unfortunate Greeks and their families lived in the outskirts of Odessa, in neighborhoods without running water or proper sanitation.[41] There was then clearly a need to take care of those people, and since the state was not doing so, private charity should take its place. For whatever reasons the leaders of the Greek community believed that the existing community charitable entities were unable to meet that need.

The last half of the nineteenth century saw a change in the composition of the Greek community in Odessa, and its counterparts in South Russia as well. A new wave of refugees from Asia Minor and other Turkish held areas came to the city. Whereas the old generation of Greek immigrants was content in their position and willing to blend with Russian society, the newcomers were intensely nationalistic and demanded the preservation of their national identity.[42] As more of those newcomers became successful and achieved leadership positions within the Greek community, they started pressuring for institutional changes. While there was never an open confrontation, it was implied that there was a need for the creation of Hellenocentric institutions which would not only serve the needs of the Greek community but also safeguard its national purity. It is interesting to note that the American Hellenic Educational Progressive Association (AHEPA), the Greek-American organization comparable to the GBAO, chose a different way of addressing the needs of its members. As it has been already stated, the Greeks of the US came under increasing pressure from official and unofficial quarters and faced dangers to life and property. After the end of the First World War a new wave of xenophobia swept the US and the Greeks found themselves under increasing pressure. The resurgence of the Ku Klux Klan especially in the American South was a watershed event. According to Theodoros Saloutos:

> Young Greek men working in the kitchens of restaurants in the South were taken, along with black workers, by the Ku Klux Klan on lynching "parties" into the woods, where the Greeks were

> roughed up and released, but the blacks were lynched. I do not know of any instances when a Greek was lynched by the Ku Klux Klan, but of many instances where they were intimidated and told to leave town. Another favorite warning of the Klan to the Greeks was not be "seen with a white girl."[43]

The creation of AHEPA was a direct result of the danger to the Greek immigrants in America but unlike the GBAO which "circled the wagons" and emphasized its Hellenic roots, the Order of AHEPA aimed to lessen the danger by promoting the Americanization of its members. Although AHEPA has come under criticism for its Americanization policy it should be noted that it did not attempt to severe all ties with Greece but rather make acceptable the notion that one can be an ethnic Greek and at the same time a loyal citizen of the United States.[44]

Besides internal pressures, the Greeks of Odessa were also under pressure from the outside. Russia had been good to the Greeks, giving them a safe home and opportunities to make money and a career. In turn the Greeks had been faithful subjects of the tsar (even those Greeks who were not Russian citizens). As a minority, the Greeks were trouble free for the state, and the only time they formed a political organization (the Friendly Society) the goal was action against a third party not the Russian state. While the Greeks as a minority in the Russian Empire were not cause for concern, that was not true for all of the empire's non-Russian subjects. In an attempt to unify the country and make it more manageable, the state came up with the idea of *Russification,* a policy which aimed at homogenizing Russian society by absorbing the various minorities in the Russian majority culture. The implementation of this policy became another reason for the creation of the GBAO.[45]

The Greek minority in Russia was an ideal target for Russification because by virtue of already being Orthodox it was already halfway closer to the governments goal of becoming Russians.[46] Within Russia's Greek community there was a schism concerning Russification. The established and powerful "old guard" was willing to go along with the Russian government's program. At the same time people, like Rodokanakis and Maraslis, well established and quite assimilated in Russian society, were nevertheless opposed to the Russification policy; the lines then were not clear cut. According to a report by the Greek consul in Taganrog (a city in South Russia with a sizable Greek population) the well to do Greeks exhibited no civic spirit and were Russified.[47] The Russification of the Greeks of Russia was not an explicitly stated government goal, but the pressure was there and although subtle it was felt keenly by the Greek community. The Russification policy vis-à-vis the Greeks took the form of refusing permission to establish new Greek schools and even closing some existing ones.[48] An example of the actions of the Russian government in regards to the Russification of Greeks and the reaction which it produced can be found in the history of the already mentioned Greek Commercial School. As it has already been mentioned the schools' goal (in 1817) was the education and training of young men who were destined to become clerks at various trading houses. By the 1880s, after the implementation of Russification measures and the take over of the school by the GBAO, its goals were changed. It became a school of general learning with emphasis on Greek education. In the 1910s, a new director was hired who drew the hostility of the local Russian educational authorities because of his overt actions to make the school more "Greek." According to reports by the Russian inspector of schools, the new director of the Greek Commercial School promoted and hired Greek teachers educated in Greece and discriminated against other teachers (also Greeks) who were graduates of Russian universities. He overemphasized the teaching of Greek language and history and even went so far as to stop the singing of the Russian national anthem in the school.[49] It is ironic that the Greek nationalist educator who attracted the attention of the Russian authorities was not an ethnic Greek but the British philhellene Charles Charlton. The pressure of Russification did not decrease over the years. Reporting to the Greek Ministry of Foreign Affairs the Greek Ambassador to St. Petersburg wrote in 1911 that:

> The Greek community of Sevastopol has a school in which, I have been told, there are enrolled about 400 students. Its normal function is endangered because the school inspector, following the directives of the Ministry of Education, is demanding that the school hire only Russian citizens as teachers and instruction in all grades, except kindergarten, should be in Russian. Such measures are in accordance with the educational reforms ordered by the nationalist government of Mr. Stolypin and is geared towards absorbing the foreign-speaking minorities such as the Poles, the Jews and the Baltic Germans. I visited the Minister of Education who took into

> consideration the fact that the school is supported solely by the Greek community, and that the Greek minority is not one of those whose Russification is a must for reasons of state. As a result the Minister agreed to my request and promised to send unofficial instructions to the local school authorities not to insist in the strict enforcement of the regulations. Such exemption to the general rule can not be accomplished with official intervention and I believe that the solution to similar problems will have to be found in similar fashion.[50]

In some areas of the Russian Empire Russification was rather successful. Thus in Transcaucasia towards the end of the nineteenth century, Russian was the language of instruction in 150 Greek schools while 100 Greek churches celebrated the liturgy in Russian.[51] It has been claimed that as a result of Russia's policy of Russification as many as half of Russia's Greeks were to an appreciable degree, assimilated by the beginning of the twentieth century.[52] Evident as it was, the pressure to Russify was not oppressive enough to account for those Greeks who became absorbed in the larger Russian society. The majority of those Greeks who chose Russification did so out of self interest. If one chose to become assimilated because he saw economic advantages in doing so, that means that there were corresponding disadvantages to remaining in a minority. The greater danger to the Greek minority of Russia was Russification not due to external pressure but through intermarriage. A large number of Greeks (mostly males but also some females) married Russians and as a result their children became Russified.[53] In the above report to the Greek Ministry of Foreign Affairs the Ambassador noted that:

> Regarding the Russification of the Greek minority...that is happening neither due to shortage of Greek schools and churches nor due to pressures from the authorities but unfortunately and inevitably due to the common religion which makes marriages between Greek men and Russian women easier. The offspring of such unions are already experiencing the lessening of their national consciousness and in the third generation, with few exemptions, the Russification is complete.

The leaders of the Greek community realized that they needed to pay more attention to Greek-oriented education as a counterbalance to the steady absorption of the younger generation of Greeks into the Russian society. The Greek Boys' School was an institution which taught its students the Greek language but by the 1870s it became clear that the Greek community should make a grater effort to educate its members. It was clear that the community needed to pay attention to the higher education of its young females and create some sort of a Greek oriented higher institution of learning for girls. Above all else, the leaders of the Greek community of Odessa reached the conclusion that they needed a new organization, more active and efficient in its approach to the needs of the community. Such organization would have to be economically independent but also inclusive in character. Equally important was the need to create an organization which could assume leadership of the community, and legitimacy in the eyes of the Russian authorities, by attracting the patronage of the leaders of Odessa's Greek population.

The Greeks of Odessa were lucky in the sense that at the time they decided to create such an important and large civic group a number of factors favorable to their cause were in existence. The most important of those factors was the attitude of the Russian state. Since the 1860s the Russian government was in the process of overhauling the structure of Russia's society with the ultimate goal of modernizing the state. Under the personal supervision of the energetic Tsar Alexander II (the Tsar Liberator), a number of far-reaching changes occurred. The end of serfdom allowed the vast majority of Russia's people to be free while a number of educational, army, and judicial reforms began to transform Russian society. As part of that overall change, the state became more tolerant of civic organization and if not actively supportive, at least was willing to allow their existence. That official "thaw" or "glasnost," to use terms made popular in the 1950s and 1980s respectively, was accompanied by a boom of civic societies with philanthropic goals. By 1901 there were about 3,700 such organizations in existence.[54] The creation of civic groups such as the GBAO can be also attributed to the frustration of the forward looking Russian middle class. That middle class, which included among its members not only the rich but also the educated professionals, was committed to change and the importance of public initiative (*samodeiatel'nost'*).[55] Since it was excluded from implementing social reforms through political participation, it channeled its efforts to social improvements through civic action.[56] Indeed, the new activism of the middle class has been called "silent bourgeois revolution" because "In the Russian context, all independent public initiative was political, even when it was not overtly opposition, because it challenged, indirectly if not directly, the autocracy's control over society."[57] Even such socially conservative groups as the merchants of Moscow, who being adherents of the Old Belief of the Russian Orthodox Church were traditionally outside the main stream of society, became involved in civic groups.[58] At the same time, the Greek government was taking a more active role in the affairs of oversees Greeks in general. Odessa and its Greeks were well known to the Greek government not only through the generous contributions that various wealthy Greeks of the city had given to Greek philanthropic causes, but also due to the fact that the wife of King George I of the Hellenes was Queen Olga, a Russian Grand Duchess by birth. The Queen visited her Russian relatives often, sometimes accompanied by the King or other members of their rapidly growing family. Most, if not all of the times, the royal party entered Russia through the port of Odessa and in the process visited with the leaders of the city's Greeks. The unelected but universally recognized leader of Odessa's Greek community was G. G. Maraslis who was not only known to both Greek and Russian officials, the former through his generous contributions and the latter through his work for the municipality of Odessa, but was also one of the main proponents of the need for a new civic organization.[59] Another link between the Greeks of Odessa and the Greek state was the Greek consul in Odessa John Voutsinas (1834–1902). This individual was not only the long serving Greek representative in Odessa but also a merchant and leader of Odessa's Greek community. Indeed, Voutsinas' interests transcended borders and subjects. Besides being a successful merchant and banker as well as a diplomat, Voutsinas was also the founder of the "Voutsineos" poetry contest in Athens, as well as cofounder of the Constantinople based Association for the Advancement of Literature. Voutsinas was also a part time newspaper columnist writing in Odessa's main newspaper (*Messenger of Odessa*).[60] Voutsinas was also a supporter of a new organization and while his actions were supposed to be that of a private individual the fact that he was also a Greek government official (and was not asked by the Greek government to avoid such conflicts of interest) shows the mixing of official approval in an ostensibly private organization. Repeatedly over the years the

Greek government intervened with the Russian authorities on behalf of the Greek minority.[61] After many private meetings among the elite of Odessa's Greek community, the Greek Benevolent Association of Odessa (Ελληνική Αγαθοεργός Κοινότης εν Οδησσώ) came into existence on August 25th 1871.[62]

III

The "birth certificate" of the GBAO appeared sometime in 1871. This was the organization's charter which was composed of forty-two articles divided into eight broad categories. Article one defined the organization's goals, article two dealt with the associations membership, articles 3-6 dealt with finances, while articles 7-13 spelled out the way the association would be governed. Articles 14-20 and 21-28 defined the authority and responsibilities of the association's elected bodies, namely, the Board of Trustees and the Board of Administrators. Articles 29-34 explained the role and authority of the General Assembly and the last articles, 35-42, outlined the association's way of operation.[63] This document was signed by over one hundred influential individuals who thus became the charter members. A closer look at both the content of the document and the people who signed it reveals much about the profile of the association itself as well as the way it was to operate.

Among the 103 founding fathers of the GABO one finds some of the *bona fide* leaders of the Greek community. The first president of the GBAO was Theodoros Rodokanakis, one of the richest man of Odessa and one who had been involved in municipal affairs for many years.[64] Among the early members of the executive committee were the wealthy property owner and official of the city of Odessa: Grigorii Maraslis, the businessman and Greek Consul John Voutsinas and a certain E. Mavros, a member of the well known family of merchants. Among the other signers of the association's charter were three members of the Petrokokkinos family, owners of Odessa's best and largest department store, and two members of the Ralli family, whose business interests at the time were to be found in four continents.[65] Having such high-power people involved in the new organization was auspicious for its future success because it gave it instant credibility both in eyes of the Greek community and the Russian authorities. Rodokanakis and Maraslis were prominent members of the establishment. The former, being the senior of the two, represented the past while the latter was already marked as the unofficial future leader of the Greek community. The fact that most of the people involved were wealthy implied that the new organization would be well endowed financially, another prerequisite for longevity and respectability. One of the founding members of the GBAO was Christos Voulodemos the author of the book *Πρώτη Πεντκονταετηρής της εν Οδησσώ Ελληνεμπορικής Σχολής 1817–1867* (The First Fifty Years of the Greek Commercial School of Odessa 1817–1867), published in Odessa the same year that the new organization was created (1871), by the Greek-owned publishing house Nitse.[66] Voulodemos (1832–1906) was a graduate of the "Rizarios" theological seminary and the School of Theology and Philosophy of the University of Athens (an institution which was named Capodistrion after Greece's first president and a personality of note among the Greeks of Russia). Voulodemos came to Odessa in 1852 and resided there until his death serving first as professor, and eventually director of the Commercial School.[67]

The charter of the GBAO provides some insight or explanation about that organization's ultimate success and longevity. The first part, composed of one article, explains the association's goals as being: a) to take care by any means of the needs of Odessa's needy Greeks both those living in the city as well as of those who are passing through it; b) to take care of the upkeep of the Greek church; c) to maintain and improve Odessa's existing Greek educational and philanthropic institutions; and d) to create, subject to government approval, such new institutions as it deemed necessary.[68] Those four short sections of article one, brief as they are, suggest the broad area of activities of the GBAO. Section one is the most straight forward of the four, describing who is eligible for the association's assistance. Being an organization created by a minority group, the GBAO made it clear that it aimed to help fellow Greeks who were in need. As it has been already noted, by the 1870s a large number of Greeks found themselves in Odessa, either living there or passing through, without work or other means of livelihood. Thus the GBAO aimed at correcting a problem which existed and presumably was becoming more and more pressing. The other three sections of article one have more far reaching consequences for the newly created organization. By declaring as a goal the upkeep and improvement of Odessa's existing Greek religious, educational and philanthropic establishments, the GBAO declared its assumption of the leading role in the city's Greek community. If one excludes political activity (a preoccupation unavailable to civic groups in nineteenth century Russia) religion, education and philanthropy were the three areas in which a group was legally allowed to operate. Thus, the new Greek organization was from its inception designed to dominate the affairs of Odessa's Greek minority. Claiming as its goal the upkeep of existing community institutions presupposes that the governing bodies of those institutions were willing to allow such interference or that they themselves had asked for such help. In many cases, people such as Rodokanaki, Maraslis, Mavros, Ralli etc, were members of the boards of those preexisting institutions; a situation which increased the GBAO power.[69] If that was indeed the case, and there is no reason to believe that it was not, then the GBAO did not come to dominate Greek community affairs in Odessa gradually and in a piecemeal fashion, but rather it was created with such an all-encompassing role in mind. It also shows that long established institutions such as the Greek Orthodox Church of the Holy Trinity (established in 1808) and the Greek Commercial School of Odessa (established in 1817) were willing to surrender part or all of their authority to a new community entity. In any case, the nine brief lines which describe the GBAO goals became the foundation for its phenomenal growth and success.

The second article of the GBAO charter dealt with the association's membership. All Greek residents of Odessa, regardless of citizenship could become members provided they paid annual dues of at least three rubles.[70] The association's General Assembly could declare honorary members people who had contributed substantially to the organization either monetarily or otherwise. All members had the right to participate fully in the association's yearly gathering and vote or be voted into GBAO office. Thus, article two of the GBAO charter made the organization inclusive in its membership accepting all Greeks of Odessa who could pay the relatively modest fee of three rubles.[71]

Part three of the charter (articles 3-6) dealt with the association's income and property.[72] These articles are mostly elaborations of the obvious, namely that the GBAO is financed by the annual dues of its members and all other property given to it as gift by individual philanthropists. Another source of income came from various theater productions, symphonies, etc., which might be performed for the association's benefit. The GBAO, being a legal entity had the right to purchase real estate or other properties as its governing body saw fit and all cash in hand should be either deposited in a Russian government bank or used to buy Russian government bonds. This last stipulation deserves comment as it was clearly designed to make sure that the Russian government would derive some benefit of the GBAO income and thus, possibly, look at the association favorably. At the same time that gesture by the new organization was also a way of demonstrating patriotic sentiments towards the host country. The last article of part three was the most important because it demonstrated good fiscal policy and became the cornerstone of the long term wealth of the association. According to that article: "One tenth (1/10) of the yearly liquid income must be deposited securely in order to built a reserve capital. Use of the reserve could be made only in case of extreme need (...*εν* κατεπειγούση μόνον ανάγκη...) and then only if the General Assembly (not the few officers of the GBAO alone) gave its consent."[73] The members of the GBAO were, generally speaking, businessmen who understood the need for cash reserves and being mindful of their responsibility as custodians of the community's properties made sure that the association was in good fiscal order. Over the years as the income of the GBAO grew so did the cash reserve which made the organization wealthy.

The fourth part of the charter (articles 7-13) defined, in general terms, the way that the association would be managed. According to this part, the General Assembly would elect a council of twelve members, as well as twelve substitutes, to act as a board of trustees. The board of trustees was elected for three years and it chose three of its members to be President, Vice-president and Treasurer of the GBAO. From the remaining nine members (the three officers mentioned excluded) the board selected three to be the administrators of the GBAO. The administrators served one-year terms but were eligible for reelection by the Trustees and could not decline to serve. The last two articles of this part provided for the hiring of one secretary who performed his duties for the administrators, trustees and the General Assembly. The secretary's salary was a matter for the trustees to decide.[74] It is worth noting that even though the GBAO grew in size and wealth over the years, its basic administrative structure remained the same down to the secretary who was the only salaried member of the GBAO bureaucracy.[75]

The scope and limits of the actions of the administrators were defined in part five (articles 14-20). The administrators took care of the day to day operation of the GBAO and executed the instructions of the General Assembly and the Trustees. They operated the GBAO office and kept regular office hours during which time the regular business of the association was transacted. They came in contact with the authorities as needed, collected dues, and made all needed payments. Once a month the administrators gave account of their actions to the Board of Trustees. The administrators kept written accounts and balance sheets which they were obliged to turn over to the board of trustees by January 15 every year in order that they could be presented to the General Assembly for audit.[76]

The next part of the charter of the GBAO (part five, articles 21-28) defined the role and function of the board of trustees. The trustees were to meet twice a month (the 1st and 15th) at a time and place determined by the president. Attendance of a least seven of the twelve members constituted a quorum. At those meetings, the trustees examined the work of the administrators and transacted other business of the GBAO. All decisions were taken by simple majority vote, and if there was a tie the president cast the tie breaker. The treasurer of the board of trustees was entrusted with the association's books and he paid all the bills provided that those bills were countersigned by two members of the board of administrators. All cash at hand was deposited in the bank and withdrawals were possible only if signed by the president, the treasurer and two members of the board of trustees.[77] The function of the board of trustees was important in providing a system of checks and balances. The charter assured that no one member of the board, however powerful, could act unilaterally, while biweekly scrutiny of the actions of the administrators assured that possible mistakes or mismanagement would be discovered quickly. Particular care was given to the administration of the association's finances. Again a system of checks and balances ensured that the possibility of embezzlement was remote. The whole system of interaction between administrators and trustees was quite efficient and businesslike, a fact that contributed to the GBAO's well-being.

Part six of the charter (articles 29-34) described the role of the GBAO General Assembly.[78] The General Assembly met once a year not later than the 1st of February. The presence of half the members constituted a quorum and all decisions were taken by simple majority. The

Assembly elected the association's officers and scrutinized the actions and financial dealings of the boards of trustees and administrators. The trustees set the agenda for the Assembly and had the right to call extraordinary meetings. If some members accused some of the administrators or the trustees for mismanagement they could petition the board of trustees which had to examine the charges and either call an extraordinary meeting of the General Assembly to deal with the charges or dismiss them. There was still room for the members to bypass the board of trustees and have the General Assembly decide on an issue. Article 29 provided authorized extraordinary meetings of the Assembly if such meetings was demanded by 1/3 of the members. As was the case with other bodies of the GBAO, its charter made sure that a mechanism of checks and balances existed which could prevent a number of officers from mismanaging the affairs of the organization. While the level of participation of the average member was minimal, there was still the possibility of forcing the officers to account for their actions if needed. The whole arrangement of the GBAO was inclusive and open.

The last part of the GBAO charter (articles 35-42) gave a general description of the association's activities. In this part there is a rehashing of the goals of the association, take care of the church, educational and other institutions as well as a detailed enumeration of the ways it could help the needy. Article 35 section A mentions eleven ways by which the needy could be helped:

1) An one-time cash payment.
2) Monthly cash payments.
3) Non-interest loans.
4) Free medical care.
5) Free or low rent housing.
6) Provide food and clothing for free or for minimal cost.
7) Find work for those who are unemployed for whatever reason.
8) Take care of the families of those who are in jail.
9) Provide legal assistance to those who are to appear in front of the court.
10) Help those who need passport or residency permit.
11) Pay for those who want to repatriate.[79]

The above ways of helping the needy were comprehensive and bring to mind the role of the welfare state as it was instituted in Western Europe, and to a lesser degree in the US, in later years. It is interesting to note that according to the GBAO charter there was no stigma attached to those who were having difficulties with the law or the families of those who were in jail. At the same time, the association stressed the fact that self help was the desired goal and for that reason was committed to find work for the able. According to the above eleven ways of helping, every Greek living or passing through Odessa no matter what kind of financial or physical need he/she might have was assured of help. In order to receive help one had to petition the administrators in written or oral form. Also, if a member of the GBAO knew of individual(s) who needed help could bring that to the attention of the administrators.[80] Petitions by the needy themselves or even recommendations for help by GBAO members did not guarantee action by the association. Article 40 stated that the administrators should investigate the situation and only if they were satisfied that the request was legitimate could proceed to action.[81] This provision made it clear that the GBAO was not going to allocate its resources without making sure that its good intentions were not being taken advantage by unscrupulous individuals. This provision was not without "teeth"; as it will be pointed later, more than once a petitioner was turned down after the Administrators investigated and found him/her not worthy of assistance.

The last two articles of the GBAO charter, 41 and 42, provided a mechanism for amending the charter and for dissolving the association. Article 41 declared that the GBAO could dissolve at any time if the General Assembly decided on such action by a two thirds (2/3) majority.[82] Changes to the charter could be proposed only by the board of trustees to the General Assembly and passage of such changes required a two thirds majority. After such changes had been decided then the GBAO should petition the Russian government to allow the changes.[83]

Thus the forty-two short articles defined the role and structure of the GBAO for the duration of its existence (1871–1917). There is no indication that the charter was ever amended or even that a proposal to amend was ever voiced.[84] It is clear from the role that the GBAO had assigned to itself that it was from its inception an organization which wanted to lead all aspects of the Greek community of Odessa. It was committed to support a number of charitable causes and thus take care of the less fortunate among Odessa's Greeks. It was also designed to take over the city's Greek religious and educational institutions, as well as create such institutions as needed. In short, the GBAO was created by its powerful founding members as a civic group which would become identified and eventually accepted as the leader of Odessa's Greek population.

V
Benevolence in Action: Creating and Operating Institutions

I accept the money which you are offering me as a token of your appreciation, under the condition that you will deposit that money for ever in a bank and from its interest you will hire a Greek teacher who will teach you and your children the Greek language.... Because it is a shame that you are Greeks but do not know your mother tongue, the most noble in the world.

Letter by John Capodistrias to the
Russian-speaking Greeks of Mariupol

The inaugural meeting of the board of trustees of the GBAO convened on December 10, 1871 in the house of G. G. Maraslis. The minutes of the meeting make it clear that the General Assembly had already met and voted the twelve members of the board, nine of whom were present at the first meeting.[1] Most of the board members were members of the wealthy mercantile class (although they might not have been engaging in trade anymore) namely: S. Ralli, G. Maraslis, I. Mavros, M. Sevastopoulos, Th. P. Podokanaki, Th. Mavrocordatos and A. Zarifis. Two members, Th. Sklavos and A. Paraskevas cannot be safely classified as members of any particular class (although given the general composition of the board they were likely to be middle class). The remaining three members were also middle class due mainly to their occupation rather than their wealth: I. Voutsinas was the Greek Consul-General; D. Dallas was a medical doctor; while E. Voulismas was a Greek Orthodox Archimandrite.[2] The board elected Rodokanaki as President, Maraslis as vice-president and Voutsinas as Treasurer. Dr. Dallas, Archimandrite Voulismas and A. Paraskevas were elected administrators for the year 1872. While there were other individuals who were elected to the board of trustees over the years, the board was dominated by a handful of individuals who were reelected time after time. Rodokanaki remained President until his death in 1882 and then Maraslis assumed the role until his death in 1907 (at some point Maraslis became honorary President for life, an office not described in the GBAO charter and which allowed him final say in important decisions while leaving the day to day work to others). I. Voutsinas was also involved in the GBAO year after year. Reelection of important members allowed for stability and continuity which contributed positively to the GBAO mission. For the purpose of this study, that mission may be divide into three general categories: A) Support of the Greek Orthodox Church and other existing Greek educational and cultural institutions; B) Creation of new educational and other institutions as needed; and C) Miscellaneous works of charity.[3]

The two Greek institutions which were already in operation when the GBAO came to existence were the Church of the Holy Trinity and the Greek Commercial School for Boys. As it has already been stated, the Church of the Holy Trinity was considered one of the best, if not the best, in Odessa and a committee of faithful was already in place charged with taking care of the needs of this institution. It is implicitly clear that the church committee not only did not object to the GBAO taking over its role but in fact accepted it gladly. The affairs of the church were a bit confusing due to overlapping jurisdictions. The church itself was Greek Orthodox in a Russian Orthodox country. Both Greeks and Russians belong to the wider family of Eastern Orthodoxy which recognizes the Patriarch of Constantinople as its spiritual leader but allows wide local autonomy. Minor differences in liturgy do exist but dogmatically all Orthodox churches are the same. The difference is mainly linguistic; while the liturgy in a Russian Orthodox Church is conducted in Russian, that of the Greek Orthodox is conducted in the Greek *koine* of the New Testament. To be sure, the Russian Holy Synod and the state kept an eye on all non-Russian Orthodox institutions but overall the Greek Church of the Holy Trinity was free from state intervention. To confuse matters even more, the Greek church of Odessa did not come under the supervision of the Russian Orthodox Archbishop of Cherson (the prelate responsible for all Russian Orthodox churches in the province) nor under the authority of the Archbishop of Athens and Greece (the head of the Autocephalous Greek Orthodox Church) nor even under the overall authority of the titular head of Orthodox Christianity, the Patriarch of

Constantinople. The Greek church of Odessa was built on the property of the Patriarchate of Antioch and the church came to be under that prelate's authority. Antioch, in present day Syria, was too far from Odessa to exercise effective control (thus the autonomy of the church and the existence of a lay committee to help) but in theory, and legally, the Patriarch of Antioch was responsible for that church.

The board of trustees of the GBAO lost no time in fulfilling their stated goal of supporting the church. During their third meeting, (January 17, 1872) the following financial arrangements were made: Out of an income of 13,208 rubles (all of it from members' dues), one tenth was put away for the creation of a reserve fund in accordance with article six of the GBAO charter.[4] Of the remaining funds (approximately 12,000 rubles) one third or 4,000 rubles, was dedicated to the church of the Holy Trinity.[5] The GBAO support to the church continued over the years at the same level. Although percentage wise the allotment to the church was never again as high, in absolute numbers it remained constant. Thus in the 1873 GBAO budget the church received 3,550.50 rubles out of the 18,099.75 spent that year.[6] Two years later the 1875 budget allocated 4,106 rubles to the church out of the 33,200.24 spent.[7] The amount allocated in 1876 was 4,285.05.[8]

From the start, the officials of the GBAO demonstrated good stewardship of the resources entrusted to them. Although their commitment to the church of the Holy Trinity was unquestioned, it was neither limitless nor unconditional. Thus when the church asked the GBAO, in March of 1872, for 11,000 rubles supplementary financial help, above the already budgeted 4,000 rubles, the board of trustees politely but firmly refused with the explanation that all the money for the year 1872 was already allotted.[9] A few months later the GBAO took over the administration of the church of the Holy Trinity.[10] This was clearly to the financial advantage of the church as its treasury contained only a total of 4,365 rubles, roughly the amount the GBAO allocated to it each year.[11] In essence, the takeover of the church administration by the GBAO meant that while the church building itself remained the property of the Patriarchate of Antioch the management of the church passed to the GBAO.

Thus within months of its inception, the GBAO became the managing entity of the Greek Orthodox Church of the Holy Trinity, a state of affairs which made the newly-formed organization the supervisor of

Greek spiritual life in Odessa. Over the years, the board of trustees of the GBAO took its role as custodian of the local church seriously. Thus, when the church needed to hire an auxiliary priest it was the board of trustees of the GBAO which conducted a search, reviewed applications of prospective employees and took the final decision.[12] The level of involvement of the GBAO in managing the church was so detailed that can be labeled "micromanaging."[13] As a result, the GBAO was perceived as the employer of the Church of the Holy Trinity, with the power to hire and fire people, allocate money, and dispense patronage. Even private donations by individuals to the church were routed through the GBAO treasury.[14] The fact that the GBAO board of trustees was the virtual "boss" of the church of the Holy Trinity was so well known that people who looked for employment in the church contacted the GBAO. In one instance, a Greek Orthodox priest serving in far away Naples, Italy inquired about a job in the Greek church of Odessa from the GBAO.[15] Even if the church wanted to regain its independence from the GBAO by 1884 it had come to depend on the yearly contribution by the GBAO to the church treasury and could not survive without it.[16] That year the Board of Trustees of the GBAO had passed a resolution establishing its financial contribution to the church to 3,600 rubles a year.[17]

This early successful fusion between the newly established GBAO and the Greek Orthodox Church of the Holy Trinity, an institution of long standing which was the focal point of the life of the Greek community of Odessa, is revealing in at least two ways. The fact that the GBAO was allowed, just a few months after its establishment, to take over the church, demonstrates that it was already considered a leading institution among the Greeks of Odessa. The well known and respected individuals who headed the GBAO, as well as its financial situation, had made the new organization an instant success. The board of trustees of the GBAO adopted a businesslike approach to their work (most of them were successful businessmen to start with) and were cognizant of the fact that their position of trust was full of responsibilities. As exciting as the prospect of running the jewel of Greek institutions of Odessa was (and the Church of the Holy Trinity was that) the Trustees did not lose sight of the fact that their main responsibility was to protect the interests of the GBAO. A case in point was the decision by the board of trustees to built some auxiliary buildings to house personnel of both the Commercial School of Odessa and later the Rodokanakio School for Girls. On November 20, 1872, the board decided that the auxiliary buildings could be built cheaper if they were erected on land owned by the church and located next to it. By that time, the GBAO was already managing church affairs but due to the original circumstances surrounding the creation of the church, the church building itself and the land around it was the property of the Patriarchate of Antioch. Projecting far into the future, and the possibility that at some point the GBAO might not be running church affairs, the board of trustees decided not to built the needed buildings unless the church could provide legal assurances that the new buildings, although standing on church property, would be owned solely by the GBAO.[18] On September 1, 1873 the board passed a resolution calling for building the new buildings but that was still subject to the church's agreement.[19] A few days later (in two separate meetings, November 16 and 22, 1873) church authorities agreed to the GBAO terms and the building commenced.[20] The GBAO board acted in similar businesslike fashion towards other institutions it controlled. Thus, when on June 29, 1875 the GBAO decided to built another auxiliary building for the Girls' school, it resolved to use the 4,365.29 rubles which it had "inherited" back in 1872 when it absorbed the church of the Holy Trinity. That decision was going to be put into effect only if the old charter of the church allowed such allocation of its funds.[21]

This early behavior of the trustees of the GBAO became the hallmark of the organization's operation. The trustees had a high sense of their mission as custodians of the GBAO financial resources. Care was always taken to ensure that actions by the board were well within the boundaries of the GBAO charter as well as legally sound.[22] Finally it should be noted that no matter how worthy a charity or institution might have been, the trustees of the GBAO were not willing to provide financial support without examining the cause or institution themselves. Even in cases when support was warranted the GBAO could and at times did decline to help if such course of action would have depleted its reserve fund. The already mentioned case of refusing additional financial support to the Church of the Holy Trinity was but one of many such instances. This was clearly a case in which businesslike approach to charity was an advantage.

Besides the Greek Orthodox Church of the Holy Trinity, the GBAO "inherited" the management of the Greek Commercial School for Boys, an educational institution of long standing and another jewel in the crown of the Greek community in Odessa. Unlike the case of the Greek church, where there is a record of the fusion between the two organizations, no GBAO record exists to note when the GBAO became responsible for the management of the school, or under what conditions such fusion took place. While no written evidence exists to confirm that the GBAO was in control of the school, the board of trustees acted as if it had such authority and its actions went unchallenged. Thus from 1872 or 1873 the Greek Commercial School for Boys was the other already established entity, together with the church, which came under the jurisdiction of the GBAO.

The relationship between the GBAO and the Greek Orthodox Church of the Holy Trinity on the one hand, and the GBAO and the Greek Commercial School for Boys on the other were fundamentally different. The reasons that caused the fusion of the GBAO and the church are clear. The church was in bad financial shape and needed financial help while the GBAO was from its inception devoted to help the church. The price that the church had to pay for financial stability was the loss of its independence. The GBAO had to subsidize the church to the tune of about 4,000 rubles a year but in return it gained the prestige of managing the Greek community's most visible institution in Odessa. Unlike the church, the Boys' School had no reason to surrender its independence of action to another organization, however prestigious it might have been. The Boys' School had been the premier Greek institution of learning in Russia for over fifty years. As such, it had received generous donations over the years; also its reputation as an institution of learning had attracted many middle class students, both Greeks and non-Greeks, who were willing to pay tuition. As a result, by the early 1870s the school was in great financial shape and had no need for help. Indeed, as it will be demonstrated shortly, the GBAO once in control of the school, diverted money from the school to its other favorite project, the creation and operation of the Rodokanakio School for Girls.[23] Although it would be unfair to accuse the GBAO of neglecting the Boys' School, it would also be accurate to say that the GBAO used the school as a "cash cow" to help its favorite project. Clearly the GBAO needed the Boys' School more than the Boys' School needed the GBAO. Thus there is no logical explanation as to the reason why the school agreed to the merger. One can only deduct that the GBAO, thanks to the community leaders it already had on its board of trustees, was able to absorb any

Greek community institution it wanted. Article one of the GBAO charter made it clear that the organization was aiming at controlling and/or directing a broad range of community activities and it seems that within months of its establishment, with the absorption of the Greek community's two most important institutions, that goal was well on its way to being achieved.

The first time that the Greek Commercial School for Boys appears in the minutes of the GBAO was on March 6, 1872.[24] At that time, the trustees resolved to ask the board of directors of the Boys' School to contribute as much money as it could for the proposed building of a Girls' School. The answer to the above request is not recorded, but the GBAO proposed budget for the year 1873 records 4,000 rubles as contribution by the Boys' School to the Girls' School.[25] Two years later, in the 1875 budget the Boys' School contributed an additional 4,600 rubles, again with the provision to help the Girls School.[26] The year after that, the Boys' School again gave 4,000 rubles to the Girls' School and 600 more to the church.[27] It appears that the contribution by the Boys School to the Girls' School became an established occurrence; thus in 1879, when the GBAO experienced a deficit problem its trustees asked, and presumably received, the directors of the Boys' School for a 2,000 rubles increase in its annual contribution to the GBAO coffers.[28] It appears that the GBAO and the Boys' School had two distinct boards (in contrast to the Church of the Holy Trinity whose board was made from the board of trustees of the GBAO) although the school routinely fulfilled the wishes of the GBAO. Also, from that point on, the contributions by the Boys' School was to the treasury of the GBAO and was not earmarked for the explicit use of the Girls' School. In 1881 the GBAO had another deficit problem (more likely a continuation of the previous financial problem)[29] and once more the Boys' School was asked to increase its regular contribution by 6,600 rubles for a total of 11,000.[30] Four months later (5/14/81) the yearly contribution by the Boys' School to the GBAO was fixed at 9,000 rubles.[31] A year and a half later the Boys' School gave the GBAO 3,400 rubles.[32] It is not clear if that amount was above the already hefty 9,000 rubles a year contribution. By 1884 the role of the Boys' School as bank roller to the GBAO needs was made more regular when the GBAO trustees fixed the Boys' School contribution to 7,000 rubles a year towards the support of the Girls' School.[33]

The record of the GBAO/Boys' School makes it clear that the former used the latter as a source of extra income to either cover its deficit and operational expenses or to help with other GBAO projects. In other words, it so happened that the Boys' School was often in position to provide financial assistance but when the situation was reversed the GBAO was willing to help the school. Thus in 1875 when the Boys' School needed money the GBAO loaned it 8,000 rubles free of interest.[34] Before that, the GBAO built a house on Boys' School property for which it paid to the school treasury 30,000 rubles in three yearly installments.[35] Ultimately, the question whether or not the GBAO was a good steward of the Greek Commercial School for Boys can be answered by looking at the financial position of the school on the eve of the Bolshevik takeover. In the balance sheet for the fiscal year 1917–1918, the Boys' School recorded its total worth (buildings, cash, etc.) at 878,636.91 rubles an amount which signifies that if the GBAO did not help the school at the least it caused no harm.[36]

The major contribution to the Boys' School by the GBAO occurred in 1875. At that time, the school was facing financial need as well as a crisis of purpose. Its expenses were too high and its enrollment was on the decline. Some years before, the school had changed from a business school to one of general purpose with emphasis on the classics. That format worked well for a while but by the 1860s and 1870s circumstances had changed. Education in Russia in general, and the cosmopolitan city of Odessa in particular, had made great leaps forward and there were many schools (both public and private) which were more successful than the Greek Commercial School in attracting pupils. As a result, the Boys' School was in danger of either closing or being taken over by the Russian public school system. At that point the GBAO intervened with dynamic action which saved the school and allowed it to exist to the end of the Imperial era. The board of trustees of the GBAO decided (another indication that the GBAO controlled the school) to turn the school back to a business school like it used to be. In its new format, the school had four grades which emphasized foreign languages (they added German to the other foreign languages taught at the school) while the teaching of Greek and Math were limited to the last grade only.[37] At the same time, the GBAO intervened with the Russian authorities who agreed to allow the Boys' School to remain a private institution.[38] It is interesting to note here the way that the GBAO chose to solve the problem. It named a five member committee which studied the problems of the Boys' School and then turn their findings to the school faculty for their input.[39] This is an indication of the open and democratic way which the GBAO often employed in its day to day affairs.

II

The fourth section of article one of the GBAO charter, stated that one of the organization's goals was the creation of such institutions as the organization thought necessary.[40] Over the years the GBAO was responsible for the creation of three new institutions which were to serve the Greek community of Odessa. Two of those institutions were created by the contribution of a particular benefactor and the GBAO agreed to take over their administration while one more institution was a GBAO creation. In 1908 a certain Mr. Paraskevas, obviously a wealthy member of the Greek community, proposed to create a craft school for Greek girls. The new school was to accept girls from the age of thirteen and above and offer a two year course in sewing. Paraskevas offered 600 rubles as start up money and then 150 rubles a month up to the amount of 6,000 rubles. The GBAO was to administer the school in cooperation with the Paraskevas family.[41] By that time the GBAO had the ability to accommodate the logistics entailed in such undertaking because it had run the Greek School for Girls for almost forty years. The GBAO had also at its disposal a number of auxiliary buildings and support personnel (janitorial assistance, etc.) to house and take care of such a school. Unfortunately, the record of the GBAO for the last decade of its existence is even more fragmented than usual and thus is not known what happened to that new school.

Another institution which the GBAO created with the cooperation of an individual was the Maraslion Nursing Home.[42] As the name suggests, the nursing home was created mainly due to the generous contribution of G. G. Maraslis. The decision for the creation of a nursing home was taken sometime in 1892. Maraslis's generous contribution was instrumental in the completion of the project and the nursing home opened its doors on August, 1896.[43] The GBAO took control of the nursing home but it allowed it to have its own separate board of administrators although the two bodies were often acting in agreement and at times had common meetings.[44] As was the case with the relationship between the GBAO and the Boys' School or the Church of the Holy Trinity, much is revealed through the financial transactions and balance sheets of those institutions. In 1896 the Maraslion Nursing Home was allocated a budget of 5,192.61 rubles for its use.[45] At the time, there were 11 people in residence.[46] In 1904 the nursing home had 31 residents and paid 96 rubles a month for personnel salaries, and almost 200 rubles per month for food related items. For that same year it was allocated 40 rubles per year for medicine and 170.45 rubles for washing the clothes and linen.[47] A year later, in 1905 the real estate value of the nursing home was estimated at 35,870.47 rubles.[48] The balance sheet of the GBAO for the year 1917 shows that the building of the nursing home was worth as much as it did in 1905 but to this was added the estimated value of the nursing home's chapel which was 70,000 rubles. This chapel, named in honor of St. Nicholas, was built with money donated by Nikolaos Mavrokordatos.[49] The monetary value of the nursing home's furniture is given as 1,710.30 rubles with another 300 rubles as the worth of its library. By the end of the era in question, the GBAO was identified with the Maraslion Nursing Home to such a degree that petitions and requests for the nursing home went straight to the GBAO board of trustees. Such was the case in 1911 when a man petitioned to become a resident of the nursing home,[50] or in 1915 when the board of trustees of the GBAO decided to hire a priest for the nursing home's chapel.[51]

Examining the record of the support by the GBAO of various community institutions, as well as the creation of others, it becomes apparent that the organization fulfilled its pledge as it was stated in its own charter. For a relatively small community of people to have achieved such lofty goals was indeed an important task. Even if the GBAO had not created any other institution, its work would have been enough to classify it as a successful civic group. That success is enhanced once the GBAO role in the creation of the Rodokanakio School for Girls is examined. Looking at the events of the late nineteenth century from the late twentieth century vantage point, one might be surprised to find that the GBAO, a bourgeois entity, run exclusively by men, had the foresight to create a girls' school. Additionally, the creation of such a school was a goal of the association from the start and to accomplice it the GBAO spent lavishly in money and energy at times, as was pointed earlier, taking money from the Boys' School. The middle class has often been characterized by a conservative outlook, but it has also been often in the vanguard of social change. All things considered, the middle class of the Greek community of Odessa represented a progressive force socially and politically.[52] Regarding education, the GBAO had two reasons to focus on women rather than men. It should be remembered that the Greek community of Odessa already had the means to provide a first class Greek education to its male members. By the 1870s, when the GBAO was formed, the Greek Commercial School for Boys was already in existence for over fifty years, had an excellent reputation for scholarship even among non Greeks. Its curriculum was more classical in nature than business oriented. Clearly, the educational needs of the Greek males of Odessa were met. Thus it was only logical that similar educational needs of females should have high priority. Finally, the peculiar conditions of the Greek community of Russia in general should be taken into account. As it has been noted, due to the common religion which the Greeks and the Russians shared, mixed marriages were common and a source of worry to the Greeks who were afraid that their children and grandchildren would be Russified. If the young Greek women were educated in a first class Greek institution it was almost assured that their children, even if their father was Russian, would be raised as Greeks culturally and linguistically. Educating the young Greek women of Odessa was not only a matter of fairness or concern for the needs of the next generation. It was also a matter of national importance and a subject of such weight that no civic group which wanted to represent the Greek community could ignore.

The educational endeavors of the GBAO are not atypical of similar attempts by the Greeks of the diaspora at the time. In nearby Bulgaria, the Greek community was also active in educational matters. Like their Russian counterpart the Greeks of Bulgaria were living in a foreign country but among people with whom they shared a common religion. The Greeks had lived in the area that became Bulgaria for centuries and had benefited economically, points shared with the Greeks of Russia. As nationalism became more and more prevalent in the late nineteenth-century Balkans, the Greeks and the Bulgarians found their respective irredentist ambitions competing with each other. Thus the position of

Bulgaria's Greeks became difficult and there was widespread fear of their being absorbed culturally in the Bulgarian state.

There are similarities in the situation facing the Greeks in both countries. As in the case of Russia, the Greeks of Bulgaria took matters into their own hands by promoting and fostering Greek education. As was the case in Russia, various Greek communities in Bulgaria had their own schools which were regulated by the government but kept their independence from the state. Naturally, the wealthy and/or educated Greek elite, together with the clergy, were at the forefront of diaspora education.[53] Also, somewhat ahead of their time, both communities fostered education for women from the outset, along with the relatively novel idea of kindergartens.[54] In contrast, the two Greek communities had certain differences in the way they financed and directed their educational institutions. Whereas Greek educational institutions in Odessa were financed by local institutions and individuals, those of Bulgaria, although also financed by local individuals and organizations, received help from other sources as well.[55] Thus in 1900, G. G. Maraslis from Odessa, whose family came from what later became Bulgaria, donated money for the creation of the Maraslion School in Bulgaria.[56] Another contributor to Greek education in Bulgaria was the Greek based Επιτροπή προς Ενίσχυσιν Εκκλησίας και Παιδείας (EEEP) (Committee for the Support of Church and Education), which was a Greek government supported institution.[57] Such intervention by the Greek government must be attributed to the inability of Bulgaria's Greek to have self-supporting educational institutions, unlike their Russian counterpart.[58] Also unlike the case in Russia, the Bulgarian government occasionally contributed money to Greek education.[59] This was not the case of enlightened policy but rather a successful attempt to influence the educational activities of its Greek minority. The Greeks of Odessa, although forced to follow governmental educational rules, were able to act independently from the Russia government due, in part, to the fact that it did not receive state funding. Finally, the role of the Greek Orthodox Church in the educational affairs of the Greeks of Bulgaria was more dynamic than was the case in Odessa. While the Greek priests were consulted and involved in the affairs of the GBAO, their role was not central (with the notable exemption of father Pefanis who became president of the GBAO in the 1910s). By contrast, throughout Bulgaria the local parish priest of the Greek community was the president of the school board.[60] The latter phenomenon, denotes the leading role of church in the affairs of the Greek diaspora in Bulgaria as opposed to the more secular leadership of Odessa's Greeks.

The decision to create a girls' school must have predated the creation of the GBAO. A little over a month after the official "birth" of the GBAO, without any other prior notice, the board of trustees allocated 2,000 rubles (out of a total of 12,000 at its disposal) to be used for the benefit of the Girls' School.[61] A few months later (May 4, 1872) the planning of starting a school had progressed to the point of looking for a someone to undertake the project. The board had decided that it would be easier to hire someone who in turn would hire teachers, buy material, etc. Prospective contractors (as those who would be commissioned to start the school were called) were to be scrutinized thoroughly before awarded the job. Many details about the school were unclear, but the members agreed that it would be a school wholly Greek in character.[62] News of the creation of a new school was already circulating and people were inquiring about jobs. Four days after the above meeting, the Girls' School was again on the agenda.[63] The board was unanimous in agreeing that it will retain close supervision over all aspects of the school's work. A three member committee would be selected to supervise the school. While the Greek language, history and geography would be taught, since some of the instruction would be in Russian (and French and German languages might also be taught), any references to the school being "wholly Greek in character" would have to be omitted. However most of the teachers were to be Greek or Greek speakers and the principal to be (if non-Greek) would have to speak some Greek. Turning to financial matters, the board agreed to allow up to fifty poor girls to study for free (the Girls' School was a boarding establishment) while the rest would pay 30 rubles per year for the lower grades and 50 rubles a year for the upper. Either the board could not find someone qualified to start the school or whoever was chosen wanted too much money. In any case, the board decided (June 20, 1872) to go ahead and get involved even more intimately by starting the school itself.[64]

Once the GBAO board took control of starting the school events proceeded at a rapid pace. First, Odessa's state educational authorities were contacted and informed about the new school. The authorities asked for more details but appeared to be supportive and a month later they approved the creation of a new school.[65] Meanwhile the GBAO

Board was moving fast. It agreed on a temporary housing for the school in the Mavrocordatos house, and agreed that the GBAO board of administrators would also be administering the school. Then it hired two Greek teachers to teach the Greek, Russian and French languages, calligraphy, mathematics, and home economics. They would be paid 50 rubles a month each and have free room and board in the school. One of the teachers agreed, for an undisclosed extra amount of money, to give German and piano lessons which would be elective subjects.[66] The subjects taught at the new school were in line with the state guidelines for secondary public education for girls. At the time Russian girls' schools offered as core curriculum: religion, Russian language, mathematics, geography, history, natural sciences and physics, handwriting, needlework and gymnastics. While French and German, drawing, music, singing and dancing were elective subjects.[67] After graduating from the second (and highest) grade of the Rodokanakio School, the young ladies were eligible to attend the third grade of any Greek gymnasium. The Greek Parliament (*Vouli*) passed law 717/1937 according to which the Rodokanakio School for Girls was recognized as equivalent to Greek secondary schools.[68] Besides the two teachers, the board hired a lady to supervise the students (mostly those who were boarders) for 25 rubles a month and a cleaning person for the same amount of money. The total budget for the school's first year amounted to 3,800 silver rubles of which 1,800 went for salaries, 1,100 for rent, 300 for operational expenses, 300 for starting costs (buying desks, blackboards, etc.) and 300 for miscellaneous. Clearly the beginning of the Girls' School was a relatively modest affair and the board of trustees was careful not to commit too many resources before it was convinced that the project had a chance to succeed. At the same time, no expenses were spared for equipment or personnel. The next time the GBAO discussed the affairs of the Girls' School there occurred an event unique in the annals of that organization. As it has been noted, the GBAO was a men's organization, its charter did not explicitly disqualify women from joining but the times being what they were, the leadership of Odessa's Greek community was an all male affair. This however was the first time that the all male GBAO had to deal with an all female institution. In order to ensure the smooth operation of the school the GBAO commissioned 20 women (presumably wives, mothers and sisters of GBAO members) to look after the school.[69]

The first year of operation must have been a good one for the Girls' School because there was already need for more space for the school. According to its balance sheet, the school received 150 rubles from tuition for the first half of the 1872–1873 academic year and 234 for the second. For the year 1873–1874 its total budget was increased to 5,280 silver rubles. Of that 1,500 rubles were for rent (up from 1,100)and 3,000 for salaries (up from 1,800). The board expected 25 students to pay 36 rubles each for tuition (the number of non paying students is not recorded).[70] Feeling good about the first year of the school, the board voted to give a 200 ruble bonus to each of the two original teachers. At the same time, it was reported that one of the teachers A. Smyrnopoulou was very sick; it was agreed to hire a replacement but continue to pay the old teacher her full salary. It is interesting to note the double role that the board of trustees had to play. Businesslike in its approach to the community's resources, it did not forget that charity and compassion for its fellow Greek was its main reason to exist.

Soon after the start of the operation of the Girls' School, it became clear that due to increasing enrollment the GBAO needed to find a permanent home for the school. It was decided to build a school building on church property (the arrangements with church authorities were described earlier) and since the Queen of Greece was passing through the city on her way to St. Petersburg (she was a Russian Grand Duchess by birth) she was invited to lay the ceremonial foundation stone.[71] While planning the long range aspects of the Girls' School's future, the board of trustees continued to be intimately involved with the day to day management of the school's affairs. Thus on October 11, 1873 the GBAO hired a music teacher for the Girls' School (they gave him a monthly salary of 50 rubles and free lodgings or 10 rubles extra in lieu of lodging accommodations). Also, due to the increasing enrollment the board hired a second teacher to teach Russian and French and simultaneously it inquired about hiring a kindergarten teacher from Athens.[72] At the time, the school had 46 paying students and an unknown number of students who studied for free. By 1878 the enrollment had increased to 168 students of which 120 were paying tuition while the rest were subsidized by the GBAO. Of that last category, 20 students received also free room and board. In 1896 the enrollment of the School for Girls had reached 232.[73] As it was noted earlier, the GBAO had budgeted 5,280 rubles for the school's operation during the academic year 1873–1874. Due to expenses related to increased enrollment, the board had to allocate another 500 rubles to balance the budget. From the balance sheet it is revealed that the school had four teachers and one principal/teacher, one student supervisor and her helper and a cleaning person.[74] For the coming academic year (1874–1875) the board of trustees planed to have a kindergarten, three lower grades and two higher. For that reason, it proposed to hire three more teachers and increase the school's annual budget to 6,640 rubles. The year of 1874 ended with two more important news regarding the Girls' School. On November 15 it was announced that the building of the new school house was almost completed and since Th. Rodokanaki was a major benefactor (he donated the total amount of construction which came to about 40,000 rubles), and the President of the GBAO during the building of the school house, the board of trustees resolved to petition the authorities to name the school "Ροδοκανακειον Ελληνικόν Παρθεναγωγείον και Νηπιαγωγείον" (Rodokanakio Greek School for Girls and Kindergarten) and place a bust of Th. Rodokanaki in the new building.[75]

The new building for the Girls' School was officially opened on June 2, 1875.[76] Soon after that big event, the financial difficulty which had forced the GBAO to economize in other areas made itself felt in the affairs of the Girls' School as well. As it has been noted, the middle 1870s was a period of economic recession and an organization like the GBAO, which derived much of its income from investments, was particularly vulnerable. On October 8, 1875 the board of trustees had to deal with cutbacks in the Girls' School.[77] The board decided to limit the total enrollment to the Girls' School to 170 students with no more than 100 of them being poor students who studied for free.[78] Also, certain generous bonuses which were promised to some of the teachers' of the Girls' School would not be given. Those budget cuts did not mean that the school's operation budget did not keep up with its increased enrollment. For the fiscal year 1876, the board increased the school's budget to 8,526 rubles.[79] At the time, the school employed the following teaching personnel: one principal, one kindergarten teacher, four teachers of Greek (not only the Greek language but also history, geography, etc.), two teachers of Russian and French, one teacher of calligraphy, and one teacher-priest without designation of his specialty, father Pefanis.[80] The school employed three more people: a doorman, a cleaning lady and a student supervisor. Soon there after the GBAO saved 300 rubles from the school budget in an unexpected way. The principal of the school, Miss E. Andoniadou, resigned due to ill health and her replacement (who was the teacher next in seniority) received a salary of 900 rubles a year as opposed to the 1,200 her predecessor received.[81] The sister of the principal, kindergarten teacher Ai. Andoniadou also quit. The reasons for the "changing of the guard" might be different from those stated by the GBAO. Both women were promised performance bonuses which they deserved but due to the GBAO financial difficulties did not receive. Also, about a month before the resignation, the board of trustees had intervene in the day to day operation of the school and nullified some directives of the principal.[82] What exactly were those measures which the principal took and the board objected is not revealed in the records. The board took exception to the principal taking action without their prior knowledge or permission. It was clear from that time, and subsequent actions confirm, that the board of trustees liked to micromanage the various operations which it financed. The tension which existed between the board and the two departing teachers resurfaced two months later, on the eve of their leaving the city. When they asked the board to pay for their travel expenses, their request was turned down not under the excuse that the financial position of the GBAO was at a delicate stage, but instead they were informed that the board was not obliged to help them in that way.[83] At the same time, they were both informed that the board will stop their salary as of March 15, 1876 (that is two weeks after the board meeting). The hard line which the board took vis-à-vis the two women had the intended effect. Some time later another teacher, Mrs. Voinof promised the board to perform her duties diligently.[84] From that time on, the board established a precedent of closely supervising the teachers and to give or withhold bonuses according to the circumstances.[85] That diligence in hiring teachers was also a necessity not only to ensure the good operation of the school but also because the Russian educational authorities paid particular attention to the credentials of the new teachers.

While the board of trustees of the GBAO was parsimonious when the organization's financial condition was in a precarious state, it did not enjoy such actions nor did it made a practice of operating in such manner. When the finances of the GBAO improved, in the late 1870s, the board was willing to loosen its purse strings. Thus, in late 1879, when the school's principal resigned, the board gave her a 250 ruble bonus.[86] Even if the overall finances of the association were relatively bad, the board recognized the need to reward the school's teachers and voted an increase of their salary.[87] In that respect, the board of trustees of the GBAO acted like a school board would; indeed, the board saw itself in that role and often the meetings of the boards of trustees (a body charged with overseeing a variety of institutions and causes) spent a good part of its time, often most, in micromanaging the affairs of the Girls' School. Some of the issues taken by the board were important enough to require its direct attention, such as the proposal to raise tuition or to look to Greece for hiring a new principal.[88] In other cases, the issues could have been decided by the teachers themselves but it seems that the board of trustees guarded its prerogatives zealously. Thus the board took the time to determine when should the school's final exams take place and how long the various classes should last as well as which particular teacher should be teaching them.[89]

Since the board of administrators of the GBAO was also the board of the Girls' School, they were the ones intimately involved in the school's day to day activities (although, as the record indicates, the board of trustees was also spending a good part of its time on school affairs). Towards the end of the century, the Rodokanakio School for Girls was such an established institution that its annual graduation ceremonies were attended by the educational and government authorities of the area, such as the mayor and the provincial governor.[90] At the same time, the school continued to be an institution where poor students (or those of modest means) were accommodated.[91] The GBAO did not only provide for the free education of poor students but also, since most of them were boarders, for other needs as well.[92] As the school was celebrating the 25th anniversary of its existence, it was clear that it was a success story and an institution that (barring a catastrophic event, such as a revolution) was going to operate for many years to come. The board had to solve certain financial problems, such as a leaky roof, but those were small compared to the ones which the school had faced early in its existence. Indeed the school became a financial asset in the community in general as it needed to procure fire wood, shoes, clothes and other essentials.[93] Thus its existence, along with those of other GBAO controlled institutions such as the Greek Commercial School for Boys and the Maraslion Nursing Home, benefited not only the Greek community of Odessa, as they were designed to do, but also the social and economic life of the whole city.

VI

Benevolence in Action: Individuals and "National" Causes

For I was hungry and you gave me something to eat,
I was thirsty and you gave me something to drink,
I was a stranger and you invited me in,
I needed clothes and you clothed me,
I was sick and you looked after me,
I was in prison and you came to visit me.
The King will reply "I tell you the truth, whatever you did
for one of the least of those brothers of mine, you did for me."

Matthew 25:35-36, 40.

As the work of the GBAO recorded in the previous chapter demonstrates, the organization's institutional activities were praiseworthy to say the least. Even if the GBAO had limited its operations to that level, its work would still be significant enough to secure the organization's place in history as one of the best Greek civic associations of the diaspora. However, the problems which the institutional activities of the GBAO addressed were not the only, nor the most important, facing Odessa's Greek community. To be sure, the Greek education of the Greek youth of the city was an important achievement as was the upkeep of the church and the operation of a nursing home for the elderly. At the same time, the founders of the GBAO were well aware of the fact that the Greek community had many other problems. For that reason, the charter of the GBAO when defining the organization's sphere of action started with attempting to address its response to the problems caused by increasing poverty among Odessa's Greeks.[1] Presumably there was some debate as to the best way which could be utilized to address poverty among the city's Greeks. The solution to that problem was rather interesting. Since the GBAO chose to create and support various institutions in order to address other problems, one might have expected a similar approach in the attempt to solve the problem of poverty among Odessa's Greeks. As it turned out, the leadership of the GBAO decided to tackle the problem of poverty differently. Instead of creating a particular institution, the GBAO dealt with various problems of poverty in an *ad hoc* manner. Instead of creating shelters or soup kitchens, the GBAO board of administrators was authorized to act according to its own judgment by examining each individual case separately. Any Greek resident of Odessa, and even those passing through the city, who found himself/herself in need of financial assistance could apply for help at the GBAO. The Trustees of the GBAO did not create guidelines and uniform criteria to help, or limit, the actions of the administrators. The board of trustees budgeted a certain amount of money every year for the benefit of the poor. If the money were spent before the end of the fiscal year there was rarely, if ever, more money allotted. The board of administrators had to investigate each petition in order to ensure that the petitioner was indeed in need. The criteria used in those examinations are not spelled out. If the petitioner could convince a member of the GBAO or some other respectable citizen or authority to vouch for their need, the request was almost automatically granted.

The direct way which the GBAO decided to use in helping the needy of the community stands in contrast to the institutional, "western" way which the organization had utilized with success in other cases. The reason for such difference has to do with the fact that modern and westernized as the Greek middle class of Odessa was, it did not sever its connection with its Eastern Orthodox roots. Unlike the beliefs of some other branches of Christianity, the Orthodox Church does not attach stigma to poverty. The vicissitudes of life, which determine wealth and poverty, are God's will and the poor are as loved by Him as the rich are. Christ is often identified with the poor and unfortunate while the rich are *obligated* to help. Another characteristic of the Orthodox ethos is the belief that direct, person to person charity is the ideal approach to almsgiving.[2] In that way the haves would come in contact with the have-nots. The western idea of indirect help in which faceless foundations give to equally faceless charity organizations who in turn help the poor was an alien concept to nineteenth-century Orthodox people.

The direct assistance which the GBAO provided to the needy can be divided into two broad categories. The first one is the more or less regular cash payments distributed to a number of poor twice a year. Usually those two times were Christmas and Easter, two religious holidays when almsgiving to the poor is a tradition. Presumably, a number of poor had applied for assistance in anticipation of those two religious holidays and the GBAO had had the time to examine and approve the petitions. The other category of assistance was that of helping individuals who were faced with a particular need. Such instances occurred throughout the year and covered a variety of areas where assistance by the GBAO was required. This second category can be divided into two sub-categories. In some cases the GBAO provided monetary assistance (more often in the form of one time payment but sometimes as a monthly stipend) while in others the organization provided the petitioner with the item he/she needed rather than cash. Examining the various petitions is an interesting exercise because it gives an idea of the number of poor needing help, the type of help needed and the way the GBAO went about providing such help while at the same time safeguarding its financial resources.

As if the GBAO wanted to reinforce the fact that it was committed to taking care of the poor, in its second meeting (December 16, 1871) it allocated 1,500 silver rubles to be distributed to the needy during Christmas.[3] There is no evidence as to who were those poor, who decided to give how much to whom and what were the criteria, if any, which the GBAO used to determined which individuals were worthy of support. In January of 1872 the Board of Trustees of the GBAO allocated 4,000 silver rubles for the needy (one third of the money budgeted for that year, more than allocated for any other cause) to be distributed as follows: 1,000 rubles given each time during three religious holidays (Easter, the feast of St. Demetrios, and Christmas) with the remaining 1,000 to be distributed as needed in between.[4] The question of who was really needy preoccupied the board of trustees which authorized the board of administrators to find out the poorest of the poor who should be helped in the coming winter.[5] While there is no way of knowing the criteria which qualified one for assistance, there is a way to see how the money was distributed and how many people needed assistance. Among the reports of the GBAO there is a catalogue of the activities of the GBAO for Easter 1892 and 1893 and Christmas 1892. If one is willing to accept that this catalogue is representative of similar activities for the rest of the year then some generalization can be made. It is interesting to note, for instance, that over the years the money allotted to the poor not only had not increased, as the fortunes of the GBAO had, but actually decreased. While the GBAO allotted 4,000 silver rubles for the poor in 1873, the same amount as the previous year, that commitment represented less than a fourth of the GBAO budget as opposed to one third the year before.[6] That number decreased both percentage wise as well as in absolute value in 1875 when the poor were allotted only 2,690 rubles in a budget of 33,200 rubles bringing the allotment to the poor down to 7-8% as opposed to the earlier 22-33%.[7] And although this percentage was somewhat increased in 1876, over 10% of the total budget, in absolute numbers the poor were still the losers as they were allotted 2,636 rubles of a total of 20,244.[8] The decline in monetary help to the poor continued over the years and it was clearly evident in 1892-93 when more details of almsgiving over Easter and Christmas are given.[9]

By 1892, the GBAO was in operation for over twenty years and thus its yearly almsgiving must have been a well-known affair thus, presumably, attracting all of the city's eligible needy Greeks. During that year's Easter, over 200 poor received monetary help totaling 711.95 rubles. During the Christmas period of the same year 207 poor received a total of 955 rubles. For the Easter of 1893 the GBAO dispensed 908.45 rubles to 345 individuals.[10] Finally, for Easter 1897 the GBAO gave to the poor 600-650 rubles.[11] The number of needy is important as it gives an idea of the Greek community's overall financial state of affairs. If one accepts even the most conservative estimates regarding the number of Greek inhabitants of Odessa (5,000), then the number of eligible poor receiving help represents under 1% of the city's Greek population (actually closer to 0.5%). Of course if one chooses to accept the higher estimations then that percentage becomes really negligible. Even allowing for the fact that other Greek organizations were also helping the poor (such as the Maraslion Nursing Home for the Elderly), the number of Greeks receiving assistance was low. Also interesting to note is the amount of help each individual received. That help was in the range of 1-10 rubles with the usual amount being 2-3 rubles. Clearly the goal of the GBAO was not to solve each individual's financial problem once and for all (an unrealistic goal) but rather to alleviate the most pressing needs of the poor. For that reason, the amount distributed during holidays was not fixed but subject to change. Thus, for Easter 1873 the amount distributed was fixed at 1,000 rubles.[12] A year later, towards the end of 1874, the GBAO board of trustees decided to give to the poor only 500 rubles since it had already given a total of 4,000 for the benefit of the poor during the year.[13] It became quite common, especially during the "lean" years of the middle and late 1870s, for the board of trustees of the GBAO to balance its books by spending cuts of which the poor were not immune. In 1876 the GBAO started dispensing money two times a year (Easter and Christmas) rather than the original three and economized even more by cutting the amount budgeted for Christmas by 50% to 500 rubles.[14] Presumably as an austerity measure, and maybe because some people might have taken advantage of the system, the GBAO decided that the needy requesting alms should provide the board of administrators with their addresses in order to verify their actual need for help.[15] By the end of 1879 the GBAO calculated its yearly commitment to helping the poor at 2,500 rubles, an amount which represented only direct cash dispersed throughout the year but excluded money spent for the benefit of the poor through institutions (scholarships, elderly care, etc.) and also the direct help provided to the poor in the form of food, clothes and other non-cash contributions.[16]

As it has been already noted the monetary help dispersed by the GBAO to the poor for Christmas and Easter was intended as a supplement to help the recipient with the increased expenses of the holidays.[17] One should keep in mind that all the recipients of seasonal financial help were not completely destitute. This fact becomes clear from the files of the GBAO where special provisions were made for those who needed financial help year-round, a number of people much smaller than the two to three hundred who received alms twice a year. It seems logical to conclude that a number of people were able to earn their living, however meager, and thus were ineligible for continuing support by the GBAO. During the holidays, the criteria for help were loosened, by design, and all those poor but not destitute could count for an one time payment. The board of trustees of the GBAO was well aware that peoples' needs were not limited to holidays (reminiscent of the contemporary slogan used by today's philanthropic organizations "need knows no season") and it did make an effort to address them. Thus in at least one instance, July 20, 1872, the board of trustees authorized the administrators to find out how many individuals and families will need extra help in the coming winter.[18] Again, as in the case of the holidays, this financial assistance was temporary in nature and supplementary rather than total. In all of the above cases the GBAO did not assume long-term full responsibility for the poor, but rather opted for temporary relief of a particular seasonal need.

The GBAO recognized that some individuals and families needed, and were worthy, of continued support. Families whose breadwinner was dead or chronically ill, and the children were still too young to earn a living, were among those needing long term support. Once again the administrators were authorized to create a list of those deserving poor who would receive monthly stipends. The total amount given could not exceed 1,500 rubles a year with another 500 rubles in reserve to cover any extraordinary need that might appear.[19] There is no other mention of this subject for many years nor is there any report as to how many families were helped or how much money each family received. The only reference to specific amounts given monthly is found in a report forty years after the one just examined. In 1915, during the First World War (when inflation was already a major factor in everyday life) the GBAO resolved to provide monthly support for five needy families at the rate of 10, 10, 7, 5 and 3 rubles respectively.[20] But the financial help which the GBAO gave to the needy that had the most impact in the community was the occasional help given to individuals throughout the year to cover a particular need of emergency.

The overwhelming number of requests for assistance refer to poverty and need in general terms without clear explanation as to the exact nature of the petitioners' need. It is not clear how many petitions were in written form and how many were oral requests. In most cases the petition was accompanied by some kind of confirmation by a member of the GBAO to the effect that the petitioner was indeed needy and worthy of assistance. As was the case with the petition itself, the supporting evidence was often oral in nature.[21] For its part the board of trustees and the board of administrators made sure that each petition was recorded in the GBAO files. With the passage of time, and as the GBAO became better known as a charitable institution, the number of petitions rose steadily.[22] In most cases the record indicates that a small amount of money was given to the petitioner for unidentified need.[23] One forms the impression that those desperate petitioners needed some extra money to keep the "wolf out of the door" due to some unforeseen event which strained even more the meager resources of Odessa's Greek poor. In some cases, the petitioner was not a typical poor (if such a category exists) but rather what would be called today "working poor," in other words working people who lived from payday to payday and who could find themselves in financial need due to an unforeseen event. For example, a man who had spent sometime in the hospital, but who had just been discharged, asked for assistance until he could start earning a living again.[24] This is similar to the case of the Greek prompter in one of Odessa's theaters who found himself in need of assistance.[25] From the way the GBAO responded to those needs one can also assume that the well off elements within Odessa's Greek community were aware of the poverty and need among their less fortunate compatriots. At the same time, the GBAO was cognizant of the fact that some people might try to take advantage of the association's generosity. The usual amount of money given to individuals was 3-5 rubles.[26] In many cases the GBAO decided that more information was needed about the individual petitioner. In such cases, the needy had to wait but in a few cases one ruble might be advanced pending the findings of the investigation.[27] Regarding most of the petitions turned down, the record of the GBAO is not illuminating. Usually petitions were turned down with no comment presumably because the investigation had turned something negative about the petitioner.[28] In a few cases, the reason for rejection was given as lack of supporting testimony by GBAO members.[29] In one memorable case, Archimandrite Pefanis turned down a woman's request for support with the terse comment that "The association gave her money many times before. There are others who are poorer."[30] Clearly, as was the case with the various institutions that the GBAO ran, the leaders of the community were careful custodians of the association's resources and each and every request for support was verified before any help was given.

Next to that general category of people who requested money to cover living expenses, the most numerous requests were by Greeks, both residents of Odessa as well as some who were passing through, who wanted to return to Greece, or to their place of residence outside Greece. Repatriation from Odessa to Greece was mainly a lower class phenomenon. In the period under examination the opportunities for overseas Greeks to transfer their business to the land of their birth were few. At best some might decide to return to Greece after retiring from active participation in commerce.[31] In many cases, especially among Greeks from Russia, even after retirement one chose to stay away from Greece due to the fact that their offspring were established in the host country. Thus, in most cases, the people who wanted to return to Greece were those who were forced to do so due to their own family and/or economic circumstances. That meant, usually, that those who wanted to leave Odessa were unable to earn a living in that city and believed that their prospects there were nil. In some cases, a family's main and/or only breadwinner had died or was incapacitated. In any case, most of those who wanted to return to Greece were poor and often did not even had the money to buy their ticket back. In a few other cases, the person(s) wanting to return to Greece were people who did not even live in Odessa but rather found themselves stranded in the city without the financial means to return home. This last category include people who came to Odessa seeking a better life but were disappointed quickly, or sailors who found themselves marooned in the city. For all those people, the GBAO made available the means to repatriate provided, as with the association's other enterprises, that their claims of need were supported and verified. In any case, the number of those applying for financial help in order to repatriate was not large. The minutes of various GBAO committee meetings, covering about twenty-five years, record about a dozen requests for such help. The first time that a request for travel expenses was brought before the GBAO was on October 23, 1896. From December 10, 1871 (when the first meeting of the GBAO Board of Trustees convened) until August 20, 1884 (when the record of board of trustees meetings ends) there was no mention of such request. The record starts again on October 17, 1896 with the minutes of the meetings of the board of administrators. One is left to speculate as to the reason why requests for travel expenses were not brought forward before. It is possible that detailed records of the board of administrators meetings existed for the period before 1896 and there one might find more requests. Those records have either disappeared (which is quite likely given the turbulent history of the city of Odessa) or are "buried" somewhere in the State Archives of the District of Odessa (GAOO) uncatalogued or classified under different file. It is also possible that the GBAO decided to finance repatriation somewhere between 1884 and 1896 and for that reason earlier records are silent about such requests.

Most of the people who requested help to repatriate were men (men were always alone while in the few cases of women asking for tickets minor children were involved) and are labeled by the GBAO as "άπορος" (destitute). In most cases the GBAO provided the petitioner with third class tickets to their destination.[32] In other cases, the GBAO gave the petitioner money to buy his/her own ticket. Thus the modern reader is informed that the trip from Odessa to Rostov did cost 5 rubles while that to Moscow cost only 3 and the fare to Constantinople was 4 rubles.[33] Finally, in at least one case, the people asking for help were well known for their need. On December 11, 1896 the GBAO gave tickets, plus three rubles extra cash each, to two Greek sailors who had survived the sinking of their ship a few days before.[34] It appears that the GBAO followed the same policy in regards to travel money that it did with all other charities it supported. If the petitioner could support his/her request by having a respectable citizen vouch for the need, then the request was granted. If such support was not forthcoming the GBAO itself was willing to conduct its own inquiry into the matter. A petition was not automatically granted and in at least two cases (involving two individuals each) request for help to travel was turned down. In one of the above cases the request was denied due to lack of support by a local trustworthy citizen.[35] In the other case the request was initially granted only to be denied a few days later, presumably after a GBAO review revealed some irregularities.[36]

Besides the help aiming at relieving poverty (in the form of biannual alms, monthly stipends or one time grants) as well as the help to those who wanted to repatriate, the GBAO was willing to help individual Greeks who had other needs. Thus various petitions appear in the GBAO records representing a miscellany of causes asking for help. A certain Telemachos Synodinos author of a book titled "Ο Ελληνισμός της Ρωσίας" (The Greeks of Russia) requested the GBAO to subsidize his work by buying a number of copies of the above book.[37] An Athens based organization dedicated to the advancement of Greek literature wrote to the GBAO asking for subsidy.[38] The Royal Chancery of the King of Greece George I thanked the GBAO for contributing 4,962.75 French gold francs for the building of an Athens hospital.[39] A young Greek who had demonstrated a talent for painting was given 120 rubles by the GBAO in order to go to St. Petersburg to study that art.[40] This young painter was lucky enough to gain favor with the GBAO. On January 10, 1876 when the GBAO was forced to cut back on its support to many worthy causes, due to money shortage, it was decided that the commitment to help the young painter would continue for four more months to the tune of 20 rubles per month.[41] The variety of petitions to the GBAO by diverse groups and individuals attest to the fact that the organization was well known among the Greeks of Russia and Greece as an entity able to dispense money and favors. That perception reveals the GBAO as an organization with several dimensions besides the obvious one of a charitable institution.[42]

As it was noted in the previous chapter, it was quite common for some wealthy individual or family to donate money to the GBAO and earmark the donation for the benefit of a particular institution, such as churches or nursing homes. In at least one case, a donation was earmarked to benefit individuals in need rather than an institution. The custom of giving a dowry to one's daughter at marriage is an ancient one which has survived into modern times.[43] This pre-modern custom, clearly sexist as it was usually applied to females and not males, was the reason for many a family tragedy.[44] Greek lore is full of stories of young ladies forced to remain unmarried due to lack of a dowry. In many cases, engagements were broken due to last minute misunderstandings about the property arrangements and there are also many stories of last minute breaking of engagements when the groom found another woman with a larger dowry. While men were the major beneficiaries of the dowry system, they were often its victims as well. Fathers had to work hard in order to provide their daughters with a respectable dowry. Also, since custom dictated that a brother should not marry before his sisters, many a young men grew to middle age before they were able to marry themselves (if indeed they married at all) after securing the dowries for their sisters. For that reason, a family with three or more daughters was considered rather unlucky. The custom of dowry, common in many cultures, "followed" the Greeks where ever they chose to live and the Greeks of Odessa were not exempted.

On December 6, 1883 the GBAO's vice-president G. G. Maraslis, came to the board of trustees with the following proposal. Maraslis owned a house on Pushkin Street number 70 which he was willing to give to the GBAO.[45] The total value of the house was not declared but the property was mortgaged to a bank for 19,864.43 rubles which would be paid by January 1, 1897 along with 2,078.33 rubles in interest. Maraslis would continue to pay the mortgage and the GBAO would pay the costs of transferring the deed. The GBAO would also be responsible for any bookkeeping associated with the property's operation. At that time, the house was rented for 209 rubles a month but that amount could be increased to 420 rubles. From the income derived from that property, the GBAO, following Maraslis' explicit instructions, was to give four (4) one hundred ruble (100) dowries a year to deserving Greek women, the money to be paid after the marriage ceremony. From that same property's income, the GBAO was to help deserving poor *regardless of the individual's nationality*. If the GBAO dissolve itself at some point in the future, then the property would be given to the city of Odessa.[46] This generous gift, which was accepted by the GBAO, was unique not only due to the type of people it sought to help, but also because is the only part of GBAO operation which, according to the donor's wishes, was designed to help Greeks and non Greeks alike. The fact that the donor wanted to help people regardless of nationality is not a surprise. Maraslis was one of the most cosmopolitan of Odessa's Greeks and during his lifetime he gave generously to various philanthropic causes in Greece, Russia and Bulgaria.[47] The reasons which prompted an elderly bachelor (Maraslis married in his sixties just a few years before his death which occurred in 1907) to provide dowries was not explained. In any case, the GBAO notified the public of the new endowment and over the years a number of women took advantage of that opportunity (usually it was the father of the prospective bride who applied for the Maraslis dowry).[48] Thus, while the GBAO could not claim that it provided "cradle to grave" assistance it did provide matrimonial help for those who qualified.

II

During its forty-five years of existence the GBAO had a good truck record as a charitable institution.[49] It is clear that the GBAO fulfilled, and even surpassed, the mandate given to it by its charter. As it turned out, the GBAO became much more than an ethnic benevolent organization. Due to its longevity, stability, wealth and institutions and individuals it supported, the GBAO became a leader of Odessa's Greek community. In that respect, the organization was political, not in the narrow definition of partisan politics (although in time it did play that role as well) but rather in the broader sense of representing a community in an informal yet real way. Clearly the GBAO did not seek to influence general Russian policy domestic or foreign. The Russian political system itself was against any type of outside input. At the same time, as was pointed earlier, the GBAO and its "agents" sought, and gained, preferential treatment from the Russian government in some important matters. Thus Greek educational institutions were unofficially exempted from the more onerous demands of the Russification policy. In this narrow sphere, the Greek diaspora of Russia as a whole became politicized and "lobbied" the government towards its own ends. The various papers of the GBAO are full of accounts which help the reader form a picture of the extent, and limit, of the organization's political maneuvers and goals. At the same time, one should be careful not to assign to the GBAO exaggerated political importance which the organization itself never had nor there is any evidence that it ever sought.

An organization like the GBAO, even if it wanted to stay non-political, still had to have some contact with the government bureaucracy in order to fulfill its obligations under the law. Also, periodically there arose certain instances when an organization, however non-political, had to make a gesture to the state as a matter of good public relations. Thus on its February 14th 1880 meeting the GBAO Board of Trustees voted unanimously to send congratulations to Emperor Alexander II on the 25th anniversary of his assuming the Russian throne.[50] In 1899 the GBAO sent an icon of St. George, along with the organization's best wishes, to Prince George of Greece who was then serving as High Commissioner in Crete.[51] Also, on January 31st 1913 the GBAO voted to send its condolences to Greece for the assassination of King George I.[52]

The GBAO, like all other civic organizations in late imperial Russia, had to follow certain rules and regulations as a prerequisite for its existence. This brought the GBAO in contact with the official Russian state.[53] That contact, although by itself did not confer any power to the organization, did give it a *de facto* role as the mouthpiece of the Greek community of Odessa as a whole. Even though the GBAO depended on the state for its existence, it attempted to follow as independent a line as was possible under the circumstances. Thus when the governor of the city of Odessa demanded that the GBAO notified the authorities in advance of its General Assembly and various board meetings, the GBAO, in essence refused to fully comply with the order. Noting that according to regulations the GBAO was obliged to report General Assembly meetings but not those of the board, the GBAO leadership wrote back to the governor promising to comply with the request about the former but omitted any reference to the latter.[54] Evidently, the authorities were satisfied and for years after that, unless asked to give some particular information, the GBAO notified the city governor only about its yearly General Assembly meetings.[55] The Russian authorities were also interested in having copies of the GBAO charter as well as its annual budgets, a request which the organization honored without any comment. [56] As the GBAO branched out to other activities, various branches of the Russian government were interested in gathering more information about this benevolent association's activities. Thus the educational authorities asked for more information on the teachers who taught at the Rodokanakio Girls' School, particularly about the credentials of those teachers.[57] The board of trustees also received inquiries from Odessa's police about the people who received poor relief from the GBAO as well as the total amount given to them. The GBAO complied with such requests but it declared its total support for the poor at 2,500 rubles a year, an amount smaller than what was usually given out by the organization. In later years (1897), the governor of Cherson province, which included Odessa, asked the director and teachers of the Girls' School to instruct their students on the subject of respecting authority.[58]

As the GBAO became better known in Odessa, it attracted the attention of other official organizations. A major part of the work of consular offices is to help its nationals who find themselves on foreign soil. It was only natural that the Greek Consulate in Odessa directed some people to the GBAO for help.[59] It is safe to assume that those individuals who turned to the Greek Consulate for help were Greek citizens traveling through Odessa. In the overwhelming number of such requests, the GBAO agreed to help but such agreement was not automatic. For instance, in keeping with its sense of fiscal responsibility, the GBAO did refuse to make long term commitment to a poor family. The GBAO agreed to give temporary help but reasoned that since the needy in question were Greek citizens the Greek state, via the consulate, should shoulder some of the responsibility.[60] This refusal by the GBAO is important not so much because it demonstrates the organization's fiscal policy, which has been already noted in more than one case, but because it illustrates the position of the GBAO vis-à-vis the Greek state. The GBAO was a "national" organization in the sense that it was created by Greeks, for the benefit of Greeks and in order to promote Greek causes. Willing as the GBAO was to help Hellenism everywhere, it made it clear that it was not an organ of the Greek state. To be sure, the Greek consular authorities were involved in the GBAO activities from the start (when Consul Voutsinas was also a member of the GBAO Board of Trustees), but the organization attempted to remain independent from both the Russian and the Greek state.[61] The Greek consulate was not the only one which utilized the good offices of the GBAO; in at least one case the Turkish consul did the same. A certain Sophia Pano, a Greek woman who was an Ottoman subject, appealed to the Turkish consulate for financial assistance. Since she was Greek the consulate recommended her to the GBAO.[62] This gesture is noteworthy. Normally, in such cases, the Turkish consul would consider it as the responsibility of the Greek authorities and would have followed diplomatic procedure and turn her over to his Greek counterpart. By choosing to address the GBAO, the Turkish consul acknowledged that organization as the natural leader of Odessa's Greeks.

Even the Russian authorities recognized by deed, if not by word, that the GBAO was a community leader in Russia in general in a incident which also demonstrates that the reputation of the organization was known far and wide. On December 12, 1881 the imperial authorities of the Black Sea port city of Batum located near the Russo-Turkish borders in present day Republic of Georgia, asked for help from the GBAO. According to the request, an unspecified number of Greeks came to Batum from the Ottoman Empire, presumably as refugees. Those people received some help from local authorities and private sources but needed supplementary support. The authorities asked the GBAO to help and the latter responded positively. Within a week, the GBAO Board of Trustees announced that the organization had collected 2,876 rubles. To that amount, there was added 500 rubles from G. G. Maraslis and 50 sacks of flour donated by Rodokanaki.[63] This event was important symbolically as it demonstrated that although the Russian authorities did not recognize the GBAO as the official representative of Odessa's Greeks, it did turn to the organization as the natural leader of that community.[64] This was not the last time that the GBAO helped Greek refugees in Russia. During the First World War, when Romania was overrun by the German army (1916–1917), a number of Greek refugees crossed the frontier to Russia to avoid being interned as nationals of a hostile power.[65] The GBAO was instrumental in helping those refugees some of whom went to Odessa, but most of whom stayed in Bessarabia.[66]

It was only natural that the Greek government would utilize the GBAO whenever it could. Sometimes it did so in matters outside the traditional sphere of action of a charitable institution. Thus in 1909 the Greek government, via its Odessa consulate, asked for help from the GBAO in locating any original papers from the old patriotic organization "Friendly Society."[67] The records of the GBAO do not indicate what steps the organization took but they must have been effective because the Greek government sent its thanks for helping locating such documents.[68] From the above interaction between the GBAO and the Greek government, one can conclude that the former was considered as an auxiliary national source by the mother country to be used in a variety of ways. This point was reinforced in July 1911 when the Greek Consulate asked the GBAO for statistical information on the Greeks of South Russia.[69] Clearly then, the Greek authorities believed that the GBAO was an organization with authority among the Greeks of Russia, and one which could be entrusted with a sensitive mission.[70]

The fact that the GBAO had assumed the position of the leader of the Greek community as a whole can also be detected by the official calls to the organization's officers by important Greek persons passing through the city. Thus when the Queen of Greece Olga, who was Russian by birth, was passing through Odessa in 1873, the GBAO was the organizer and host of her reception. The officers of the GBAO as well as the students of the various GBAO controlled institutions welcomed the queen who dedicated the foundation of the Girls' School new building. Besides a gift of flowers and some icons, the GBAO gave Olga 10,000 rubles to be used by her for charities in Greece.[71] Since Olga made the same trip many times on her visits to her Russian relatives, the GBAO played the host repeatedly.[72] The GBAO hosted welcoming ceremonies on the occasion of other visits by VIPs to Odessa. A case in point was the visit of the Patriarch of Jerusalem Nicodemus. Again the GBAO was the one which either volunteered or asked to be the host.[73] Lastly, there were the occasions when the Greek community of Odessa came together to celebrate a Greek national event. Such was the case with the annual celebration of Greece's Independence Day (March 25th). Since the GBAO "controlled" the church and the Greek schools, the organization was again both the organizer and host of the celebration.[74]

As the record indicates, the GBAO assumed, almost from the moment of its creation, the leading position in Odessa's Greek community even though this was never spelled out in the organization's charter and was not recognized officially by any authority. Be that as it may, the GBAO was treated by Greeks and non-Greeks alike, as well as by officials from various countries, as the real representative of Odessa's Greeks. One forms the impression that had a visitor arrived in Odessa and uttered the words "Take me to your leader" to any of the thousands of Odessa's Greeks, that visitor would have been directed to the offices of the GBAO. Such an assessment of the organization's role was not limited to the Greek community. As has been demonstrated earlier, Russian and other authorities treated the GBAO as the leader of Odessa's Greeks. Also, the GBAO itself acted as the leader of the community from the start which makes one suspect that the organization did not grow in the role of the leader, nor did it assume such position by default. Instead, it appears that the leadership of Odessa's Greeks was a GBAO goal from the start, a goal which had to remain unstated given the political realities of Russia at the time which made any declared attempts for minority leadership problematic, to say the least. Thus the GBAO combined its general leadership position with that of a charitable institution, the former covering the latter, and achieved its own private aims by going around the rules and regulations of the host state.

The GBAO was from the start receptive to requests for support of Greek "national causes." Thus, on November 20, 1872 the Board of Trustees of the GBAO received an interesting request for support. The Ecumenical Patriarch of Constantinople Anthimus (being the spiritual leader of all Orthodox Christians) wanted financial support in order to create what he called a "National Treasury." The Board of Trustees took a "wait and see" stance vis-à-vis the above request. It noted that such allocation of GBAO funds would need the permission of the Russian authorities (a difficult undertaking at best), but at the same time it did not drop the matter entirely.[75] Ten years later the Patriarch sent a circular to all Orthodox Christians asking for contributions in order to establish and maintain a theological seminary. In this case the GBAO appeared willing to contribute.[76]

In many instances the requests for support were clearly intended for Greek national causes. This was the case in 1911, when the government of independent Crete solicited help from the GBAO and other Greeks of the diaspora.[77] The connection between the Greeks of Odessa and Crete predate the creation of the GBAO. During the Cretan revolt of 1866–1869 the Greeks of Odessa provided generous financial support to the Cretan insurgents. There was even a committee created whose sole purpose was the support of the Cretan revolution, more accurately the victims of that war. Among its members were some individuals such as Rodokanaki, Voutsinas, Sklavos, Paraskevas, Manzavinos, and Mavrocordatos who became the founding fathers of the GBAO.[78] Other future GBAO founders such as Maraslis, Ralli, and Mavros appear as generous contributors to the Cretan cause.[79] Another call for help came from Greek Orthodox Metropolitan Chrysanthos, the spiritual and political leader of the Greeks living on Turkey's Black Sea littoral. The Pontic Greeks had formed an independent entity during the First World War with Chrysanthos as their leader.[80] The level of support of national causes by the GBAO becomes clear from the hand written letter sent to the organization by Greece's Prime Minister Eleftherios Venizelos. The letter is dated 31 January 1913 which means that it was sent during the height of the First Balkan War when Greece and her allies (Montenegro, Serbia, Bulgaria) were victorious against the Turks. Venizelos took time out of his busy schedule (besides being premier he was also minister of defense) to thank the GBAO for its generous contribution of 90,000 gold French francs donated to cover "national needs."[81]

Besides the direct way with which the GBAO helped Greek national causes, there were also indirect ways by which it continued to provide assistance. Over the years, whenever Greece found itself involved in wars aiming at irredentist goals the GBAO was active in offering "humanitarian" aid, which did help the combatants. Quite often the GBAO, and Odessa's Greek community as a whole, financed transportation of volunteers from Russia to Greece in order to fight on the side of the regular Greek army. Also, the GBAO made sure that the families of those volunteers did not suffer financially while their breadwinner was away. This was the case in 1878 when, during the Russo-Turkish War, a number of Greeks from Russia joined the Russian Army as well as Greek paramilitary units.[82] Similarly, after the disastrous (for Greece) Greek-Turkish War of 1897, the GBAO opened its coffers and helped a number of Greeks of Odessa who volunteered and fought in that war.[83] The GBAO and Odessa's Greeks as a whole were also involved in helping volunteers join the Greek army during the First

World War.[84] The fact that in 1878 and 1917 the Russian government favored Greece's involvement in the wars made the work of the GBAO easier as it did not have to operate covertly.

During the First World War the GBAO became involved in Greek political affairs in an unprecedented way. Political events in both Russia and Greece created a climate in which the Greeks of Odessa could voice their political beliefs openly, even though Russia was still governed by an autocratic regime. In order to understand better how such political gestures were allowed to manifest themselves, one has to look into events prior to the beginning of the war. During the nineteenth century, Greece had gone through a number of political transformations which culminated, by the early twentieth century, in the creation of a system of constitutional monarchy in which the king retained a number of powers but an elected parliament conducted most of the state's affairs. The political parties of the day were controlled by a few wealthy and well known individuals centered in Athens with a long family tradition of office holding. In 1909 a military coup toppled the old order and power shifted to the new emerging middle class with Eleftherios Venizelos and his Liberal Party as their champions.[85] Venizelos undertook an extensive program of political and administrative modernization with the aim of rejuvenating the country and challenge the Ottoman Empire.[86] As a result, Greece and its Balkan allies fought successfully against Turkey in 1912–1913 and the country tripled in territory almost overnight. Political as well as personal differences between Venizelos and King Constantine I came to a head at the beginning of the First World War. Venizelos, a known admire of France and Britain, pointed to the fact that Greece through treaties (with Serbia) and national interests should enter the war on the side of the Western Allies. Constantine (who had studied at the German Military Academy and was married to the Kaiser's sister) favored neutrality. Constantine believed that the constitution gave authority for defense and foreign affairs to the king while Venizelos pointed to his electoral success as proof of his popular mandate. Eventually the country was split into two (first ideologically and then literally) creating a "National Schism" (Εθνικός Διχασμός) which never really healed. That schism transcended national boundaries and appeared wherever Greek communities of the diaspora existed. Odessa was no exception, but the local political climate made the situation even more interesting. The Russian Emperor Nicholas II had many ideological and personal ties with the Greek Royal family. As an autocrat, Nicholas understood the "right" of kings to govern independently from parliaments. On a personal level, Constantine was related to the Romanovs through his mother Queen Olga who was a Russian Grand Duchess. At the same time Russia was at war with Germany and Constantine's pro-German sentiments put him at odds with his Russian relatives. This ambivalent official position allowed interest groups, such as Odessa's Greek community, to voice their preference for one or the other of Greece's two opposing factions.

The Greek community of Odessa had a history of supporting Venizelos' program of political and economic change. The traditional view of historians who have dealt with Odessa's Greeks is that the wealthy leaders of the community were conservative in their political and social views.[87] While it is true that those pillars of the community were not revolutionaries, they were not reactionaries either. The Greek Liberal Party advocated constitutional monarchy, economic freedom, and wider political participation. Those were goals which the middle classes all over Europe understood and supported.[88] Odessa's mainstream Greek newspaper *Κόσμος* (The World) added its editorial support for the 1909 coup less than a week after that event took place. On 21 August 1909 *Κόσμος* criticized Greece's old style politicians (against whom the coup was aimed) as being responsible for Greece's bad governments and also for not allowing new men with progressive ideas to achieve their goals.[89] After the successful conclusion of the First Balkan War, the newspaper was hailing Venizelos as Greece's leader and noted that the Greek Premier's efforts not only rejuvenated Greece itself but that the new spirit spilled over to the Greeks of the diaspora and the Greek community of Odessa.[90]

During the time of the "National Schism," Odessa's Greek community was not as divided as other communities of the Greek diaspora.[91] To be sure, differences did exist and some individuals did attempt to "take over" community institutions. The Venizelist newspaper *Αναγέννησις* reported that on 11 June 1917 some unnamed individuals registered a number of new parishioners in the local Greek Orthodox Church with the aim of influencing upcoming elections.[92] A few months later, the same newspaper claimed that the priests of the Greek Orthodox Church of the Holy Trinity were royalists in their political beliefs (even going so far as to want the re-establishment of tsardom), and they manipulated the just concluded elections for Church Board.[93] Complains about the above mentioned elections were not limited to the press. According to the GBAO records a number of the organization's members charged that the elections were "rigged" not only because a number of people were registered overnight, but also because some of them were not even Greeks.[94] With the exception of the above mentioned incident, it seems that the majority of Odessa's Greek society was either neutral about political events in Greece (an unlikely possibility given the traditional level of politicization among Greeks, as well as the fact that the "National Schism" was an event of monumental interest and importance among Greeks) or supported Venizelos' Liberal Party.[95]

The GBAO, the leader of Odessa's Greek community (and itself governed by the elite of that group), was at the forefront of support for Venizelos' program. On March 4, 1915, when Venizelos was still Premier but Greece remained neutral due to royal insistence, the Board of Trustees of the GBAO passed a resolution asking Greece to abandon its neutrality and enter the war on the side of the Western Powers (Russia being an ally of the British and the French).[96] This clear political stance of the GBAO (even for a cause favorable to Russia) was a dynamic move which points to the overwhelming support for Venizelos among Odessa's Greeks.[97] Later that year, when the disagreement between king and Venizelos lead to the premier's resignation, the GBAO came out openly for Venizelos by sending him a telegraph of support.[98] In the next few years, up to the communist victory in the Russian Civil War, the GBAO (while maintaining its character as a benevolent organization) came to assume the characteristics of a political organization.[99] Using its excellent relations with Greece's Consul General Kapsambelis, the GBAO was able to achieve its ends with the help of the local Russian authorities. Thus when the Greek language newspaper *Ελληνικός Αστήρ* (Greek Star) displeased the GBAO, the organization requested from Kapsambelis to close the newspaper. Within a few days the military commander of Odessa, using his special powers under the marshal law which existed at the time, ordered the closing of that newspaper.[100] But the action which clearly demonstrates the politicization of the GBAO took place in late 1915. Greece was still neutral in the war and many communities of the Greek diaspora clamored for their country's entrance in the war at the side of the Western Powers. Some of those Greek communities decided to act independently of the Greek government and convene in a representative body composed of Greeks from different communities. That body, which would be clearly pro-western, would coordinate the actions of the Greeks of the diaspora, show the West that there were Greeks who supported their side and bring pressure on the King of Greece to change his policy. The Greek community of Odessa was invited to send representatives to Paris, the site of the proposed gathering.[101] It is interesting to note that the Greeks of Paris (who were the ones contacting their Odessa counterparts) sent the telegram to the GBAO, again underlying the fact that the organization was the leader of Odessa's Greeks. On December 21st the Board of Trustees of the GBAO agreed to designate as their representatives to Paris Messrs. Ralli and Triandaffilides who had the advantage of being two GBAO members who were already in that city.[102] The indication from the GBAO record is that the association acted independently without asking the permission of the Russian authorities or the advise of the Greek Consul.[103]

The above described actions are hardly those of conservative individuals and illustrate that the GBAO was a progressive entity. A conservative institution (such as the GBAO has been portrayed by some), does not take a position against the established political order and the king. It certainly does not side with a liberal party which, although not revolutionary, advocated important social and political changes. During the First World War the GBAO behaved in a way that a political organization would. It advocated a particular course of political action and pursued its aims independently from both Greek and Russian governments. One could say that during that period, the GBAO came "out of the closet" and revealed itself to be a national organization with goals going beyond the narrow ones which its charter described.

VII
End of an Era

The year 1917 was one of critical importance for Russia and for the world as a whole. The First World War was in full swing and besides the carnage it had created in the various fronts among the combatants, its effects were felt among civilians as well. Blockades and new types of "total war" had brought commerce to a standstill while inflation and food shortages hit the civilian populations more than at any other time before in the history of warfare. Generally speaking, wars are bad for most businesses and the people of Odessa felt the impact of the war acutely. Since Turkey had entered the war on the German side, the Dardanelles were closed to navigation and trade to and from Odessa came to a standstill. As a result, the economy of the city suffered and even people not directly engaged in trade felt the pinch. Shortages of food and other goods caused by the war added to the discomfort of the people while worries over loved ones in combat and military reversals taxed the tranquility even of the most patient individuals. The Greeks of Odessa were doubly hit during this turmoil. Most of them anxiously followed the events of the war not only in Russia but in Greece as well. All in all while life in 1917 Odessa was not unbearable it was far from being pleasant.

The GBAO felt the impact of the war mainly in its financial affairs. Due to the fact that war-caused inflation had driven prices high, the GBAO had to increase the dues collected from individual members.[1] There was also some political friction between those GBAO members (the majority) who supported the pro-western Greek Premier Venizelos and those who remained loyal to pro-German King Constantine I. To those differences were soon to be added political antipathies between those who supported Russia's new liberal regime versus those who supported the tsar.[2] Those difficulties aside, the GBAO had every reason to be pleased with its general condition and in fact looked to the future with some confidence.

The year 1917 marked the forty-fifth anniversary of the existence of the GBAO. By all measures, the organization was well-established, indeed the GBAO at forty-five was the longest existing Greek organization in Russia. The fact that the Who's Who of Odessa's Greeks belonged to the GBAO, and also that all Greek institutions in that city were either owned or controlled by the organization, signified that entity's importance. It was quite logical for the GBAO members, and for everyone else for that matter, to assume that the organization would continue to exist as long as Greeks continue to reside in Odessa. As has been chronicled in the previous chapters, after the initial problems of establishing the organization and creating various institutions, the GBAO had entered a period of relatively smooth sailing. The organization had even become overtly political in nature and attempted (with some success) to influence both Russian and Greek policies. Political developments in Russia during the early part of 1917 were also favorable for that country's Greeks. The February Revolution did away with the tsar and a western-style democratic government was established which was willing to allow Russia's ethnic minorities a larger degree of freedom and participation in the government. Unlike some other minorities of the empire (such as the Poles and the Finns), the Greeks were not expecting self-determination but were hopeful of more freedom to administer their educational and other community affairs. Due to war and revolutionary developments, the Greeks of Russia were optimistic about the future and made a rather belated attempt (discussed earlier in this work) to organize in all-encompassing union of Russian Greeks with political, educational, religious and financial goals.[3] These aspirations remained unfulfilled. As it turned out the well established GBAO as well as the vast majority of Russia's Greeks were forced out of the country due to the monumental events of October 1917. Hellenism in Russia was almost wiped out and the GBAO became a footnote in history as a result of Russia's change of regime following the October Bolshevik Revolution, the civil war and foreign intervention. Ironically enough, that tragic outcome came when the GBAO was at the pinnacle of its power.

By 1917 the GBAO was clearly the focal point of Greek life in Odessa. Its support of the church, schools, nursing home and special needs of individuals as well as its foray into political representation had made the organization the representative of Hellenism in the area. The first budget of the GBAO for the year 1873 shows an income of

27,689.66 rubles and an equal amount of expenses.[4] Compared to that the GBAO balance sheet (Γενικός Ισολογισμός) for the year 1917 shows receipts of 98,647.46 rubles and expenses of 95,731.75 rubles.[5] The surplus of 2,915.71 rubles was transferred to the new budget starting January 1, 1918. The total worth (gross) of the GBAO assets came to 529,693.18 rubles.[6] Of that amount 228,320 rubles was in real estate (the building of the Girls' School, the nursing home for the elderly, etc.), while another 272,200 rubles were in stocks, bonds and government securities. At the same time the GBAO had outstanding debts of 4,139.40 rubles.[7] From the above mentioned balance sheet, the Greek Orthodox Church of the Holy Trinity and the Boys' School were omitted because they, although controlled by the GBAO, had separate boards of administrators and budgets. The 1917–1918 balance sheet of the Boys' School shows gross worth of 878,634.91 rubles.[8] Its projected operational budget for the 1919–1920 school year was 229,262.32 rubles.[9] From the numbers in the GBAO budget, and those of related institutions, one can come to the logical conclusion that the organization was solid and, barring an extraordinary event, would have continued to exist and prosper.

The GBAO was not only beneficial to Odessa's Greeks (which was after all the reason for its existence) but to the population of Odessa as a whole. Such benefits were both direct and indirect, financial as well as other intangible ones. By taking care of poor Greeks, the GBAO relieved other charities (private or church led) from that burden thus freeing up community resources for other purposes. At the same time, the money that the GBAO gave to the poor were spent in the community while items provided (such as tickets for repatriation or clothes) were locally bought thus adding to the local economy. Also, the dowry which the GBAO provided for needy women (four grants a year per person of 100 rubles each) did not remain in the Greek community. Naturally it was spent locally, but also since the original donor (G. G. Maraslis) had stipulated that the dowry should be given to Greeks and non-Greeks alike, the money was given directly to non-Greeks. The various institutions supported by the GBAO had to have furniture, and other equipment, which was bought locally. In 1917 the GBAO listed in its balance sheet 7,138.70 rubles worth of furniture and books for the Girls' School and the nursing home for the elderly. To that amount one should add the equally, if not more, expensive furniture and books of the Boys' School and those of the church of the Holy Trinity. Besides furniture the various

GBAO institutions had operational expenses which were also spent in the community. The salaries of personnel, heating of buildings, clothing of students were only some of the money contributed to Odessa's economy. The GBAO itself, although run frugally, had monthly operational expenses in the neighborhood of 500 rubles.[10] The already mentioned 272,200 rubles in stocks, bonds and government securities were also an important GBAO contribution to the economic growth of the city as a whole.[11] The various buildings which the GBAO erected, notably the Girls' School but also the nursing home, were also a source of monetary contribution to Odessa's economy. Money for material and wages of workers was spent in the community, while the buildings themselves added to Odessa's beautification.

Besides the purely financial contribution, the existence of the GBAO benefited Odessa in a non-monetary way. Providing for the poor, besides being "good" in a moral sense, also adds to a city's quality of life. While poverty can never be eradicated, measures can be taken to limit its most onerous manifestations. The quality of life of even that of the wealthiest suffers if their homes and/or businesses are surrounded by poverty and squalor. The various GBAO buildings were also an asset to the community. The well kept church and the building of the Girls' School, situated on Pushkin Street which connects the railroad station to the city center, created an aesthetically pleasing environment. Both of the GBAO supported educational institutions, the Girls' and the Boys' Schools, contributed to the community by educating Odessa's Greeks. Since most of those young men and women remained in Russia, their education was in some way used for their adoptive country's benefit. At the same time, a number of non-Greeks also received a first-rate education in the GBAO supported schools (more non-Greeks attended the Boys' School than did the Girls') thus the Greek community's resources were utilized, for a fee, by the rest of the community. The contributions which the GBAO made to Odessa's society and economy was multifaceted and manifested in many different ways.

The GBAO compares favorably with the various civic charity groups in existence at the time. A brief overview will help illustrate the level of success of the GBAO in terms of finances as well as its membership. The GBAO was a typical Russian volunteer charitable organization in a number of ways. Like the vast majority of Russia's private charities the GBAO was located in an urban center. Over half of the urban-based charities were in cities with a population of at least 20,000 inhabitants.[12] The overwhelming majority of those associations demanded relatively low annual dues in order to attract more participants. According to Russian government sources most charities' dues were between 1.5-3 rubles per year.[13] The GBAO as an association of an ethnic minority was a rare, but not a unique, phenomenon in the Russian Empire. Although only 3.5% of charitable associations were composed of minority ethnic groups, in absolute numbers 130 such entities existed.[14] Understandably, ethnic organizations were located in urban areas, like Odessa, with a cosmopolitan population. While the GBAO was in many ways a typical Russian charitable association, when it came to membership and wealth it was quite atypical.

A number of historians have claim that although the GBAO was powerful and beneficial to the community, its membership was low, indicating that the organization was an elite institution. The position of this writer is quite the opposite. Far from being the preserve of the few, the GBAO was an open organization with a large membership. As it has already been noted, according to the 1897 Russian census there were 5,013 Greek speakers in the city.[15] At about the same time (1896) the GBAO membership stood at 334, about 7% of the total Greek speaking population.[16] Given the fact that the GBAO membership was limited, not by rule but by custom to males, one should calculate the members as a percentage of Odessa's Greek speaking males. Out of a total of 3,166 Greek speaking males in Odessa 334 (9.5%) belonged to the GBAO.[17] Clearly not all Greek speaking males of Odessa were of adult age or had the financial means to pay the 3 ruble a year membership fee. Thus, the percentage of eligible Greeks who joined the GBAO might have been as high as 20% or even higher. In absolute numbers, the membership of the GBAO was large compared with the average number of participants in other Russian charitable organizations. In 1901 3,258 charitable associations had a total membership of almost 450,000. The membership of those entities is broken down in Table 6 below.[18]

The average membership for all associations was 138. The GBAO membership (334) was almost two and a half (2.5) times larger than the national average and almost four (4) times larger than the average membership for associations which, like the GBAO, were based in district towns. Clearly then, the GBAO, was quite representative of the Greek community of Odessa.

TABLE 6
Size of Charitable Associations by Location, circa 1901

Location	Number of Associations	Average Membership
Provincial capitals	1,419	194
District towns	1,283	86
Other towns	195	156
Countryside	361	94

As it has been already noted the GBAO was a relatively wealthy organization with a substantial income from endowments. A sizable amount of its income each year was devoted to various charitable enterprises. A comparison with other Russian organizations of the same type reflects the GBAO's relative impact on society.

TABLE 7
Capital Assets of Charitable Associations Circa 1901[19]

Capital Assets	Number of Societies Reporting	Percentage
No capital assets	216	6.5
1,000 rubles or less	942	28.2
1,000-3,000	643	19.2
3,000-5,000	298	8.9
5,000-10,000	403	12.1
10,000-50,000	612	18.3
Over 50,000 rubles	227	6.8

The GBAO with capital assets of almost 530,000 rubles (in 1917) belonged to the few, less than 7% of better to do Russian charitable associations.[20] Besides assets, the GBAO belonged among the few Russian charitable organizations which enjoyed high income which in turn enabled them to engage in several charitable activities.

TABLE 8
Charitable Associations' Income and Expenditure Circa 1901[21]

Income	**Number of Societies Reporting**	**Percentage**
500 rubles or less	779	23.3
500-2,500	1,320	39.6
2,500-10,000	827	24.8
Over 10,000	410	12.3
Expenditure		
500 rubles or less	1,073	32.2
500-2,500	1,227	36.9
2,500-10,000	681	20.5
Over 10,000	348	10.4

The GBAO belonged, again it will be noticed, among those charitable associations which enjoyed high income (12.3% of the total) as well as spending more money (10.4%). Total GBAO income for 1917 came to a little over 44,000 rubles while expenditures for the same year totaled over 54,000 rubles.[22] From these figures, one forms the opinion that the GBAO was secure in its position as one of Russia's top charitable associations, an organization which was well established and viewed the future with confidence.

At the organization's apogee of power and prestige, calamity struck swiftly and hard. The Bolshevik coup and the eventual victory of the Reds against the Whites, spelled the end of the GBAO. Given the events of 1917–1920s, the end of the GBAO was inevitable. The communists were ideologically opposed to non-governmental charity organizations, wanted to control the property of such institutions, and distrusted all types of non-communist led civic groups. The Bolsheviks tolerated private charitable institutions and allowed them to operate during the 1921–1922 famine but banned them soon after.[23] Thus when the Soviets were firmly established in Odessa the end of the GBAO became imminent.

The fact that the Greek community of South Russia was identified with the anti-Communist camp was another reason to abolish that minority's independent institutions. While it is true that a number of Russia's Greeks were sympathetic to the communist cause, the most prominent and vocal members of the community were identified with the Whites. Consequently, the whole Greek community of Russia was labeled hostile to the new regime. The Greeks of Russia became the victims not only of the political events of their host country, but also of political decisions taken as far away as Paris. The victors of WW I, mainly Britain and France, decided that it was beneficial to their interests to defeat communism in Russia. France's Premier George Clemenceau was particularly active in that cause and decided to send French troops to South Russia to intervene in that country's civil war and help the Whites defeat the Reds. The expedition was far from popular in France and Clemenceau looked for allies who were willing to shoulder part of the responsibility of fighting communism. The Greek Premier E. Venizelos agreed to provide over 40,000 Greek troops in support of their French allies.[24] The most common misconception surrounding the Greek participation, a misconception supported by memoirs of Greek military commanders, is that the Greeks (both the government and the common soldiers) were motivated by their love for Russia, a fellow Orthodox nation which had helped Greece in the past.[25] While such feelings might have existed, they were of minor importance as motives for military action. Venizelos wanted Greece to annex extensive territories belonging to the defeated Ottoman Empire, territories which were of strategic and economic importance for Greece. Most importantly, these territories were populated by a substantial number of ethnic Greeks. Inclusion of those areas in Greece proper would have also fulfilled Greece's age old irredentist goals. Clemenceau promised Venizelos that in exchange for Greek participation in the Russian campaign, France would support Greek expectations in Thrace and Asia Minor (provided that Britain and the USA would also support the Asia Minor transfer).[26] Even the common soldiers knew that Greek participation in Ukraine meant possible gains elsewhere and a song of the barracks proclaimed that "The road to Smyrna runs through Russia."[27] The story of the allied intervention in South Russia is not particularly glorious. The western powers overestimated the popular support for the White cause. At the same time, they underestimated the power of the Bolsheviks. This, coupled with bad planning and low morale, spelled the doom of the expedition. However, the short period of time which the western allies spent in Ukraine, January to summer 1919, was enough to turn the local population and the communist regime against the Greeks in general and the Greeks of Russia in particular.

Due to difficulties in transporting the troops, Greece was able to send a little over 23,000 troops out of the 42,000 originally planed. Even with that reduced number the Greeks were the most numerous non-Russian troops in the area. To have a Great Power like France intervene in the national affairs of another major power is one thing, to have a tiny country like Greece assume such role was considered totally unacceptable. The Russians felt humiliated and reserved some of their enmity for the Greeks.[28] The Greeks of Russia, and particularly those of Odessa, welcomed the Greek troops enthusiastically. Such demonstrations of support for the invaders embittered the Russian population and turned it against the local Greeks.[29] In some other parts of Russia, the local Greeks became even more identified with those who opposed the Bolsheviks. The Greek Central National Committee of Transcaucasia set up an army brigade composed by local Greeks and commanded by Greek officers of the Russian Army with Major-General Ananias as its commander.[30] As part of the military operations, the Greek army had to arrest and disarm Bolshevik sympathizers among the civilian population, a state of affairs which alienated the Russia public. In some instances, such as the one which occurred in the city of Kherson in March of 1919, a large number of Russian civilians were killed when the people of that city attacked the citadel which was defended by Greek army units.[31] The Ukrainian Soviet complained to the Greek government and threatened the Greeks of Ukraine with reprisals.[32] The Greek government, which had come to realize that the expedition will fail and that the Greeks of Russia could not be protected, was able to pacify the Bolsheviks who promised not to harm Russia's Greeks.[33] The Bolsheviks have often been accused of not honoring their word but in this case they did and when the foreign troops left Russia there was no wholesale reprisals against the Greeks. That might have also been due to the fact that a number of Greeks had joined the Bolshevik ranks. The Reds attempted to use those like-minded Greeks to spread defeatist propaganda to the Greek Army but the overall results were mixed at best.[34] In some cases, the reprisals were local in nature as when the people of Kherson turned against the city's Greek population once the Greek army had withdrawn.[35] With the supremacy of the communist regime established, the leaders of the Greek community and the GBAO, being themselves wealthy capitalists, escaped to the West leaving the field open to those communist or communist sympathizer Greeks who were now in position to assert their leadership on the community. [36] Soon after, on an unspecified date, the GBAO (as quietly as it was created about fifty years before) ceased to exist.

Those Greeks who left Odessa (like other wealthy groups) faced financial difficulties to which they were unaccustomed. Given the fact that the overwhelming majority of the wealth of the well to do Greeks was in real estate and Russian stocks and bonds, huge fortunes were lost overnight.[37] According to some estimates the Greeks of Odessa collectively lost property worth 6,500,000 British pounds sterling.[38] Collectively the Greeks of Russia lost property worth 25,470,000 British pounds. The Greeks of the Odessa-Kherson-Nikolaev region lost 7,150,000 (that amount includes the already mentioned 6,500,000). Other loses by region included. Kuban 3,940,000; Don-Azov 2,570,000; Black Sea 3,450,000; Siberia 430,000; Turkmenistan 350,000; Manchuria-Vladivostok 500,000, etc.[39] Many formerly wealthy individuals had to end their lives in reduced circumstances. Thus one member of the famous Ralli family ended his life in a small Athens apartment, a long way from his multi-level mansion in Odessa which took the space of almost a whole city block.[40] Considering the hardship of many other Greeks from Russia, the aforementioned Ralli was lucky. The widow of G. G. Maraslis, a former mayor of Odessa and founding member and president of GBAO, found herself destitute and was discovered in 1928 living in Athens in a basement room of the "Maraslion Teachers' School" (ironically built with funds donated by her late husband). Fortunately for her, her plight came to the attention of Greek Premier E. Venizelos who drafted a special law giving her an "honorary pension for life" which helped her live in some comfort until her death in 1935.[41] Since almost to a person those repatriated Greeks spoke Greek they were soon absorbed into the main stream of Greek society.

A large number of Greeks (overwhelmingly Russian speakers) found themselves in the USSR either because they did not want to leave or because they couldn't do so. In the early 1920s, the Ukrainian government attempted to win over the Greek minority by reviving some of the advantages which Catherine the Great had used to entice the Greeks to South Russia in the first place. According to official Ukrainian sources, in 1926 there were about 104,000 Greeks in the Republic 93,000 of whom were farmers.[42] As Greek-Soviet relations normalized in the late 1920s, about 40,000 more Greeks were able to leave. In those years, Odessa became the destination of many Greeks from inside the USSR who saw the city as the first leg of their trip to Greece.[43] Although there was official pressure to integrate into Soviet society, the Greeks were allowed to use their own language, publish books in Greek and even transmit radio programs in Greek (there was an Odessa radio station which broadcasted in Greek three times a week until about 1935).[44] During the early 1930s, when Ukraine was forcibly collectivized by Stalin, the Greeks were hit hard. About 7% of them were labeled *kulaks* (rich peasants) and were "liquidated" while the rest were collectivized.[45] In 1928–1929 a wave of xenophobia swept the country which culminated in the so-called "engineers' plot." In that incident a number of foreigners working in the Soviet Union as specialists in mining and industry (hence the name of the affair) were accused of actually sabotaging production. Among the many foreigners caught in the middle was a certain Voutsinas who was accused of "economic espionage" and sentenced to ten years imprisonment but eventually was allowed to return to Greece.[46] During the middle and late 1930s, at the height of the Stalinist purges, the Greeks, like all national minorities, were a target. There were wild stories circulating about the conspiracy to create a "Greater Greek Republic" in Ukraine, a puppet state supported by Greece and other western nations. Greeks who were not Soviet citizens or who did not live in Greek communities in the Soviet Union were arrested and exiled to Siberia or forced to leave the country.[47] Odessa's Greek Church of the Holy Trinity escaped destruction but a number of Greek churches in other places were closed and the Greek priests were required to obtain Soviet citizenship. At that time the various ethnic-based Soviets, including the Greek, were dissolved.[48]

A measured assessment of the impact and legacy of the GBAO has to take into account the political and social conditions during the period of the organization's existence. In many respects, its work was pioneering, especially when one keeps in mind that at the time the state was not considered responsible for the physical well being of individual citizens. That problem was gradually being addressed by emerging charity organizations mainly church-sponsored ones. The GBAO was one of the pioneers in Russia of civic sponsored charity. They recognized the need and usefulness of organized charity, and foresaw the time when the state itself would take up that role. In time the GBAO went beyond its stated mandate and expanded its activities becoming a spokesman of the concerns of the Greek community of Odessa and Russia in general. Perhaps they viewed themselves as a type of pressure group attempting, and at times succeeding in modifying official tsarist policy. In that respect the GBAO became the ancestor of such special interest groups championing the causes of national minorities.[49] Also pioneering were the attempts by the GBAO, in 1917, to organize all Greek associations into an umbrella group with clear cut political goals; goals which Russia's Provisional Government, more tolerant than the tsarist regime it replaced, was willing to accommodate. Considering the authoritarian regime which existed in Russia throughout most of the GBAO existence, the organization made great strides and its accomplishments can be described as significant, especially in the social and educational fields.

The GBAO's internal organization and dynamics are also an interesting subject. The organization itself was governed by the few who were willing and/or able to spend the required time and effort. While the Greek community of Odessa was primarily Russian-speaking, the leaders of the GBAO were almost exclusively Greek-speaking and, if not rich, at least members of the professional and/or educated middle class. The most impressive fact in the GBAO story is the exemplary way with which the organization's finances were handled, avoiding improprieties and insuring good returns in every sense of the word.[50] Claims for assistance were thoroughly examined in order to assure that the needy were helped but the ones who wanted to take advantage of the community's good would be turned away. The result was financial and administrative success, which was translated in fulfillment of the goals of the association. It is not surprising that an organization run by businessmen was businesslike in its day to day work. It is also interesting to note that the GBAO was less judgmental of people's failings (middle class organizations of that era have been often portrayed as highly critical and judgmental of the less fortunate). Thus the fact that one had been found guilty of a crime and imprisoned did not disqualify him or her from receiving a helping hand from his fellow Greeks. Needless to say, the GBAO had its shortcomings. It was clearly a paternalistic entity in its approach to charity. It decided who deserved charity, how much and what kind of help would be given. However, in the final analysis all private charity has a paternalistic side to it. Occasionally, the GBAO was accused of not fulfilling its goals properly. Such accusations were anonymous and general in nature and can be dismissed as unsubstantiated. A rare eponymous accusation, and one which had some merit, was leveled at the GBAO in 1908.[51] The writer, a certain Ch. Kourtides, was not an outsider as he was elected a non-voting member of the GBAO board in 1910. While applauding the GBAO educational policies, the author noted that if the organization's goal was to provide Greek education for Odessa's Greek youth it should establish small grammar schools in the outer suburbs of the city. Those were the areas where Odessa's poor Greeks lived. Since they were numerous and most of them Russian speakers the author's suggestion made sense. However, the GBAO did not seem to have taken up the challenge. This failure was indeed serious for an organization which claimed to represent all of Odessa's Greeks and had as its goal the survival of the Greek language. Important as the operation of the Boys' Commercial School as well as the Girls' School was, it still did not address the basic educational needs of the city's Greeks. What was clearly needed was free elementary Greek education for the vast majority of the city's poor Greeks. For a variety of reasons the GBAO failed to do anything about this major issue

Odessa was never a "Greek" city and it is much less so today. The few Greeks that are left in the city today are either elderly Greek speakers or young Russian speakers. Both categories are assimilated to the Russian way of life.[52] Most common are the people who know that a great-grandparent was Greek but that is about all they know of their ethnic past. Some old mansions of Greek merchants survive, dilapidated, sad reminders of past glories and of the days when the city was rich and important. Some of the surviving buildings have been converted to institutional use: the Maraslis house has become part of a medical school; other homes have been subdivided into apartments.[53] The Greek Orthodox Church of the Holy Trinity is still in use, an old magnificent building serving a dwindling, mainly Russian, number of faithful. Recent grants by the Greek government have restored an old Maraslis property, supposedly the meeting place of the old Greek patriotic organization "Friendly Society," and now it houses the offices and library of the Athens based Foundation for Hellenic Culture. The tourist to the city, the one who does not know its ethnic history, would be surprised to find that in Odessa's center there is a "Greek Square" and a "Greek Street," reminders of a time when Greek merchant houses controlled the city's economy and young men from all over the Greek world came to Russia, as later they would go to America, to make their fortune.

Notes

Chapter I
The Historical Background

1. See John Boardman, *The Greeks Overseas* (Baltimore: Penguin Books, 1964), 245-275. Also, William H. McNeill, *History of Western Civilization* (Chicago: University of Chicago Press, 1969), pp. 41-45. According to McNeill most of the ancient Greek colonization occurred between 750-550 B.C.

2. In a recent study, *Global Diasporas: An Introduction* (Seattle: University of Washington Press, 1997), Robin Cohen differentiates between the classical meaning of the word *Diaspora*, which signified migration and colonization, versus the modern term which (taking into account the Jewish, African, Palestinian, and Armenian experiences) signifies "...a collective trauma, a banishment, where one dreamed of home but lived in exile" (p. ix). Clearly the ancient Greek settlers of the Black Sea littoral confirm Cohen's thesis. On the other hand, as will be explained later, one could argue that even the Greek diaspora in Russia of the late eighteenth century was closer to the ancient rather than the modern model.

3. Cohen, p. xii.

4. Neal Ascherson's *Black Sea* (London: Jonathan Cape, 1995), though a popular history, gives a good account of the relationships between the various peoples of the Black Sea from ancient times to the present. See also, E. I. Levi, *Nadpisi Ol'vii* (The Inscriptions of Olvia). (Leningrad: Nauka, 1968) and *Ol'viia. Gorod epohi ellinisma* (Olvia. A City of the Hellenistic Era) (Leningrad: Nauka, 1985) which deal with archeological evidence from the ancient Greek settlements in the Black Sea littoral. The pre-revolutionary works of V. V. Latyshev deal with the plethora of archeological evidence pointing to the strong presence of Greeks in the area. See especially his *Isliedovaniia ob Istorii i gosudarstvennom stroie goroda Ol'vii* (Study of the History and the Political System of the City of Olvia) (St. Petersburg: Balasheva, 1887); and *Sbornik Grecheskich Nadpisej Christianskich Vremen iz Juznoj Rossii* (Collection of Greek Inscriptions of the Christian Times from Southern Russia) (St. Petersburg: Imperial Academy of Sciences, 1896).

5. For a panoramic and diachronic description of the Greek presence in the region, see Marina Koromila, ed., *The Greeks in the Black Sea* (Athens: Panorama, 1991).

6. When Greek refugees from Greece proper met their Crimean compatriots, who by that time (1774) were living in Mariupol, the two groups could not communicate as the former spoke Greek while the latter spoke a Turkish/Tartar dialect. See Patricia Herlihy, *Odessa: A History, 1794-1914* (Cambridge, Mass: Harvard University Press, 1986), p. 28. Also, Grigorii Arsh, "Grecheskaia emigratsiia v Rossiiu v kontse xviii-natsale xix v." (Greek Emigration to Russia at the end of the Eighteenth to the Beginning of the Nineteenth Centuries), *Sovetskaia ethnografiia* 3 (1969), p. 87; and A. Fisher *The Russian Annexation of the Crimea 1772-1783* (Cambridge: Cambridge University Press, 1970), p. 13.

7. Francis House, *Millennium of Faith: Christianity in Russia, AD 988-1988* (Crestwood, NY: St. Vladimir's Seminary Press, 1988), pp. 5-6.

8. Vladimir was a pragmatist looking to gain advantage by his conversion rather than a man who was looking for spiritual guidance. Reportedly he rejected Islam due to that religion's prohibition of wine consumption (a sacrifice that Vladimir was not prepared to make), Judaism was rejected because the prince reasoned that a god who has allowed his chosen

people to be uprooted was not much of a protector. Janet Martin, *Medieval Russia 980-1584* (Cambridge, Cambridge University Press, 1995), pp. 6-7.

9. George Vernadsky, *A History of Russia* (New Haven: Yale University Press, 1951), pp. 32-34. Also Basil Dmytryshyn, ed., *Medieval Russia: A Source Book, 900-1700* (New York: Holt, Rinehart and Winston, Inc., 1967), pp. 11-23 and 32-37.

10. During the heyday of its power, the Byzantine Empire was notorious for refusing to marry princesses to anyone but Orthodox Christians. It seems that Vladimir wanted the prestige of being the husband of a Byzantine princess enough to consider conversion. Dimitri Obolensky, ed., *The Byzantine Inheritance of Eastern Europe* (London: Variorum Reprints, 1982), p. 131.

11. John Meyendorff, *Byzantium and the Rise of Russia* (Cambridge: Cambridge University Press, 1981), p. 21.

12. Martin, pp. 10, 46, 66.

13. Obolensky, *Byzantine Inheritance*, p. 11.

14. The artistic presence of Greeks in Russia continued even after the Byzantine period. In one interesting case two Greek brothers, Ioannes and Georgios, (last name unknown) wrote to Patriarch Nikon of Moscow asking for his patronage. The brothers were painters specializing in church iconography, especially frescoes. In their letter to Nikon the brothers noted that Russian painters were not proficient in fresco painting and proposed to go to Moscow for a year in order to paint and teach their craft to Russian painters. They directed the patriarch to ask information about their artwork from those who had seen some other works by the brothers in the church of St. Vladimir in Kiev as well as in a number of monasteries in Wallachia and Moldavia. See B. L. Fonkich, ed., *Graeco-Russian Contacts from the middle of the XVI century up to the beginning of the XVIII century* (Moscow: USSR Academy of Sciences, 1991), pp. 51-52. The letter is dated 1665, and if the word of the brothers is to be believed, Russian artists were still behind their Greek counterparts in some areas. The fact that the brothers had worked outside the boundaries of Greece is a testament to their skill and/or the good reputation enjoyed by Greek artists throughout the Orthodox world.

15. Meyendorff, p. 17. In some cases the Patriarch appointed Russian prelates without consulting the Russian ecclesiastical or lay authorities. Martin, p. 255.

16. See Dimitry Obolensky, ed., *Byzantium and the Slavs: Collected Studies* (London: Variorum Reprints, 1971), p. 271.

17. One instance which illustrates the complexity of Greek-Russian church relations is the story of the cleric Maksim the Greek. In the early sixteenth century the Grand Prince of Muscovy requested from the Patriarch of Constantinople to sent an educated theologian who could help the Russian church in matters of dogma. Maksim the Greek was sent to Moscow and devoted his energy and vast knowledge not only to matters of dogma, but also in translating works from Greek into Russian. In time Maksim fell into disfavor and spent the remaining of his life a virtual prisoner. See Jack V. Haney, *From Italy to Muscovy. The Life and Works of Maxim the Greek* (Munich: Wilhelm Fink Verlag, 1973). Also, Hugh Olmsted, "A Learned Greek Monk in Muscovite Exile: Maksim Grek and the Old Testament Prophets" *Modern Greek Studies Yearbook* 3 (1987): pp. 1-74.

18. For centuries the leader of the Orthodox Church in Russia was often a Greek. Between the time of Vladimir's conversion (late tenth century) and the "Mongol Yoke" (early to middle thirteenth century) there were twenty-three leaders of the Russian Church of which seventeen were Greeks. Meyendorff, p. 19.

19. The rulers of Moldavia and Wallachia, although Orthodox do not count as they were already vassals of the Ottoman Sultan. Muscovy's claim as successor to Byzantium

was strengthened in 1472 when Ivan III married Zoe Paleologos, niece of the last emperor of Constantinople.

20. At least one scholar speculates that Isidor was allowed to escape because the Russian authorities "...had little enthusiasm for carrying out the mandatory penalty for apostasy, death by burning at the stake or burial alive." Martin, pp. 255-256.

21. George Majeska, "Russia's Perception of Byzantium After the Fall" in Lowell Clucas, ed., *The Byzantine Legacy in Eastern Europe* (Boulder: East European Monographs, 1988), p. 19.

22. For a detailed account of the impact of the Council of Florence on Russian Church affairs see John Fennell, *A History of the Russian Church to 1448* (New York: Longman, 1995), pp. 170-188.

23. Martin, pp. 258, 262.

24. Michael Cherniavsky, *Tsar and People: Studies in Russian Myths* (New York: Random House, 1961), p. 51. Also Majeska, p. 23.

25. Obolensky, *Byzantium and the Slavs*, 272. The Russian Orthodox Church became officially autocephalous only in 1589 but for over a century it was able to manage its own affairs. For a comprehensive study of the role of the Orthodox Church in the culture and society of Eastern Europe see Obolensky's classic work *The Byzantine Commonwealth. Eastern Europe, 500-1453* (London: Weidenfeld and Nicolson, 1971).

26. Fonkich, 9. The tsar was petitioned for help from, among others, the Metropolitan of Thessaloniki (1631), the Metropolitan of Paleopatras (1644) and the Patriarch of Jerusalem (1645). See Fonkich, pp. 21-24, 29, 32. In the last two cases the tsar responded by sending money. The Metropolitan of Thessaloniki received money as well as religious books. This last case is interesting as it demonstrates that by that time Russia had become not only a political but also an intellectual center for Orthodoxy.

27. Fonkich, p. 11.

28. See Theofanis G. Stavrou, *Russian Interests in Palestine 1882-1914* (Thessaloniki: Institute for Balkan Studies, 1963), p. 10.

29. Fonkich, 54-59. The tsar could, and did, act independently in this matter but the fact that he felt the need to have his actions "blessed" by non-Russian (mainly Greek) church authorities demonstrate the prestige which the religious heirs to Byzantium enjoyed in Russia and in the Orthodox world at large.

30. L. S. Stavrianos, *The Balkans Since 1453* (New York: Rinehart, 1958), pp. 150, 270-272.

31. C. Th. Dimaras, *Modern Greek Literature*, trans. Mary P. Gianos (Albany, NY: State University of New York Press, 1972), p. 127.

32. B. H. Sumner, *Peter the Great and the Emergence of Russia* (New York: Macmillan, 1962), pp. 72-75.

33. See Franco Venturi, *The End of the Old Regime in Europe, 1768-1776*, trans. R. Burr Litchfield (Princeton: Princeton University Press, 1989), pp. 3-22.

34. See *Ιστορία του Ελληνικού Έθνους* (History of the Greek Nation) 16 vols. (Athens: Ekdotiki Athenon, 1978) IA: 86-89. And, George Roussos, *Νεώτερη Ιστορία του Ελληνικού Έθνους 1826-1974* (Modern History of the Greek Nation, 1826-1974), 7 vols. (Athens: Hellenic Educational House, 1975) 1:128-145. Also, Isabel de Madariaga, *Russia in the Age of Catherine the Great* (New Haven: Yale University Press, 1981), p. 349.

35. Madariaga, pp. 383-384. This grandson of Catherine was the one who later served as Russia's viceroy in Poland (1815-1831) and whose refusal to succeed his older brother Alexander I to the throne sparked the 1825 Decembrist revolt.

36. Madariaga, p. 349. At different times Potemkin dreamed of becoming sovereign of Moldavia, Walachia, Crimea or Curland.

37. Venturi, *1768-1776*, p. 5.

38. Venturi, *1768-1776*, p. 28. Among those who commented on the Greek hope that the Russians will help them was Giacomo Casanova.

39. Venturi, *1768-1776*, pp. 29-35. While those Greeks in Russian service were, to some extent, role models for their compatriots they, and others in the service of foreign powers, were not above criticism. As a popular song of the time proclaimed: "Καλλιά γιά την πατρίδα κανένας να χαθή, η να κρεμάση φούντα γιά ξένον στο σπαθί. (Better to lose one's life for the Fatherland, than hang a foreign tassel to one's sword." See G. Tertzetis, *Th. Kolokotronis: Memoirs from the Greek War of Independence, 1821-1833*, trans. E. M. Edmonds (Chicago: Argonaut Publishers, 1969), p. xxii n.

40. Venturi, *1768-1776*, p. 106.

41. *Ιστορια* IA: 58-83. Also, Roussos 1:117-127, Madariaga, pp. 208-209, and Theophilus Prousis, *Russian Society and the Greek Revolution* (DeKalb: Northern Illinois University Press, 1994), p. 7.

42. An individual who played an important role in the actual fighting was Alexander Pushkin's great-uncle Brigadier Ivan Abramovich Hannibal or Gannibal, son of "Peter the Great's Moor."

43. See G. Tertzetis, p. 83.

44. See Katsonis' biography by Elias Georgiou, *Ο Θαλασσομάχος Λάμβρος Κατσώνης* (The Naval Warrior Lambros Katsonis) (Athens: n.p., 1971).

45. Georgiou, p. 19.

46. Georgiou, pp. 19-20.

47. Georgiou, p. 20.

48. Georgiou, p. 43.

49. Georgiou, p. 292.

50. Georgiou, pp. 349-362.

51. Georgiou, p. 363. It is not clear why Paul acted in such a manner. It is possible that as he did in other cases the new emperor acted diametrically opposite to what he thought his mother would have done.

52. Georgiou, p. 363. A note on the value of money: Between the 1870s and 1914 the value of major currencies remained more or less stable. According to Baedeker's travel guide, 1902 edition, the Russian ruble was worth about $0.5. There is no precise method to adjust for inflation over a long period of time. A general "rule of thumb" is that pre-World War I currencies have to be multiplied by 10-20 in order to approximate their late twentieth century equivalent.

53. Georgiou, p. 371. Some years after Katsonis' death the Russian royal family built a palace in Levadia which in 1943 became the site of some of the meetings of the "Big Three" during the Yalta Conference.

54. See E. I. Druzhinina, *Kiuchuk-Kainardzhiskii Mir 1774 goda (Ego Podgotovka Zakliuchenie)* (The Kutchuk-Kainardji Peace of 1774) (Its Preparation and Signing) (Moscow: Nauka, 1955). Also, *Ιστορια* IA: 83-85. Article 7 of the treaty stated that:

> "The Sublime Porte pledges to give the Christian faith and its churches firm protection and it grants the Ministers of the Russian Imperial Court {the right} to protect all interests of the church built in Constantinople and mentioned below, in Article 14, and those whom it serves, and it {the Porte} will accept

any complaints respectfully, since these are being made by a trusted person of a neighboring and truly friendly country."

Article 14 stated that:

"The Imperial Court of Russia, similarly as other countries, has the right, in addition to a private chapel in the quarters of the Minister, to built in the Galat Part {of Constantinople} on Bei Ogl Street, a public Greek Orthodox Church, which shall remain always under the protection of Ministers of that Empire, and it shall not be subjected to any persecution or insult...."

See Basil Dmytryshyn, ed., *Imperial Russia: A Source Book, 1700-1917*, 3rd ed. (Orlando, FL: Harcourt Brace Jovanovich, 1990), pp. 109-111.

55. See Grigorii Arsh, *Οι Έλληνες της Ρωσ'ιας* (The Greeks in Russia) (Athens: Foundation for Hellenic Culture, 1994), pp. 13-16.

56. Sumner, pp. 37-38. Also, Eric Morris, *The Russian Navy: Myth and Reality* (London: Hamish Hamilton Ltd., 1977), pp. 3-15. According to a recent study there were at least 66 Greeks who joined the Russian Navy around 1700. Of them 62 were sailors, one boatswain (a non-commissioned officer with expertise in running a ship's deck crew), one navigator and two ship's captains. See Edward J. Phillips, *The Founding of Russia's Navy. Peter the Great and the Azov Fleet, 1688-1714* (Westport, CT: Greenwood Press, 1995), p. 138.

57. One eponymous Greek footnote in Russian history of that period occurred when Eudoxia Dioper, daughter of a Greek sea captain became the first wife of Abram Petrovich Hannibal, Alexander Pushkin's African ancestor. Joseph Wieczynski *The Modern Encyclopedia of Russian and Soviet History*, 59 vols. (USA: Academic International Press, 1983), 12:82.

58. The Greeks of the Crimea were considered by Russian authorities to be vital to the areas' agriculture. See Peter Simon Pallas, *Travels Through the Southern Provinces of the Russian Empire in the Years 1793 and 1794*, 2nd ed. (London: Stockdale, 1812), p. 346.

59. Arsh, "The Greeks of Russia," p. 18.

60. Madariaga, p. 363.

61. For details on Catherine's efforts to colonize the South of her empire, see Franco Venturi, *The End of the Old Regime in Europe, 1776-1789*, 2 vols., trans. R. Burr Litchfield (Princeton: Princeton University Press, 1991), vol. 2, pp. 768-773.

62. Roger Bartlett, *Human Capital: The Settlement of Foreigners in Russia 1762-1804* (Cambridge: Cambridge University Press, 1979). Also, Joseph H. Height, *Homesteaders on the Steppe: Cultural History of the Evangelical-Lutheran Colonies in the Region of Odessa 1804-1945* (Bismarck ND: North Dakota Historical Society of Germans from Russia, 1975). On October 1, 1996 the Historical Section of the State Archives of the District of Odessa, in cooperation with that city's Museum of Literature, organized an exhibit with the life of the early Mennonite pioneers as its theme. The exhibit coincided with a visit to the city of a group composed of descendants of Russia's Mennonites who left the country after the 1917 October revolution and settled in the US and Canada.

63. Venturi, *1768-1776*, p. 46-55.

64. Venturi, *1776-1789*, vol. 2, p. 776.

65. Venturi, *1776-1789*, vol. 2, pp. 774-775.

66. Arsh, "The Greeks of Russia," pp. 17-18.

67. C. Papoulides, "Οι Έλληνες της Ρωσίας τον 19ο και στις αρχές του 20ου αιώνα" (The Greeks of Russia in the Nineteenth and the Beginning of the Twentieth Century) *Balkan Miscellany* 4 (1992): p. 110.

68. Papoulides, "The Greeks of Russia," pp. 110-111.

69. Tzelina Harlafti, "Ελληνικά Εμπορονατηλιακά δίκτυα στη νότιο Ρωσία 1830-1914" (Greek Merchant Marine Networks in South Russia, 1830-1914), Conference "The Greeks in Ukraine (18th-20th Century) Social Life, Trade, Culture" Foundation for Hellenic Culture, Institute for Balkan Studies, Odessa State University. Odessa, 27 Sept. 1996.

Chapter II
Odessa: Profile of a City

1. It has also been stated that cities were essential for New Russia because many of the newly arrived refugees from the Balkans, mainly Greeks, were city dwellers. Marc Raeff, "In the Imperial Manner," *Catherine the Great: A Profile*, ed. Marc Raeff (New York: Hill and Wang, 1972), p. 210.

2. Patricia Herlihy, *Odessa: A History, 1794-1914* (Cambridge, MA: Harvard University Press, 1986), pp. 6-7. This is arguably the best book written on the subject of Odessa, its people and the economy of the city in pre-Revolutionary Russia.

3. Frederick W. Skinner, "Trends in Planning Practices: The Building of Odessa, 1794-1917," *The City in Russian History*, ed. Michael F. Hamm (Lexington, KY: The University Press of Kentucky, 1976), p. 139.

4. Herlihy, *Odessa*, p. 10. Like the city he helped to create de Ribas was a man of cosmopolitan outlook having been born in Italy from a Spanish father and an Irish mother. Don Joseph de Ribas was also a colorful character even by the standards of that colorful era. After his exploits in the South of Russia, he became one of the main conspirators who planned and executed the overthrow and murder of Emperor Paul.

5. Herlihy, *Odessa*, p. 7.

6. Herlihy, *Odessa*, pp. 58-60.

7. Herlihy, *Odessa*, pp. 49-51.

8. Herlihy, *Odessa*, pp. 54-56.

9. Herlihy, *Odessa*, p. 19. Herlihy provides a number of tables (utilized for this study) which help to quantify Odessa's population and economic success.

10. Robert Lyall, *Travels in Russia, the Crimea, the Caucasus and Georgia,* 2 vols. (London: T. Cadell, 1825), vol. 1, p. 186. Lyall's numbers for the year 1802 are slightly different from those provided by Herlihy.

11. See report by John Ralli in *Dispatches from US Consuls in Odessa, 1834-1906* (Washington, DC: National Archives and Records Service, 1963.) Microfilm Publications Roll 1, Vol. 2, Microcopy No. 459. John Ralli served for many years as unpaid US Consul to Odessa. He was a member of the famous Greek mercantile family with connections all over Europe and the rest of the world.

12. Herlihy, *Odessa*, pp. 204-231.

13. *Dispatches*, Roll 7, No. 863, 872.

14. Occasionally, as in 1897, traffic in and out of the port of Odessa surpassed even that of the country's most busy harbor St. Petersburg. See V. I. Kovalevskii, ed., *Rossia v kontsie XIX veka* (Russia at the End of the Nineteenth Century) (St. Petersburg: Brockhous-Efron, 1900), p. 717. The importance of Odessa as a port would have come as a surprise to the British traveler Lyall who on visiting the city in 1825 predicted that it would never amount to much. Lyall warned his British readers not to plan starting businesses in the city and claimed that those merchants who were planning to stay in Odessa for good will be faced with financial disaster. See Lyall, vol. 2, pp. 476-478.

15. Skinner, "Trends in Planning," p. 139.

16. Between 1870 and the 1890s, Odessa averaged one industrial strike per year. This number might not be large by today's standards but one should keep in mind that in tsarist Russia strikes were illegal, thus the ones that actually took place manifested great social and political upheaval. Frederick W. Skinner, "Odessa and the Problem of Urban Modernization," in *The City in Late Imperial Russia*, ed. Michael F. Hamm (Bloomington: Indiana University Press, 1986), p. 232.

17. Isabel de Madariaga, *Russia in the Age of Catherine the Great* (New Haven: Yale University Press, 1981), 359-376. Both men were Catherine's lovers and instruments of her policy. While Zubov was not a formidable individual, Potemkin wielded great power through his personal relationship to the empress (who allowed him almost complete autonomy of action in New Russia) but also because he was a capable man and an early supporter of the development of New Russia.

18. For a biography of Richelieu in English see Cynthia Cox, *Talleyrand's Successor: Armand-Emmanuel du Plessis, Duc de Richelieu (1766-1822)* (London: Arthur Baker Ltd., 1959). Also, Joseph Wieczynski, *The Modern Encyclopedia of Russian and Soviet History*, 59 vols. (USA: Academic International Press, 1983), vol. 31, pp. 88-89.

19. Herlihy, *Odessa*, pp. 20-30.

20. Mose Lofley Harvey, "The Development of Russian Commerce on the Black Sea and its Significance," Ph.D. dissertation, University of California, 1938, p. 76.

21. Herlihy, *Odessa*, p. 234.

22. According to the 1902 edition of Baedecker's guide, Odessa's population was about 430,000 a number which does not compute with the official estimates. See Karl Baedecker, *La Russie: Manuel du Voyageur* (Paris: Paul Ollendorff, 1902), p. 347.

23. That old pessimist Lyall would have been impressed by Odessa's growth as a city. Back in 1825 the overcritical Englishman dismissed predictions that by 1923 the city might have as many as 200,000 inhabitants. Lyall, vol. 2, pp. 476-477.

24. To this day the part of the city he helped to develop, and which is situated behind his statue on top of the famous Potemkin steps, is one of Odessa's architectural treasures.

25. Herlihy, *Odessa*, p. 276.

26. Grigorii Moskvich, *Illustrirovannyi practicheskii putevoditel' po Odessie* (A Practical Illustrated Guide to Odessa) (Odessa: Technik, 1908), p. 111.

27. It has been estimated that Odessa was populated by as many as one thousand (1,000) French émigrés, most of them in Russian state service. Cox, p. 90.

28. Although an able administrator, Langeron was not as tireless a worker as Richelieu. Furthermore, the office of governor-general was separated from that of the city leader. See Wieczynski, vol. 19, pp. 31-33.

29. Herlihy, *Odessa*, p. 39.

30. Harvey, p. 71.

31. See Dimitri von Mohrenschildt, *Russia in the Intellectual Life of Eighteenth Century France* (New York: Columbia University Press, 1936), pp. 123-124.

32. For an excellent biography of Vorontsov, see Anthony Rhinelander, *Prince Michael Vorontsov: Viceroy to the Tsar* (Montreal: McGill-Queens University Press, 1982).

33. During the time of his governorship of New Russia, Vorontsov invested large sums from his personal fortune in land acquisition and development, introduction of new crops, etc. As a result while he was already a rich man when he went to Odessa, he left the city as one of the richest Russians of his time. It should be noted that neither then nor now,

has ever been even a hint of wrong doing. It seems that Vorontsov enriched himself by legal methods.

34. Harvey, p. 61.

35. After 1861, the government placed restrictions against foreigners (as well as certain domestic ethnic groups, mainly Jews) owning certain types of businesses. Thomas C. Owen, *Russian Corporate Capitalism from Peter the Great to Perestroika* (New York: Oxford University Press, 1995), p. 53. Patricia Herlihy underscores (maybe subconsciously) the point of how important foreigners were for the development of Odessa. In her already mentioned book on the history of Odessa, Herlihy includes a few pictures. Most of them are pictures of buildings and streets and only two are depicting individuals (facing page 175). One is the portrait of the Duc de Richelieu, the Frenchman who was one of the area's most able governor. The other depicts the Greek merchant Stephen Ralli, founder of the great merchant house of the same name. The fact that from all the possible individuals that could have been included, Herlihy chose two foreigners is suggestive of the importance of foreigners in Odessa's development. The fact that she chose a Greek merchant as one of the two pictures is testament to the influence the Greek commercial interests had in he city.

36. Skinner "Odessa," 212.

37. Skinner "Odessa," 217.

38. Lyall, vol. 1, p. 172.

39. Mary Holderness, *New Russia: Journey from Riga to the Crimea by Way of Kiev* (London: Sherwood, Jones and Co., 1823), pp. 78-79.

40. Holderness, p. 77.

41. Special thanks to Professor Patricia Herlihy for sharing with me her unpublished essay "Commerce and Architecture in Odessa in Late Imperial Russia," p. 3.

42. Lyall, vol. 2, p. 475, Appendix 1; Holderness, p. 103.

43. K. G. Avgitides, *Οι Έλληνες της Οδησσού και η Επανάσταση του 1821*(The Greeks of Odessa and the Revolution of 1821) (Athens: Dodoni, 1994). At the end of the book the author includes a number of rare pictures of some private homes and stores in nineteenth-century Odessa.

44. Herlihy, "Commerce and Architecture," p. 6.

45. Herlihy, *Odessa*, p. 36.

46. Herlihy, "Commerce and Architecture," pp. 6, 11. This "style police" continued its work in later years and is thus responsible for the relative continuity of architectural style of the city.

47. Herlihy, "Commerce and Architecture," p. 6.

48. Herlihy, "Commerce and Architecture," p. 8.

49. Herlihy, "Commerce and Architecture," pp. 7-8.

50. Herlihy, *Odessa*, pp. 133-136.

51. Herlihy, *Odessa*, 35.

52. See Konstantinos Papoulides, *Γρηγόριος Γ.Μαρασλής (1831-1907) Η Ζωή και το Έργο του* (Gregory G. Maraslis [1831-1907] His Life and Work) (Thessaloniki: Institute for Balkan Studies, 1989), pp. 44-47.

53. Herlihy, *Odessa*, p. 141.

54. In the fifteen years between 1878 and 1892 Odessa's city budget showed a deficit seven times. See Papoulides, *Maraslis*, p. 40.

55. Herlihy, "Commerce and Architecture," p.4.

56. Herlihy, "Commerce and Architecture," p. 9.

57. Herlihy, *Odessa*, p. 140.

59. Herlihy, "Commerce and Architecture," p. 9.
59. Herlihy, "Commerce and Architecture," p. 9.
60. Baedecker, p. 393.
61. Herlihy, *Odessa*, pp. 264-265.
62. Herlihy, "Commerce and Architecture," p. 21.
63. Skinner, "Odessa," pp. 217-218. Some of the short stories of the writer Isaac Babel, a long time Odessa resident, describe the two sides of the city. Isaac Babel, *Lyubka the Cossack and Other Stories,* trans. Andrew MacAndrew (New York: New American Library, 1963).

Chapter III
The Greeks of Odessa

1. Andrew Zapantis, *Greek-Soviet Relations, 1917-1941* (New York: Columbia University Press, 1982), p. 6.
2. Grigorii Arsh, "Οι Έλληνες της Ρωσίας" (The Greeks of Russia) *Μουσείο Φιλικής Εταιρείας* (Athens: Foundation for Hellenic Culture, 1994), p. 21. From the time of Peter the Great and up to the end of the Imperial era all people in state service were ranked according to the Table of Ranks. Divided into fourteen levels with corresponding positions for military, naval and civilian personnel the Table of Ranks denoted one's position in state and society. The fourteenth rank (equivalent to that of an army second lieutenant) conferred nobility to the holder for his lifetime only. If one reached the eight rank (army major or its equivalent in other services) one became a hereditary noble, a great advantage in a country with the hierarchical structure of Imperial Russia. Reaching one of the four highest ranks (the so-called Generalitet) was a great achievement. Besides those Greeks who reached the Generalitet in the armed forces, there were others who achieved the equivalent rank in civil service. Count Capodistrias, while acting foreign minister, became a privy counselor (equivalent to an army lieutenant general) a rank also achieved by Gregorii Maraslis later in the century. For more on the Table of Ranks see Basil Dmytryshyn, ed., *Imperial Russia: A Source Book, 1700-1917* (Philadelphia: Holt, Rinehart and Winston, Inc., 1990), pp. 19-20.
3. Arsh, "The Greeks of Russia," p. 21.
4. Arsh, "The Greeks of Russia," p. 24.
5. For more information on the life and career of this remarkable individual see Stephen Batalden, *Catherine II's Greek Prelate: Eugenios Voulgaris in Russia, 1771-1806* (Boulder, CO: East European Monographs, 1982).
6. See Gregory Bruess, "Catherine II's Imperial Manner and Eastern Orthodoxy: The Case of Nikiforos Theotokis, 1779-1800," Ph.D. dissertation, University of Minnesota, 1992. This dissertation was revised and published as *Religion, Identity and Empire: A Greek Archbishop in the Russia of Catherine the Great* (Boulder, CO: East European Monographs, 1997). Also by the same author, "Crossing Boundaries: Nikiforos Theotokis in the Russia of Catherine II," *Modern Greek Studies Yearbook* 9 (1993): pp. 51-74.
7. Isabel de Madariaga, *Russia in the Age of Catherine the Great* (New Haven: Yale University Press, 1981), pp. 521, 527.
8. See G. Arsh, "On the Life of the Greek Patriotic Family of Ypsilanti," *Balkan Studies* 26:1 (1985): pp. 73-90. Also, Nicholas Pappas, *Greeks in Russian Military Service in the Late Eighteenth and Early Nineteenth Centuries* (Thessaloniki: Institute for Balkan Studies, 1991).

9. Nicolas de Basili, *Diplomat of Imperial Russia 1903-1917. Memoirs* (Stanford: Hoover Institution Press, 1973), pp. 4-7, 187-189; and Joseph Wieczynski, *The Modern Encyclopedia of Russian and Soviet History*, 59 vols. (USA: Academic International Press, 1983), vol. 3, p. 181.

10. Theophilus Prousis, "The Destunis Collection in the Manuscript Section of the Saltykov-Shchedrin State Public Library in Leningrad," *Modern Greek Studies Yearbook* 5 (1989) 395-452. Also, Konstantinos Papoulides, "Οι Έλληνες της Ρωσίας τον 19ο και στις αρχές του 20ου αιώνα" (The Greeks of Russia at the End of the Nineteenth and the Beginning of the Twentieth Century), *Βαλκανικα Συμμεικτα* 4 (1992): p.127. The Destounis were also noted Byzantinists. See I. P. Medvedev, *Arkhivi Russkikh Byzantinistov v Sankt-Peterburge* (The Archives of Russian Byzantinists in St. Petersburg) (St. Petersburg: Russian Academy of Sciences, 1995), pp. 22-35.

11. C. M. Woodhouse, *Capodistria: The Founder of Greek Independence* (London: Oxford University Press, 1973), p. 52. Also, Papoulides, "The Greeks of Russia," p. 127.

12. Papoulides, "The Greeks of Russia," pp. 113.

13. Patricia Grimsted, *The Foreign Ministers of Alexander I* (Berkeley: University of California Press, 1969).

14. Better known among the Greek university professors were G. S. Destounis (formerly a diplomat) and A. Papadopoulos-Keramevs. Papoulides, "The Greeks of Russia," p. 125. Like Destounis, Papadopoulos-Keramevs was also a noted Byzantinist. See Medvedev, pp. 430-445. Two Mavrocordatos cousins became an admiral (and prince of the empire) and chamberlain to the tsar respectively. Patricia Herlihy, "The Greek Community in Odessa, 1861-1917," *Journal of Modern Greek Studies* 7 (1989): p. 243. During the early twentieth century, General Konstantas was military governor of the Russian capital and member of the upper chamber of Russia's legislature. Dominic Lieven, *Russia's Rulers Under the Old Regime* (New Haven: Yale University Press, 1989), pp. 386, 388. Besides Konstantas, another Greek, A. Vlangali was also a member of the Russian Empire's Upper House. Konstantas was involved in the following incident which illustrates the fact that Greeks were indeed a nation of immigrants. During the Russo-Turkish War of 1878 General Konstantas was ordered to coordinate his operations with those of a unit of the Rumanian Army (Rumania being Russia's ally). Konstantas and his staff contacted the Romanian general and his staff. As soon as the two generals were introduced they started conversing in a language which the rest of the officers could not understand. As it happened, the Romanian commander General Kandiles was also an ethnic Greek and like Konstantas a fluent speaker of the Greek language. Emmanouel Kapsambelis, *Αναμνήσεις Διπλωμάτου* (Memoirs of a Diplomat) (Athens: n.p., 1939), p. 38.

15. Theophilus Prousis, "Demetrios S. Inglezes: Greek Merchant and City Leader in Odessa," *Slavic Review* 50:3 (1991): pp. 672-246. Greek participation in Odessa's municipal affairs starts even earlier than Inglezes's appointment. Between 1797-1801 there were two Odessa city councils. Besides the one in which Russian citizens could participate, there was also the so called "Municipal Council of Non-citizens" in which Greeks were prominent members. Eight of its fourteen members were Greeks and its four successive presidents were A. Kesoglou, I. Destounis, C. Saibel and L. Berdonis. See K. Avgitides, *Οι Έλληνες της Οδησσού και η Επανάσταση του 1821* (The Greeks of Odessa and the Revolt of 1821) (Athens: Dodoni, 1994), p. 92.

16. See K. Papoulides, *Γρηγόριος Γ. Μαρασλής (1831-1907) Η Ζωή και το Έργο του* (Gregory G. Maraslis [1831-1907] His Life and Work) (Thessaloniki: Institute for Balkan Studies, 1989).

17. Emmanouel Kapsambelis, *Διπλωματικά Παρασκήνια* (Diplomacy Behind the Scenes) (Athens: n.p., 1946), p. 34.

18. S. Kiouze-Pezas, *[Έκθεσις Περί Γεωργίας, Εμπορίας, Βιομηχανίας και Ναυτιλίας ανα την Προξενική Περιφέριαν Ταιγανίου 1910-1911* (Report on the Agriculture, Trade, Industry and Merchant Marine in the District of Taganrog, 1910-1911) (Athens: National Press, 1912), pp. 10-11.

19. E. M. Sacharova, *Vokrug Chehova* (About Chekhov) (Moscow: Pravda, 1990), pp. 39, 48.

20. Michael Hamm, *Kiev: A Portrait, 1800-1917* (Princeton: Princeton University Press, 1993), p. 38.

21. *Κοσμος*, 30 March 1911: 2.

22. Robin Cohen, *Global Diasporas: An Introduction* (Seattle: University of Washington Press, 1997), p. 26.

23. George Leber, *The History of the Order of Ahepa: (The American Hellenic Educational Progressive Association) 1922-1972* (Washington: The Order of AHEPA, 1972), pp. 69-78.

24. Michael Hamm, *Kiev: A Portrait, 1800-1917* (Princeton: Princeton University Press, 1993), p. 192.

25. Leber, pp. 95-100.

26. Konstantinos Papoulides, "Η Εκπαιδευτική και Πολιτιστική Δραστηριότητα Των Ελλήνων της Οδησσού τον 19ο και 20ο Αιωνα" (The Educational and Cultural Activities of the Greeks of Odessa During the Nineteenth and Twentieth Centuries), *Yearbook of the University of Thessaloniki Divinity School* (1988): pp. 653-654; and Papoulides, "The Greeks of Russia," p. 129; also Kapsambelis, *Memoirs*, p. 34.

27. Avgitides, p. 85.

28. A number of Greeks left the war ravaged Caucasus for the safety of Russia.

29. Arsh, "The Greeks of Russia," pp. 22-23.

30. Avgitides, pp. 89-91.

31. Yannis Kordatos, *Ιστορία της Ελλάδας* (History of Greece), 5 vols. (Athens: 20th Century, 1957), vol. 1, p. 260. If the number sounds too excessive, it probably is. Kordatos often allows his Marxist ideology to color his presentation of facts. In this particular instance he offers no evidence to support his claim.

32. Avgitides, p. 192.

33. Robert Weinberg, *The Revolution of 1905 in Odessa* (Bloomington: Indiana University Press, 1993), p. 13.

34. Herlihy, *Odessa*, p. 242.

35. Papoulides, "The Greeks of Russia," p. 111.

36. Herlihy, "The Greek Community of Odessa," p. 237.

37. Herlihy, "The Greek Community of Odessa," pp. 247-248. While on page 237 Herlihy did not consider the possibility that many Greek men might have been married to non-Greek women, a few pages later (247) she notes that a large number of Greek men did in fact intermarry.

38. Herlihy, "The Greek Community," p. 237.

39. Emmanouel Kapsambelis, *[έκθεσις περί Γεωργίας, Εμπορίας, Βιομηχανίας και Ναυτιλίας εν Ρωσία εν γένη καιι ιδίαν εν Οδησσώ* (Report on the Agriculture, Trade, industry and Merchant Marine in Russia and Particularly in Odessa) (Reports of the Ministry of Foreign Affairs) (Athens: National Press, 1912), p. 12.

40. Eleftherios Pavlides, ed., *Ο Ελληνισμός της Ρωσίας* (Greeks in Russia) (Athens: Union of Greeks from Russia, 1953), p. 38.

41. Zapantis, p. 11.

42. Papoulides, "The Greeks of Russia," p. 111.

43. Grigorii Arsh, "Grecheskaia emigratsiia v Rossiiu v kontse xviii-nachale xix v." (Greek Emigration to Russia at the end of the Eighteenth to the Beginning of the Nineteenth Centuries), *Sovetskaia ethnografiia* 3 (1969): p. 85.

44. See James S. Olson, ed., *An Ethnohistorical Dictionary of the Russian and Soviet Empires* (Westport, CT: Greenwood Press, 1994), p. 267.

45. Natalia Terentjeva, "Οι 'Έλληνες στην Ουκρανία, 1920-1940" (The Greeks in Ukraine, 1920-1940), Conference "The Greeks in Ukraine (18th-20th Century): Social Life, Trade, Culture." Foundation for Hellenic Culture, Institute for Balkan Studies, Odessa State University. Odessa, 30 Sept. 1996.

46. Papoulides, "The Greeks of Russia," p. 111.

47. Zapantis, p. 11; also Herlihy, *Odessa*, p. 234.

48. Papoulides, "The Educational and Cultural Activities," p. 648.

49. G. L. Rees, *Britain's Commodity Markets* (London: Paul Elek Books, 1972), p. 127.

50. The archives of the commercial firm Ralli Bros. Ltd. would have been a treasure of information. Unfortunately, they were damaged and many papers lost in the firm's offices in London during the German Blitz of 1940. Letter to the author by Sir Godfrey Ralli Bt. February 9, 1996. Sir Godfrey was the last director of the family firm which closed in the middle of the 1960s.

51. As a result of the close knit system of operation, the families involved in major trade were relatively few. During the first period (1830-1870), there were about sixty families most of them from the Aegean islands especially Chios. During the second period (1870-1900), there were about 140 families mostly from Asia Minor. Gelina Harlaftis, "Ελληνικά εμποροναυτιλιακά δίκτυα στη νότιο Ρωσία, 1830-1914" (Greek Merchant Marine Networks in South Russia, 1830-1917), Conference "The Greeks in Ukraine (18th-20th Century): Social Life, Trade, Culture." Foundation for Hellenic Culture, Institute for Balkan Studies, Odessa State University. Odessa, 27 Sept. 1996. Also, S. D. Chapman, "The International Houses: The Continental Contribution to British Commerce 1800-1860," *Journal of European Economic History* 6:1 (1977): pp. 37-38.

52. See biographical notes in Λυντια Τριχα, *Διπλωματία και Πολιτική. Χαρίλαος Τρικούπης-Ιωάννης Γεννάδιος. Αλληλογραφία 1863-1894* (Diplomacy and Politics. The Correspondence of Charilaos Trikoupis and John Gennadios, 1863-1894) (Athens: Association of Greek Archives of Literature and History, 1991). In her book, *A History of Greek-Owned Shipping. The Making of an International Tramp Fleet, 1830 to the Present Day* (London: Routledge, 1996), Gelina Harlaftis catalogues the first degree kinship between some of the most important Greek merchants. See Appendix 2.2, pp. 316-320.

53. George Soures, *Άπαντα Σουρή* (The Collected Works of Soures), ed. G. Valetas, 5 vols. (Athens: Ch. Yovanes, 1966), vol. 1, pp. 70-84. Incidentally, Soures was not the only Greek man of letters associated, however briefly, with the Greek international trading houses. The poets Alexander Pallis and Argyres Eftaliotes were successful merchants who worked for years for the Ralli Brothers first in India and then in England.

54. Dan Morgan, *Merchants of Grain* (New York: The Viking Press, 1979), p. 29.

55. Rees, p. 127.

56. Avgitides, p. 123. This is not the only instance of Greek contribution to a Russian war effort. According to Kordatos, G. I. Maraslis offered to the tsar 550,000 rubles during the Crimean War for the rebuilding of the church of Hagia Sophia in Constantinople if Russia succeeded in taking control of the City. Kordatos 3:601. During the Russo-Turkish War of 1878 the Greeks of Odessa contributed materially to Russia's war effort and a number of Greeks volunteered for service in the Russian army. One P.S. Ralli was the recipient of the St. George Cross, Imperial Russia's highest award for valor. See Grigorij M. Piatigorskij, "Οι εξεγέρσεις στις ελληνικές επαρχίες της Οθωμανικής αυτοκρατορίας το 1878 καιι οι Έλληνες της Οδησσού" (The Uprisings in the Greek Provinces of the Ottoman Empire in 1878 and the Greeks of Odessa), Conference "The Greeks in Ukraine (18th-20th Century): Social Life, Trade, Culture," Foundation for Hellenic Culture, Institute for Balkan Studies, Odessa State University. Odessa 28 Sept. 1996. It is interesting to note that during the First World war, America's Greek immigrants contributed generously to the US war effort by purchasing war bonds. Between 1917-1918 the Greeks purchased ten million dollars (10,000,000) worth of "liberty" bonds. The Greeks of Chicago alone contributed two million dollars (2,000,000). According to the local press, the Greeks of Chicago contributed on an average of $167.83 per capita, the highest amount of any national group. See Leber, p. 101.

57. Patricia Herlihy, "Greek Merchants in Odessa in the Nineteenth Century," *Harvard Ukrainian Studies* 3/4.1 (1979-1980): p. 401. Also Steven Zipperstein, *The Jews of Odessa: A Cultural History, 1794-1881* (Stanford CA: Stanford University Press, 1985), p. 171.

58. Herlihy, *Odessa*, pp. 258-259.

59. That is the impression left by the reports of the United States Consul in Odessa when he relayed to the State Department the information that the famous House of Ralli closed its doors (12/3/1905) and that other well known Greek businesses were in trouble (4/30/1906). *Dispatches*, Roll 7, Enclosure 1, # 863 & 872.

60. Alfred Rieber, *Merchants and Entrepreneurs in Imperial Russia* (Chapel Hill: University of North Carolina Press, 1982), p. 113.

61. Harlaftis, "Greek Merchant Marine Networks."

62. Kiouze-Pezas, p. 79.

63. Harlaftis, "Greek Merchant Marine Networks."

64. Kiouze-Pezas, p. 41.

65. Konstantinos Papoulides, "Γύρω απο την Οικονομική Δραστηριότητα Ωρισμένων Ελλήνων στη Ρωσία κατά τα Τέλη του 19ου Αιώνα (Regarding the Financial Activities of Some Greeks in Russia at the End of the Nineteenth Century), *Balkan Bibliography* 7 (1978).

66. In Imperial Russia the whole society was organized in various classes according to the function of the people. Thus there was the Imperial family (since 1796 considered to be a special class) the aristocracy, merchant class, city dwellers and peasants. Even within classes there existed sub-groups. The merchant class was divided into merchants of first, second and third order. The different merchants paid a fee depending on the order in which they belonged. Merchants of the third order were modest entrepreneurs while those of the first order were the ones who owned big import/export firms and factories. The merchants of the second order were somewhere between the other two. Although not as rich as their first order colleagues they could still get involved in foreign trade, a privilege denied to third order merchants. Papoulides' list records only merchants of the first order; the number of prosperous Greek shopkeepers, who belonged to the second order is unknown but must have

been considerable. Those who point to Greek mercantile decline in Odessa do not, as a rule, deal with merchants other than those of the first order.

67. Papoulides, "Financial Activities of Greeks in Russia," pp. 109-111.

68. Kiouze-Pezas, p. 55. Also, Kapsambelis, *Report on Agriculture*, p. 27. It seems that the drinking habits of the people of Odessa have not changed much over the years. Metaxa brandy remained popular and following the collapse of the Soviet regime, it can be found all over the city.

69. Papoulides, "Financial Activities of Greeks in Russia," pp. 106-109.

70. Kiouze-Pezas, p. 68. Also Emmanouel Kapsambelis, *Τι οφείλει η Ρωσία στην Ελλάδα* (Russia's Debt to Greece) (Athens: n.p., 1947), p. 14.

71. Herlihy, "The Greek Community," p. 244.

72. Herlihy, "The Greek Community," p. 240.

73. *Dispatches*, Roll 7, vol. 13, No. 770.

74. Herlihy, "Commerce and Architecture," pp. 14-15.

75. *Κοσμος*, 69 May 5, 1907.

76. Herlihy, "The Greek Community," p. 238.

77. Harlaftis, "Greek Merchant Marine Networks."

78. George Leon, "The Greek Merchant Marine (1453-1850)" in *The Greek Merchant Marine (1453-1850)*, ed. Stelios Papadopoulos (Athens: National Bank of Greece, 1972).

79. *Dispatches*, vol. 1 May 30, 1831-Jan. 12, 1858.

80. *Dispatches*, vol. 9, # 246.

81. Kiouze-Pezas, p. 71. Also, Kapsambelis, *Report on the Agriculture*, pp. 34-37.

82. Michael Dendias, *Αι Ελληνικαί Παροικίαι ανα τον Κόσμον* (Greek Communities Throughout the World) (Athens: Sideris, 1919), p. 26.

83. Kiouze-Pezas, p. 81.

84. David Cannadine, *The Decline and Fall of the British Aristocracy* (New Haven, CT: Yale University Press, 1990). Also, Dominic Lieven, *The Aristocracy in Europe 1815-1914* (New York: Columbia University Press, 1993).

85. Papoulides, "Financial Activities of Greeks in Russia," pp. 103-106. Papoulides records the various landholdings in stremmata, the Greek unit of measuring area. This writer made the conversion to acres (one stremma = 0.247 acres) and added the total landholdings by all the Greek owners on the list.

86. Herlihy, "The Greek Community in Odessa," pp. 246-247. One Ralli from Odessa married the sister of Count Theotokis, a Greek politician; their son George Rallis (the branch of the family still in Greece spells the name with an "s" at the end) is a former Prime Minister of Greece (1980-1981).

87. Herlihy, *Odessa*, pp. 258-259.

88. See Melville Henry Massue Marquis of Ruvigny and Raineval, ed., *The Titled Nobility of Europe* (London: Harrison, 1914). For the English branch of the Ralli family, see *Debrett's Peerage and Baronetage* (Kingston upon Thames: Kelly's Directories, 1980).

89. Vasilis Kardasis, "Νότια Ρωσία τον 19ο αιώνα Οι Έλληνες ομογενείς" (South Russia in the Nineteenth Century: The Greek Diaspora), Conference "The Greeks in Ukraine (18th-20th Century): Social Life, Trade, Culture," Foundation for Hellenic Culture, Institute for Balkan Studies, Odessa State University. Odessa, 27 Sept. 1996.

Chapter IV
The Greek Benevolent Association of Odessa

1. Adele Lindenmeyr, "The Rise of Voluntary Associations During the Great Reforms: The Case of Charity," in *Russia's Great Reforms 1851–1881*, ed. Ben Eklof (Bloomington, Indiana University Press 1994), p. 267.

2. Th. Panagiotides, *Ο εν Ρωσία Ελληνισμός* (The Greeks of Russia) (Athens: Trembela, 1919), p. 25.

For that reason the various Greek organizations used philanthropy as their main purpose for existence even though not all of them were true philanthropic associations.

3. Adele Lindenmeyr, *Poverty Is Not a Vice. Charity, Society, and the State in Imperial Russia* (Princeton: Princeton University Press, 1996), pp. 26-33.

4. Lindenmeyr, *Poverty*, p. 99.

5. Lindenmeyr, *Poverty*, p. 106. According to the same author (pp. 110-111) other early charitable associations were also heavily subsidized and controlled by the Russian government. As late as 1893 Odessa was the main beneficiary, after St. Petersburg and Moscow, of monetary support from those semi-private organizations. See V. I. Kovalebskii, ed., *Rossia v Kontsie XIX veka* (Russia at the end of the Nineteenth Century) (St. Petersburg: Brockhous-Efron, 1900), p. 939.

6. Lindenmeyr, *Poverty*, p.109.

7. Lindenmeyr, *Poverty*, pp. 116-122.

8. Lindenmeyr, *Poverty*, p. 204.

9. Once again, the parallel between the Greek immigrants of Russia in the early nineteenth century, and those of the US later in time holds true. Before the founding of the American Hellenic Educational Progressive Association (AHEPA) there were a number of other Greek organizations founded which attempted to cater to the needs of the immigrants. See George Leber, *The History of the Order of AHEPA: (The American Hellenic Educational Association) 1922–1972* (Washington: The Order of AHEPA, 1972), pp. 113-115.

10. E. Chrysogelos, *Grecheskaia Tserkov Sv. Troitsi v Odesse 1808–1908* (The Greek Church of the Holy Trinity in Odessa 1808–1908) (Odessa: n.p., 1908).

11. K. Papoulides, "Η Εκπαιδευτική και Πολιτιστική Δραστηριότητα των Ελλήνων της Οδησσού τον 19ο και 20ο Αιώνα" (The Educational and Cultural Activities of the Greeks of Odessa During the Nineteenth and Twentieth Centuries), *Yearbook of the Divinity School, University of Thessaloniki* (1988): p. 654.

12. E. Kapsambelis, *[Έκθεσις περί Γεωργίας, Εμπορίας, Βιομηχανίας και Ναυτιλίας εν Ρωσία εν γένη και ιδίαν εν Οδησσώ* (Report on the Agriculture, Trade, Industry and Merchant Marine in Russia and Particularly in Odessa) (Athens: National Press, Reports of the Ministry of Foreign Affairs, 1912), p. 13. Also, Grigorii Moskvich, *Illustrirovannyi prakticheskii putevoditel' po Odessie* (A Practical Illustrated Guide to Odessa) (Odessa: Technik, 1908), p. 122. According to the guide, the Greek church was not only one of the most beautiful in the city but also one of the oldest and richest.

13. I would like to express my appreciation for Mr. Sofronis Paradissopoulos for permitting me to quote from his unpublished paper "Activities of the Greek Charity Society in Odessa 1871–1896," p 2.

14. Papoulides, "The Educational and Cultural Activities," p. 651.

15. Vasilis Kardasis, "Νότια Ρωσία τον 19ο αιώνα Οι Έλληνες ομογενείς (South Russia in the Nineteenth Century: The Greek Immigrants), Conference "The Greeks in

Ukraine (18th-20th Century) Social Life, Trade, Culture." Odessa: Foundation for Hellenic Culture, Institute for Balkan Studies, Odessa State University, 27 September 1996.

16. There are many works written about the Friendly Society a number of them by Academician Grigorii Arsh. His work *Eteristkoe dvizhenie v Rosii* (The Friendly Society Movement in Russia) (Moscow: Nauka, 1972) is considered classic on the subject.

17. E. Pavlides, ed., *Ο Ελληνισμός της Ρωσίας* (The Greeks in Russia) (Athens: Union of Greeks from Russia, 1953), pp. 162-163.

18. K. Papoulides, "Οι Ελληνες της Ρωσιας τον 19ο και στις αρχες του 20ου Αιωνος" (The Greeks of Russia in the Nineteenth and the Beginning of the Twentieth Centuries), *Balkan Miscellany* 4 (1992): p. 115. Also, Marina Koromila, ed., *The Greeks in the Black Sea* (Athens: Panorama, 1991), p. 257.

19. K. Avgitides, *Οι Έλληνες της Οδησσού και η Επανάσταση του 1821* (The Greeks of Odessa and the Revolution of 1821) (Athens: Dodoni, 1994), pp. 179-182. Avgitide's main thesis is that while the West paid lip service to Greek independence, the Russian people and to a lesser extend the government, were genuinely hoping and helping their coreligionists.

20. Needless to say Langeron did not know that the Society of Friends even existed. Avgitides, p. 210.

21. Konstantinos Papoulides, "Η Ελληνεμπορική Σχολή της Οδησσού 1817–1917" (The Greek Commercial School of Odessa 1817–1917), *Pontic Greek Archive* 37 (1982): p. 148.

22. Papoulides, "The Greek Commercial School," pp. 144, 151.

23. See Avgitides, p. 213.

24. Papoulides, "The Greek Commercial School," p. 147.

25. Herlihy, "Greek Merchants," pp. 402-403. The best known was the Graeco-Russian Insurance Co. which started giving 10% of its net earnings in 1808. Koromila, p. 251. S. Kiouze-Pezas, *[Έκθεσις Περί Γεωργίας, Εμπορίας, Βιομηχανίας και Ναυτιλίας ανά την Προξενική Περιφέριαν Ταιγανίου 1910–1911* (Report on the Agriculture, Trade, Industry and merchant Marine in the District of Taganrog 1910–1911) (Athens: National Press, Reports of the Ministry of Foreign Affairs, 1912), p. 12.

26. Paradissopoulos, "Activities…," p. 2.

27. Kapsambelis in his detailed works about the Greeks of Russia mentions two Greek philanthropic organizations in Odessa but he only names GBAO. See Kapsambelis, *Report*, p. 12. The same is true for other such works. See *Ημερολόγιον των Ελληνικών Φιλανθροπικών Καταστημάτων* (Almanac of National Philanthropic Institutions) (Constantinople: n.p., 1905), p. 207.

28. See Papoulides, "The Educational and Cultural Activities," p. 654.

29. There are no details about the membership and function of the social clubs. One of them was named Ομονεια (Concord) and was considered respectable enough by the leadership of the Greek community. *Αναγέννησις*, 20 Aug. 1917: p. 3. Other clubs were not as respectable. In one case the police closed down one of the social clubs because its premises were used for gambling. See *Κοσμος*, 1 Nov. 1909: p. 3.

30. The Greek Students' Union "*Ενωσις*" was created in May of 1917. *Αναγεννησι*, 7 May 1917: p. 3, also 28 May 1917: p. 4. And Kapsambelis, *Αναμνήσεις Διπλωμάτου* (Memoirs of a Diplomat) (Athens: n.p., 1939), p. 38. An example of the hostility to the student union occurred on May 8, 1917, when the members of Ενωσις after asking and obtaining permission from the Board of Directors of the Rodokanaki School for Girls to meet at the school building were forcibly removed from the school by the school principal. See

Gosudarstvennyi arkhiv Odesskoi oblasti (State Archives of Odessa Province [henceforth: GAOO]), Odessa, Ukraine, font 765, opis 1, delo 26, list 75.

31. It is reported that the vice-president of the GBAO E. Pavlides called for a Pan-Hellenic meeting of the Greeks of Russia with the goal of creating an umbrella organization. *Αναγεννησις*, 14 May 1917: pp. 1-2.

32. *Αναγεννησις*, 2 July 1917: p. 1.

33. Michael Dendias, *Αι Ελληνικαί Παροικίαι ανά τον Κόσμον* (Greek Communities Throughout the World) (Athens: Sideri, 1919), p. 24.

34. Kardasis holds that view and believes that Odessa's Greek community was always led and controlled by its wealthy leaders.

35. *Κοσμος*, 25 March 1908: p. 3, and 2 April 1908.

36. *Κοσμος*, 27 Sept. 1909: p. 1.

37. All Greek organizations but the GBAO were criticized for working in relative secrecy without public record of their budget. *Κοσμος* 2 Sept. 1909: p. 3.

38. *Κοσμος*, 5 May 1913, special edition.

39. The yearly dues for members of the GBAO were 3 rubles. In 1917 the organization announced that since its expenses had increased due to the war it would increase its dues (but it was not clear by how much). *Αναγεννησις*, 20 Sept. 1917: p. 4.

40. The only fund raising activity of the GBAO was a yearly amateur theater production which was always sold out. *Κοσμος*, 9 Jan. 1908: p. 2, and 27 Nov. 1909: p. 3, also 6 Dec. 1909: p. 3.

41. While a little less than 50% of the Greeks of Odessa lived in the city's two best neighborhoods, another 25% was living in the city's five worst where many homes had no sewage. Herlihy, "The Greek Community," p. 239

42. The earlier Greek immigrants were comfortable in Russia and believed that Russification was a desirable goal. By contrast, the newer immigrants form the Ottoman Empire were more nationalistic and insisted on keeping their Greek identity. Papoulides, "The Greek Commercial School," pp. 149-150.

43. See Leber, p. 100.

44. Leber, pp. 161-162.

45. "Russification in Tsarist Russia" in *The Modern Encyclopedia of Russian and Soviet History*, 1983 ed., vol. 32: pp. 205-211.

46. Th. Panagiotides, *Ο εν Ρωσία Ελληνισμός* (The Greeks of Russia) (Athens: Trembela, 1919), p. 11. The author reiterates the fact that the Greeks of Russia became a prime target of Russification due to their religious and cultural proximity to the ideas of that policy.

47. S. Kiouze-Pezas, p. 8.

48. S. Loukatos, *Ο Ελληνισμός της Διασποράς 1830–1914* (The Greeks of the Diaspora 1830–1914) (Athens: Center for Southeastern European Studies, 1994), p. 70. See also Dendias, p. 19.

49. Papoulides, "The Greek Commercial School," pp. 146, 149-150.

50. Ιστορικό Αρχείο Υπουργίου Εξωτερικών (Historical Archives of the Ministry of Foreign Affairs) Athens, Greece (AYE) Gen. Διεθ. Β, Τμήμα Γ, Φάκελλος 175 No. 015,692 June 2, 1911.

51. N. Petsalis-Diomidis, "Hellenism in Southern Russia and the Ukrainian Campaign: Their Effect on the Pontus Question (1919)," *Balkan Studies* 13:2: pp. 223-224.

52. See Panagiotides, p. 15.

53. E. Kapsambelis, *Memoirs*, p. 27.

54. Lindenmeyr, "The Rise of Volunteer Associations," p. 265. As the same author notes in page 269, the new freedoms did not mean that a civic organization would be automatically allowed to exist. Russian Poland was explicitly excluded from the general relaxation of government vigilance regarding civic groups. Even in the rest of the empire, if the authorities were suspicious of a proposed organization they would refer the matter either to the Committee of Ministers or reject the proposal outright.

55. Lindenmeyr, *Poverty*, p. 123.

56. Lindenmeyr, "The Rise of Volunteer Associations," pp. 270-271. This was the case with many other Russian organizations of the same type as the GBAO which found support both among the bourgeoisie and among the radicals.

57. Lindenmeyr, *Poverty*, p. 196.

58. See Joseph Bradley, "Merchant Moscow After Hours: Voluntary Associations and Leisure" in James West and Iurii Petrov, eds., *Merchant Moscow. Images of Russia's Vanished Bourgeoisie* (Princeton: Princeton University Press, 1998), pp. 133, 135.

59. The patronage of such social stalwarts as Maraslis and Rodokanakis indicate that the founding fathers of the GBAO were not exclusively those newcomers who opposed Russification outright. Maraslis was a leading member of the old guard and his career in the Russian administration made him one of those Greeks who had done well in life through cooperation with the Russian state. Both Maraslis and Rodokanakis, though assimilated into the mainstream of Russian society, remained Greek patriots. Time after time (1878, 1897) they gave generously to Greek patriotic causes.

60. *Μεγάλη Ελληνική Ενγκυκλοπαίδεια* (Great Greek Encyclopedia) 28 vols. (Athens: Phoenix, n.d.), vol. 7: p. 798. The Greek poet, and sometime resident of Taganrog, George Soures (see Chapter 3, note 51) won the Voutsineos poetry contest in 1876.

61. The Greek government and its representatives in Odessa were intimately involved with the affairs of the city's Greek community. Thus on February 22, 1880, the Greek Foreign Ministry expressed interest in the philanthropic activities of Odessa's Greeks in general and G. G. Maraslis in particular and advised John Voutsinas, who was for many years the Greek consul in the city, to encourage such good works. AYE 77/2/1606. According to K. Papoulides, in 1874, after many years of "lobbying" the Russian government, Voutsinas succeeded and the Greek Merchant School was recognized as an independent legal entity (*νομικον προσωπο*). Papoulides, "The Greek Commercial School," pp. 144-145. However, six years after the status of the Commercial School was supposed to have been resolved, Voutsinas wrote to his superiors in Athens (August 23, 1880):

> "Σκοπός της εις Πετρουπόλιν μεταβασεώς μου ην να εξομαλύνω...υποθέσεις τινάς της εν Οδησσώ Ελληνικής Κοινότητος, προ πάντων δε την υπό της Αυτοκρατορικής Κυβερνήσεως αναγνώρισιν της ενταύθα Ελληνικής Εμπορικής Σχολής και της Ελληνικής Εκκλησίας ως προσώπων νομικών και ανεξαρτήτων." (The reason for my trip to St. Petersburg was to smooth out...some business of the Greek Community of Odessa and in particular the recognition by the Imperial Government of the Greek Commercial School and the Greek Church as legal and independent organizations.)

According to Voutsinas, he had been promised many times that his request would be granted but for political reasons it had not. The reason for wanting the recognition was financial. If the two organizations were not officially sanctioned their property might be at the mercy of some local bureaucrat who might or might not be sympathetic to the Greek community. Voutsinas was optimistic about his last appeal partly because the King of Greece George I was visiting St. Petersburg at the time and his presence added weight to the request. AYE 77/2/7209. Voutsinas was not the only Greek official who was intimately involved in the affairs of Odessa's Greeks. On April 30, 1911, the then Greek Consul in Odessa E. Kapsambelis sent the following telegram to the Greek Foreign Ministry: "...κατά χθεσινήν γενικήν Συνέλευσιν Ελλήνων υπό την Προεδρίαν εμού απεφασίσθη ανέγερσις μεγαλοπρεπών οικοδομών δια Ελληνικόν Σχολείον αρρένων και Λέσχην...." (...during yesterday's general assembly of Greeks under my chairmanship it was decided to built substantial buildings for a Greek Boys' School and a Club.) AYE ΒΓ/175/10923. Kapsambelis' report is important for two reasons. In the first place he wrote that the meeting was that of *all* the Greeks in Odessa, not just the GBAO and that he (Kapsambelis) was presiding. That shows that the Greek Foreign Ministry was the driving force behind the events taking place. Secondly, unlike Voutsinas, who was a merchant and resident of Odessa who also acted as Greek Consul, Kapsambelis was a career diplomat. Whereas the former could be involved in community affairs in his capacity as resident of the city, albeit one with official ties, the latter did not have such excuse and his involvement was clearly part of his professional duties. The incident illustrates how the Greek government was involved in the affairs of overseas Greeks.

62. The leaders of the Greek community petitioned the city authorities in 1867 for permission to form an association. Due to various legal and bureaucratic problems the petition took four years to be approved. Paradissopoulos, "Activities," p. 3.

63. GAOO, f. 765, op. 1, d. 1, ll. 12-19.

64. Herlihy, *Odessa*, p. 151.

65. GAOO, f. 765, op. 1, d. 1, ll. 18ob-19.

66. Nitse was one of seven Greek-owned publishing houses in Odessa. See Papoulides, "The Greeks of Russia," p. 123, and "The Educational and Cultural Activities," p. 655.

67. *Greek Encyclopedia*. vol. 7: p. 699.

68. GAOO, f. 765, op. 1, d. 1, l. 12.

69. Paradissopoulos, "Activities," p. 6.

70. GAOO, f. 765, op. 1, d. 1, l. 12.

71. While three rubles a year was not a large amount of money it was not too small either. People from the middle and even lower middle class could easily participate but one has to assume that the vast majority of Greek proletariat was in essence kept out of the GBAO. Civic groups with philanthropic aims tend to be creatures of the middle class, a case of "for the people" but not "by the people." Although not explicitly barred from participation, Greek women were not involved in the GBAO. This was normal in an era before women had achieved a degree of equality and when documents and proclamations which referred to: "all Greeks" or French, Americans, etc. was understood to mean "all *male* Greeks," French, Americans, etc. What is not as easy to ascertain is if non-Greek speaking Greeks were included in the GBAO membership. The charter says nothing about language so presumably Russian-speaking Greeks could become members. It should be noted though that all of the association's business (meetings of the Assembly and officers, minutes of those meetings, correspondence, etc.) was in Greek (with the obvious exemption of reports to the Russian authorities) which meant that non-Greek speakers would be forced to a passive role even if they chose to attend.

72. The GBAO is referred to as "κοινότης" which can be translated as association but also as community. This last term is confusing as the GBAO was not synonymous with the Greek community of Odessa as a whole until later when it assumed the leading role *de facto*.

73. GAOO, f. 765, op. 1, d. 1, l. 12ob.

74. GAOO, f. 765. op. 1, d. 1, ll. 12ob-13ob.

75. A long-suffering secretary complained of being overworked especially due to the fact that he had to catalogue the GBAO archives. Also, as a result of his job description he had to be present in all kinds of committee meetings. As an example he noted that in August of that year (1902) he attended nine committee meetings. See GAOO, f. 765, op. 1, d. 10, l. 93.

76. GAOO, f. 765, op. 1, d. 1, ll. 13ob-14ob.

77. GAOO, f. 765, op. 1, d. 1, ll. 14ob-15ob.

78. GAOO, f. 765, op. 1, d. 1, ll. 16-16ob.

79. GAOO, f. 765, op. 1, d. 1, l. 17.

80. GAOO, f. 765, op. 1, d. 1, l. 17ob, article 37.

81. GAOO, f. 765. op. 1, d. 1, l. 18.

82. GAOO, f. 765, op. 1, d. 1, l. 18.

83. GAOO, f. 765, op. 1, d. 1, ll. 18-18ob.

84. Unlike the charter of the GBAO, that of AHEPA is composed of just six articles explaining, in general terms the goals of the organization and the eligibility of those who can join. AHEPA is a national organization (indeed international since Canada and the Caribbean are also included). While the GBAO was limited to Odessa alone, the Greeks of Russia had created a multi purpose organization with clearly defined goals. In contrast, the AHEPA charter was less precise leaving the task of "painting" the details to the regular meetings of the organization which followed. Leber, pp. 150-160.

Chapter V
Benevolence in Action: Creating and Operating Institutions

1. Gosudarstvennyi arkhiv Odesskoi oblasti (State Archives of Odessa Province [henceforth: GAOO]), Odessa, Ukraine, f. 765, op. 1, d. 2, l. 1.

2. Voulismas came from a family with a tradition of providing clerics and scholars to the Greek Orthodox Church. *Μεγάλη Ελληνική Εγκυκλοπαίδεια* (Great Greek Encyclopedia), 28 vols. (Athens: Phoenix, n.d.), vol. 7: p. 694.

3. The existing record of the GBAO is fragmented. The State Archives of the District of Odessa contain the minutes of the biweekly meetings of the Board of Trustees between the years 1871–1884. After that, there is a gap of twelve years and the record starts again with the meetings of the Board of Administrators for the years 1896–1898. After that, there are only bits and pieces of information (such as balance sheets, petitions and correspondence) up to 1919. The fate of the missing archives is unknown. The fact that Odessa was occupied by foreign powers in both World Wars, as well as the upheavals of the Bolshevik revolution and the Russian Civil War, might be the reason for the disappeared documents. In any case, the existing record is enough to demonstrate a pattern of operation of the GBAO which can be taken as typical of the overall work of that organization.

4. GAOO, f. 765, op. 1, d. 1, l. 12ob.

5. GAOO, f. 765, op. 1, d. 2, l. 1ob.

6. GAOO, f. 2, op. 1, d. 857, l. 56.

7. GAOO, f. 2, op. 1, d. 857, l. 157.

8. GAOO, f. 274, op. 2, d. 13, l. 18. Clearly this is not a complete list of the GBAO budgets but rather a collection of those found to date. Although they might not give a com-

plete picture they do give an indication of the financial relationship between the GBAO and the church of the Holy Trinity.

9. GAOO, f. 765, op. 1, d. 2, l. 3.

10. A consistent problem with the GBAO records is that they record official meetings of the Board of Trustees but say nothing about actions and events which might have started outside the board. Thus the decision to merge is reported as a *fait accompli* without explanation, but there must have been a sequence of events which is not followed here. Someone proposed the merger. Was it the church board or the GBAO? Someone approached the GBAO and made the proposal, and meetings and negotiations must have followed. The assumption is that besides the formal biweekly meetings, the leaders of the GBAO were in informal communication with each other. GAOO, f. 765, op. 1, d. 2, ll. 5ob-6. While there is no direct evidence, it seems that the whole affair was a case of "friendly takeover" by the GBAO. This, by the way, was not the only instance in which the GBAO absorbed another Greek civic body. In October of 1873 the GBAO took over the affairs of the old Philanthropic Society. GAOO, f. 765, op. 1, d. 2. ll. 15ob-16.

11. GAOO, f. 765, op. 1, d. 2, l. 10ob. The actual amount might have been even smaller. In the various GBAO documents amounts of money are referred to simply as rubles. In this instance the 4,365 are specifically labeled "paper rubles." Paper rubles were exchanged at the rate of 3.5-4.5 to the silver ruble.

12. On February 8, 1874 the GBAO hired the newly ordained A. Pefanis as auxiliary priest with yearly salary of 200 rubles. GAOO, f. 765, op. 1, d. 2, ll. 16ob-17. Pefanis, who was originally from the island of Cephalonia, went to Odessa and remained there for the rest of his life eventually being promoted to Archimandrite and director of the church of the Holy Trinity (1884). GAOO, f. 765, op. 1, d. 2, ll. 45-46. In the final years of the GBAO, Pefanis, who had been for many years a member of the Board of Trustees, became President of the organization. This was not the only case of the GBAO hiring clergy for the church. In 1917 it hired a deacon to help the rest of the church's clergy. GAOO, f. 765, op. 1, d. 26, l. 130.

13. GAOO, f. 765, op. 1, d. 2, ll. 28-28ob.

14. As was the case, by no means the only one, of 5,000 rubles left in a will to the church but entrusted to the GBAO. GAOO, f. 765, op. 1, d. 2, l. 11ob. Actually the deceased a Mr. Theodorides stipulated that G. G. Maraslis should be the one who would decide when and how the money should be used for the benefit of the church.

15. GAOO, f. 765, op. 1, d. 22, l. 86.

16. GAOO, f. 765, op. 1, d. 3, ll. 54-54ob.

17. GAOO, f. 765, op. 1, d. 2, ll. 43-43ob.

18. GAOO, f. 765, op. 1, d. 2, ll. 9ob-10.

19. GAOO, f. 765, op. 1, d. 2, ll. 13ob-14.

20. GAOO, f. 765, op. 1, d. 2, ll. 14ob-15.

21. GAOO, f. 765, op. 1, d. 2, ll. 22ob-23. Apparently the charter of the defunct Holy Trinity Brotherhood did not object to the use of its money in the manner the GBAO wanted to use them and thus the building went on.

22. As it has already being pointed out the GBAO was mindful of its own as well as other organizations' charters. The same caution was exhibited in the way the Trustees administered donations to the GBAO by individuals. If the donor stipulated that his/her money should be used for a particular goal the GBAO complied.

23. This situation might be a first. Usually one would expect nineteenth-century organizations (dominated by males) to pay more attention to schools for boys rather than those for girls. In this case, the roles are reversed. The Boys' School was well established and the

GBAO was committed to the Greek education of women to the point that the former was made to serve the later.

24. GAOO, f. 765, op. 1, d. 2, l. 2ob.

25. GAOO, f. 2, op. 1, d. 857, l. 56.

26. GAOO, f. 2, op. 1, d. 857, l. 157.

27. GAOO, f. 274, op. 2, d. 13, ll. 17ob-18.

28. GAOO, f. 765, op. 1, d. 2, ll. 32-32ob.

29. The GBAO ran into financial difficulties from 1875 to the early 1880s. The reason for that was threefold: The economy experienced a recessionary period in the middle and late 1870s and thus the GBAO lost some of its income due to lower interest rates and returns from stocks and securities. At the same time the building of the Girls' School meant increased expenditures. Finally, while many Greeks contributed generously to the GBAO their contributions were usually earmarked by the benefactors for specific projects and could not be used by the Board of Trustees in any way they saw fit. GAOO, f. 765, op. 1, d. 2, ll. 20ob-21ob.

30. GAOO, f. 765, op. 1, d. 2, ll. 34-34ob.

31. GAOO, f. 765, op. 1, d. 2, ll. 35-35ob.

32. GAOO, f. 765, op. 1, d. 2, ll. 39-39ob.

33. GAOO, f. 765, op. 1, d. 2, l. 44ob.

34. GAOO, f. 765, op. 1, d. 2, l. 20.

35. GAOO, f. 765, op. 1, d. 2, ll. 19ob-20.

36. GAOO, f. 765, op. 1, d. 24, l. 124. The Boys' School contributed to the GBAO to the end. In that year, the contribution to the GBAO by the school is recorded as being 6,000 rubles. l. 187.

37. GAOO, f. 765, op. 1, d. 2, l. 22ob.

38. GAOO, f. 765, op. 1, d. 2, l. 23ob.

39. GAOO, f. 765, op. 1, d. 2, ll. 23-23ob.

40. GAOO, f. 765, op. 1, d. 1, l. 12.

41. GAOO, f. 765, op. 1, d. 10, ll. 68-68ob.

42. The role of the nursing home in Greek society is different from that of its western counterpart. The nursing home, in the Greek scheme of things, is not a place where older people go when they are unable physically to take care of themselves either due to illness or due to infirmities brought about by old age. Old people, however sick or infirm, stay with their families (most likely with one of their children) who considered it part of their duty to take care of their parents. A nursing home is the place where old people who have no family, and usually no money, find themselves. A Greek family however poor will consider it a point of pride to take care of its own. To allow one's parents to go to a nursing home is to this day considered an improper action which brings about social stigma. Thus, Greek nursing homes cater to the poorest of the poor, it needs financial assistance from the government, the Church, civic groups or individual donors in order to survive as the residents themselves are unable to contribute to their own upkeep. The need for a nursing home for the Greeks of Odessa seems to suggest that the poor Greeks of the city were numerous and there was a need to take care of the elderly.

43. See Sofronis Paradissopoulos, "Activities of the Greek Charity Society in Odessa 1871–1896," unpublished essay, p. 9.

44. GAOO, f. 765, op. 1, d. 8, l. 36, 58.

45. GAOO, f. 765, op. 1, d. 10. l. 267.

46. Paradissopoulos, p. 10.

47. GAOO, f. 765, op. 1, d. 17, ll. 38-59.
48. GAOO, f. 765, op. 1, d. 13, ll. 1-4.
49. Paradissopoulos, p. 9.
50. GAOO, f. 765, op. 1, d. 19, l. 15.
51. GAOO, f. 765, op. 1, d. 24, ll. 19-20.
52. Although the Greeks of Odessa were careful not to become involved in the political affairs of their host country, they were eagerly observing the political affairs in Greece and their sympathy was with the reformist Liberal Party of E. Venizelos. *Κόσμος*, 21 September 1909: p. 1 and 5 May 1913: p. 1; also, *Αναγέννησις*, 30 April 1917: p. 1.
53. See Xanthipi Kotzageorgi-Zymari, *Η ελληνική εκπαίδευση στη Βουλγαρ'ια (1800–1914)* (Greek Education in Bulgaria [1800–1914]) (Thessaloniki: Festos, 1997), pp. 27-38.
54. Zymari, 54-57.
55. Zymari, 69, 73.
56. Zymari, 67.
57. Zymari, 131.
58. The Greeks of Odessa received the Greek government's help in running their school from an organization called "Society for the Support of Greek Science and Education." In that case, the help took the form of supplying text books and recruiting teachers for the Rodokanaki Girls' School. See Paradissopoulos, p. 7.
59. Zymari, 137.
60. Zymari, 143.
61. GAOO, f. 765, op. 1, d. 2, l. 1ob. January 17, 1872. For some time, the school was simply referred to as "Girls' School" (Παρθεναγωγείον) later the title Rodokanakion was added to honor the GBAO president and the school's major benefactor Th. Rodokanaki.
62. GAOO, f. 765, op. 1, d. 2, l. 3ob.
63. GAOO, f. 765, op. 1, d. 2, ll. 4-5.
64. GAOO, f. 765, op. 1, d. 2, ll. 5ob-6.
65. GAOO, f. 765, op. 1, d. 2, ll. 7, 9.
66. GAOO, f. 765, op. 1, d. 2, ll. 7ob-8ob.
67. See Nicholas Hans, *History of Russian Educational Policy (1701–1917)* (New York: Russell and Russell, 1964), pp. 127-128.
68. Paradissopoulos, pp. 7-8.
69. GAOO, f. 765, op. 1, d. 2, ll. 9ob-10. Eventually the number was reduced to ten. Among the first women charged with that duty were: E. Sevastopoulou, E. Rodokanaki, P. Paspali, A. Papoudof, A. Rodokanaki, Mrs. Voutsina, Ageliki, Ariadni and Xeni Mavrocordatou, M. Ralli, M. Sklavou, M. Paraskeva, etc. It is clear from the names that the women involved were indeed representatives of the upper strata of Odessa's Greek society. GAOO, f. 765, op. 1, d. 2, l. 24ob.
70. GAOO, f. 765, op. 1, d. 2, ll. 12-13. This meeting of the GBAO Board of Trustees was the only one on record to end not because the agenda was completed but due to an emergency. The meeting took place on July 27, 1873 not in the house of Maraslis in Odessa, as most of the meetings had up to that time, but at the summer home of Th. Rodokanaki outside the city. The meeting started at 7:30 p.m. but later Mrs. Rodokanaki interrupted to announce that there was a fire reported in Odessa and naturally the members left in a hurry to see if their families and properties were in danger.
71. GAOO, f. 765, op. 1, d. 2, ll. 13ob-14, 18-18ob.
72. GAOO, f. 765, op. 1, d. 2, ll. 15ob-17.
73. Paradissopoulos, p. 7.

74. GAOO, f. 765, op. 1, d. 2, ll. 18ob-19. The exact role of the supervisor and her helper (all of the personnel of the school were female with the exemption of father Pefanis the parish priest and second grade teacher) is not clear. Her title was "Επιμελήτρια" which indicates that her role was to supervise the non academic aspects of the girls' lives, a crucial role since many of the girls were boarders.

75. GAOO, f. 765, op. 1, d. 2, ll. 19ob-20.

76. GAOO, f. 765, op. 1, d. 2, ll. 21ob-22.

77. Besides the general economic difficulties which the GBAO experienced there were also some associated with the school itself. The newly finished building must have put extra strains on the GBAO budget. Also, the fact that the school was growing rapidly meant extra teachers, personnel, supplies, etc. The fact that the school was a success might have also worked against it financially because the board noted that not enough donations are given by the public for the school's benefit. The board's reaction to the school's financial difficulties was to cut expenses, borrow or shift money from other sources (notably the Boys' School). There were some attempts to organize lottery, selling of handicrafts, etc., but although successful, those endeavors could not generate nearly as much income as was needed. GAOO, f.765, op. 1, d. 2, ll. 28, 29.

78. GAOO, f. 765, op. 1, d. 2, ll. 23ob-24.

79. GAOO, f.765, op. 1, d. 2, l. 25ob.

80. The principal earned 1,200 rubles a year, the kindergarten and one other teacher earned 800, while the rest of the teachers earned 600 each. Father Pefanis earned 700 while the teacher of calligraphy earned only 240.

81. GAOO, f. 765, op. 1, d. 2, ll. 25ob-26.

82. GAOO, f. 765, op. 1, d. 2, l. 25.

83. GAOO, f. 765, op. 1, d. 2, ll. 26-26ob. The conclusion that the parting of the ways between the teachers and the board was less than amicable is deducted from circumstantial evidence. The language used to refuse the request was too harsh. Also, the two women were ostensibly traveling to a better climate in order for one of them to find a cure for whatever illness she was suffering. Under such conditions, one would expect a charitable organization to be understanding. To be sure, the financial condition of the school was not great. At the same meeting, the board decided to investigate the financial position of the parents of poor students before giving them free clothes.

84. GAOO, f. 765, op. 1, d. 2, l. 30.

85. GAOO, f. 765, op. 1, d. 2, ll. 31-32ob.

86. GAOO, f. 765, op. 1, d. 2, ll. 32-32ob.

87. GAOO, f. 765, op. 1, d. 2, ll. 33ob-34.

88. GAOO, f. 765, op. 1, d. 2, ll. 39ob, 41.

89. GAOO, f. 765, op. 1, d. 2, ll. 35-36, 42-42ob.

90. GAOO, f. 765, op. 1, d. 8, ll. 14-15.

91. GAOO, f. 765, op. 1, d. 8, ll. 12-13, 69.

92. The assistance to poor students went farther than just free room and board. Periodically the GBAO invited doctors to examine the students and to assure the board that their general health condition was good. GAOO, f. 765, op. 1, d. 8, l. 14.

93. One case deserves special mention because it was interesting but also because it illustrates the extent to which the Girls' School could and did impact Odessa as a whole. A certain dentist named Poliakov contacted the GBAO asking for the contract to become the school's dentist, his request was denied but the school did provide health services to its poor students as needed. GAOO, f. 765, op. 1, d. 8, ll. 53, 69.

Chapter VI
Benevolence in Action: Individuals and "National" Causes

1. Gosudarstvennyi arkhiv Odesskoi oblasti (State Archives of Odessa Province [henceforth: GAOO]), Odessa, f. 765, op. 1, d. 1, l. 17.

2. Adele Lindenmeyr, *Poverty Is Not a Vice: Charity, Society and the State in Imperial Russia* (Princeton: Princeton University Press, 1996), pp. 9-12.

3. GAOO, f. 765, op. 1, d. 2, l. 1.

4. GAOO, f. 765, op. 1, d. 2, ll. 1ob-2.

5. GAOO, f. 765, op. 1, d. 2, ll. 5ob-6.

6. GAOO, f. 2, op. 1, d. 857, l. 56.

7. GAOO, f. 2, op. 1, d. 857, l. 57.

8. GAOO, f. 274, op. 2, d. 13, ll. 17ob-18.

9. It should be noted that sometimes the numbers which appear on the balance sheet are not the total amount spent. Thus, while in 1875 the GBAO spent less than 3,000 rubles for the poor, it also used the interest of a 3,000 rubles endowment left by a D. Theodorides who specified that such interest should be given to the poor every Easter. GAOO, f. 765, op. 1, d. 2, ll. 20ob-21ob.

10. GAOO, f. 765, op. 1, d. 7, ll. 1-12.

11. GAOO, f. 765, op. 1, d. 8, l. 27.

12. GAOO, f. 765, op. 1, d. 2, l. 11ob.

13. GAOO, f. 765, op. 1, d. 2, ll. 19ob-20.

14. GAOO, f. 765, op. 1, d. 2, ll. 26ob-27ob. That year the GBAO gave 1,000 rubles for Easter.

15. GAOO, f. 765, op. 1, d. 2, ll. 28-28ob. That year, 1877, the GBAO fixed the amount dispensed for Easter to 500 rubles.

16. GAOO, f. 765, op. 1, d. 2, ll. 32-32ob. The above amount was declared by the GBAO to Odessa's police which wrote requesting information about the money spent on the poor as well as on the poor themselves. The reason for such official request was neither given nor asked.

17. Both Easter and Christmas are seasons in which people traditionally consume better food, desserts, etc. In the Greek Orthodox tradition Easter is even more important than Christmas and along with the usual increased expenses people buy spring and summer clothes thus stretching their budgets even more.

18. GAOO, f. 765, op. 1, d. 2, ll. 5ob-6. The exact nature of the need is not stated but since the concern of the Board revolves around "...winter conditions..." (...εν καιρώ χειμώνος...) it is safe to assume that any money given were targeted at warm clothes and/or heating fuel.

19. GAOO, f. 765, op. 1, d. 2, ll. 23ob-24.

20. GAOO, f. 765, op. 1, d. 24.

21. Both the petitions and the support, even when in written form, were not elaborate affairs. In some instances the GBAO member wrote a brief note in the back of his business card vouching for the petitioner.

22. Thus the GBAO file for the year 1903 contains about 250 pages out of a total of 260 (11 x 8 inches) of petitions. GAOO, f. 765, op. 1, d. 16.

23. GAOO, f. 765, op. 1, d. 8, ll. 33-34, 59, 67-68, 71, 73-73ob.

24. GAOO, f. 765, op. 1, d. 7, l. 66.

25. GAOO, f. 765, op. 1, d. 18, l. 19.

26. GAOO, f. 765, op. 1, d. 8, ll. 2-3, 21-23. In a few cases the amounts given were larger (25 rubles to a priests widow and 12 rubles to an unidentified individual were only two such cases) GAOO, f. 765, op. 1, d. 2, l. 30, and d. 8, l. 1.

27. GAOO, f. 765, op. 1, d. 8, ll. 4-7. The Greek Orthodox priest was the one entrusted with investigating the petitioners as well as the periodic updating and verification of the association's list of needy. GAOO, f. 765, op. 1, d. 8, ll. 25-26.

28. In one case the petitioner, who was unemployed and his wife was sick with tuberculosis, was refused help to return to Greece. One would expect a comment regarding such action but none was given. GAOO, f. 765, op. 1, d. 18, l. 25.

29. GAOO, f. 765, op. 1, d. 24. Dated July 11, 1915. In this case two individuals had asked for help to leave Odessa for Athens and Moscow respectively. The refusal underscores the importance of networking and convincing some influential Greek to sponsor one's petition.

30. GAOO, f. 765, op. 1, d. 20, l. 55.

31. The best example of such return to Greece was that of the fabulously wealthy Emmanuel Benakis who made a fortune in Egypt's cotton trade. Benakis returned to Greece and became involved in politics serving as member of parliament, cabinet minister, and mayor of Athens.

32. Thus a certain Maria Theodorou with four small children was given four third class tickets (presumably one of the children was so young that traveled for free). A male petitioner, Vasilios Athanasiou Dalopoulos (who arrived in Odessa from Taganrog) received a third class ticket to Braila (Rumania) in order to return to the town of Mesologgi in Greece. Another petitioner, George Gerakites from the island of Syros, was to receive a ticket home after furnishing proof that his passport was ready. GAOO, f. 765. op. 1, d. 8, ll. 3-5 and 38-39.

33. Why the trip to Rostov (a city on the Black Sea) was more expensive than that to Moscow or Constantinople is never explained. Also why some petitioners received tickets while others were trusted with cash is also a mystery. Clearly not all Greeks leaving Odessa wanted to return to Greece, presumably those who did not have relatives or other prospects in some other land. GAOO f. 765, op. 1, d. 8, ll. 9, and 35-36.

34. The extra help of three rubles each was conditional upon the Greek Consul's recommendation. GAOO, f. 765, op. 1, d. 8, ll. 14-15.

35. GAOO, f. 765, op. 1, d. 24. Dated September 18, 1915.

36. GAOO, f. 765, op. 1, d. 22, ll. 11, 14-17.

37. GAOO, f. 765, op. 1, d. 22, ll. 58, 60. The answer that the GBAO gave to the above request is not recorded.

38. GAOO, f. 765, op. 1, d. 2, l. 3. Once again there is no record of the GBAO giving any money to that particular cause.

39. GAOO, f. 765, op. 1, d. 3, ll. 53-53ob. The document is dated May 10 1884, the hospital in question is the well known, and still in existence, "Ευαγγελισμός".

40. GAOO, f. 765, op. 1, d. 2, l. 19ob. By coincidence the young painter's name was Painter (Κωνσταντίνος Ζωγράφος)

41. GAOO, f. 765, op. 1, d. 2, ll. 25ob-26.

42. That aspect of the GBAO and a number of diverse petitions from different individuals and groups will be examined in the second part of this chapter.

43. Up to the early 1980s the Greek Military Regulations stipulated that an officer was required to receive a dowry of a house or its cash equivalent otherwise permission to marry would be denied.

44. In some areas of Greece, such as Thessaly, the groom as well as the bride is expected to have a dowry usually in the form of clothes, linen, etc.

45. Pushkin Street was, and is, located in Odessa's best district and runs in a North-South direction from the city's city hall, by the sea, to Odessa's main train station. If the numbering of streets has not changed drastically over the years, Maraslis' property was located a city block north of today's Pushkin Museum.

46. GAOO, f. 765, op. 1, d. 2, ll. 41ob-42.

47. The Maraslis family, Greek by nationality, came from the area of the Ottoman Empire that eventually became Bulgaria.

48. GAOO, f. 765, op. 1, d. 8, ll. 40-41. Also d. 7, l. 6. In the first instance, the GBAO wanted proof of marriage before giving the 100 rubles.

49. The GBAO did not dissolve until some time in 1919–1920; however after the October Revolution of 1917 its integrity as an independent organization was compromised.

50. GAOO, f. 765, op. 1, d. 2, ll. 33-33ob.

51. The prince acknowledge the present on March 28, 1899. GAOO, f. 765, op. 1, d. 7, l. 64. Prince George was the second son of King George I of the Hellenes as well as a cousin and close friend of Russian Emperor Nicholas II. Just prior to his assuming the throne then Grand Duke Nicholas went on a world tour accompanied by his Greek cousin. During a visit to Japan someone tried to kill Nicholas but the attempt failed when Prince George hit the would be assassin on the head with a walking stick. The prince served as High Commissioner of semi-independent Crete from 1897–1905. At the time, most Greeks welcomed such a move as a first step towards eventual union of Crete with Greece as well as a paradigm of future incorporation of lands to the Greek kingdom. Thus the gesture of the GBAO had clear patriotic overtones, although it was done in a "safe" way designed not to offend and alarm the Russian authorities.

52. GAOO, f. 765, op. 1, d. 22, ll. 66-67.

53. Part of that contact with the Russian state was the annual invitation of city and educational authorities to attend the Rodokanakion School's graduation ceremonies. Such contacts, although not substantive in their nature did help create a spirit of good will between the GBAO and Odessa's authorities. GAOO, f. 765, op. 1, d. 8, ll. 14-15. The GBAO did not fail to cultivate Russian and Greek authorities when the opportunity presented it self. Thus when celebrating the 25th anniversary of the organization's founding, the Greek Consular authorities were invited to the festivities. GAOO, f. 765, op. 1, d. 8, ll. 57-58.

54. GAOO, f. 765, op. 1, d. 2, ll. 1ob-2.

55. Most of those routine reports can be found in GAOO, f. 2, op. 1, d. 857.

56. GAOO, f. 765, op. 1, d. 2, ll. 12-13.

57. GAOO, f. 765, op. 1, d. 2, ll. 32-32ob. This was a reasonable request since a number of the teachers had earned their degrees in non-Russian universities, mainly in Greece, and thus the authorities had no record of their qualification to teach.

58. GAOO, f. 765, op. 1, d. 8, ll. 25-26. There is no information as to the reasons for such a request. It is not known if it was part of a routine instruction sent to all schools or if it was one directed to the Greek School for Girls alone.

59. GAOO, f. 765, op. 1, d. 10, ll. 53, 114.

60. GAOO, f. 765, op. 1, d. 8, ll. 33-36.

61. By the early twentieth century, a number of Odessa's Greeks criticized the actions of the Greek state especially when it came to the state's policy towards the Greek diaspora. *Κόσμος*, November 1, 1909: p. 1.

62. GAOO, f. 765, op. 1, d. 10, l. 59.

63. GAOO, f. 765, op. 1, d. 2, ll. 36ob-37.

64. To be sure such request came from the regional authorities and not from St. Petersburg but the fact remains that the authorities of Batum chose to turn to the GBAO for help rather than the church, the authorities in the capital, or the Greek Embassy.

65. Romania declared war on Germany and Austria-Hungary on August, 1916 and capitulated in December of the same year. Many Greeks living in Romania found themselves in a difficult position. Even though Greece did not enter the war officially until the summer of 1917, by August of 1916 the country was already split into two with Venizelos established in the North. Thus although Germany and Greece were not at war, the two countries were not friendly either.

66. GAOO, f. 765, op. 1, d. 10, ll. 271-282.

67. GAOO, f. 765, op. 1, d. 10, ll. 60-61.

68. GAOO, f. 765, op. 1, d. 10, l. 137. There is no clue as to the number or nature of the documents found.

69. GAOO, f. 765, op. 1, d. 19, ll. 2-3.

70. Clearly the Greek government did not trust the official Russian statistics on the number of Greeks in the area and believed that the GBAO was in position to provide a more accurate number. Given the fact that the Russian government was sensitive about its minorities, one could assume that the request to the GBAO was made behind the Russian government's back.

71. GAOO, f. 765, op. 1, d. 2, ll. 13-14. The various expenses connected with the royal visit (more of a stopover actually) taxed the GBAO resources and for that reason the organization had to dip into its capital to balance its books. This 2,000 ruble capital expenditure is the *only time* on record that the GBAO had to resort to such extremes. GAOO, f. 765, op. 1, d. 2, l. 15ob.

72. GAOO, f. 765, op. 1, d. 2, ll. 43-43ob.

73. GAOO, f. 765, op. 1, d. 2, l. 41ob.

74. *Κόσμος*, March 25, 1908: p. 3.

75. GAOO, f. 765, op. 1, d. 1, ll. 9ob-10. There is no other record on the subject; clearly the GBAO did not want to be identified (in the eyes of the local authorities) as a nationalist organization like the "Friendly Society" because such identification would cause closer scrutiny. At the same time, it did not refuse its help. Most likely, wealthy individuals of the GBAO sent money to the National Treasury thus circumventing the Russian law about organizations declaring such contributions.

76. GAOO, f. 765, op. 1, d. 2, ll. 37-37ob. Again there is no more records on the subject.

77. GAOO, f. 765, op. 1, d. 19, ll. 89-96. Crete was semi-independent from 1897 until its union with Greece in 1912.

78. Once more I am indebted to a scholar for permission to site unpublished work. In this instance the credit is due to Professor Grigorij Piatigorskij, formerly of Odessa State University but now living in Germany, and his work "Kritskoje vosstanije 1866–1869 i greki Odessi" (The Cretan Revolt of 1866–1869 and the Greeks of Odessa) unpublished essay, 1992. 11; scheduled for publication in the *Modern Greek Studies Yearbook*, vol. 14 (1998).

79. Piatigorskij, p. 12.

80. GAOO, f. 765, op. 1, d. 26, l. 144. Chrysanthos was a warrior-priest. He fought for the good of his nation and paid the ultimate price for it as he was killed in 1922 by the victorious Turks. In 1992 Chrysanthos, together with Metropolitan Chrysostomos of Smyrna

(who was also killed by the Turks in 1922), and five other martyred prelates, was declared a saint by the autocephalous Orthodox Church of Greece.

81. GAOO, f. 765, op. 1, d. 22, l. 62. The letter by Venizelos confirms that the GBAO was indeed a national organization preoccupied with the plight of Greeks in general and not focused only on charitable work.

82. The activities of Odessa's Greeks during that war have only recently been examined by professor Piatigorskij utilizing the post-communist opening of state archives. Grigorij Piatigoskij, "Οι εξεγέρσεις στις ελληνικές επαρχίες της Οθωμανικής αυτοκρατορίας το 1878 και οι Έλληνες της Οδησσού" (The Revolts in the Greek Provinces of the Ottoman Empire in 1878 and the Greeks of Odessa), Conference "The Greeks in Ukraine (18th–20th Century): Social Life, Trade, Culture." Foundation for Hellenic Culture, Institute for Balkan Studies, Odessa State University. Odessa, 28 Sept. 1996.

83. GAOO, f. 765, op. 1, d. 8, ll. 43-44.

84. *Αναέεννησις*, June 4, 1917: p. 3.

85. Eleftherios Venizelos (1864–1936) was liberal in the classical sense of the term advocating democratic and economic freedoms and limiting royal authority. At the same time the Liberals were not republicans by conviction (although in time they became republicans due to circumstances) and some of their political and social beliefs put them squarely in the middle of the political spectrum.

86. The GBAO helped Greece's reorganization by donating generously. See footnote 74 above.

87. This is clearly the view of Papoulides, Avgitides and Kardasis all of whom place Odessa's Greek leaders to the right of the political spectrum.

88. Even in Russia, which was years behind western Europe in its political development, the Constitutional Democrats (Kadets) had captured the majority of seats in Parliament (Duma) by advocating measures similar to those of other European liberal parties.

89. *Κόσμος*, August 21, 1909, no. 359: p. 1.

90. *Κόσμος*, May 5, 1913, no. 483: p. 1. It should be noted that this newspaper was not partisan Venizelist having often editorialized that Greece needed the royal family. See no. 362, p. 1.

91. The Greeks of the United States became notorious for their physical confrontations which often necessitated police intervention. The most common apple of discord was which side controlled the local Greek Orthodox Church (a symbol of the community).

92. *Αναγέννησις*, June 16, 1917, no. 8: p. 4.

93. *Αναγέννησις*, September 27, 1917, no. 22: p. 4.

94. GAOO, f. 765, op. 1, d. 26, l. 100. The record, and the press, do not mention names, thus it is not known who were the leaders of the main factions. It is not known what steps, if any, the GBAO took to address the alleged electoral irregularities. This is the only time when non-Greeks are alleged to have become GBAO members.

95. The royalists were clearly the minority and kept a relatively low profile. There was a royalist newspaper called *Ήλιος* (The Sun) but its circulation and importance appears to have been limited. See *Αναγέννησις*, June 4, 1917, no. 6: p. 11.

96. GAOO, f. 765, op. 1, d. 24.

97. Some of Greece's grandiose war aims, such as occupation of Constantinople, were unacceptable to Russia who had the same expectations. Thus the move of support by the GBAO can not be seen as having the endorsement of official Russia.

98. GAOO, f. 765, op. 1, d. 24, l. 21, dated September 18, 1915. The telegraph was sent after unanimous vote by the GBAO Board of Trustees. This gesture put the GBAO, and

the Greek community of Odessa which the organization clearly represented, on the liberal side and openly against the wishes of the King of Greece.

99. In earlier chapters of this work, it was explained how the GBAO and its energetic vice-president E. Pavlides were the force behind the creation of an umbrella organization representing all the Greeks of South Russia. *Αναγεννησις*, June 25, 1917, no.9: p. 3 and July 23, 1917, no. 13: p. 1. Pavlides was the most active member of the Board of Trustees of the GBAO and the sponsor of the earlier resolution supporting Venizelos. After the Russian Revolution, Pavlides went to Greece where he became the leader of Greece's community of Greek refugees from Russia and long time president of their union.

100. Ιστορικό Αρχείο Υπουργίου Εξωτερικών (Historical Archives of the Ministry of Foreign Affairs, AYE) Athens B/49 pp. 4-5, March 3, 1916. The request to Kapsambelis by the GBAO claims that the editor of the newspaper slandered people of the Greek community and had become the organ of a few meddling individuals. In the military governor's order the editor of the newspaper is labeled "irresponsible".

101. GAOO, f. 765, op. 1, d. 24, l. 22. The Board of Trustees of the GBAO discussed the telegram for the first time on December 8, 1915.

102. GAOO, f. 765, op. 1, d. 24, l. 23.

103. Kapsambelis, although personally sympathetic to Venizelos, was still the representative of the Greek government and thus could not be contacted officially (it would not be surprising if the leaders of the GBAO contacted Kapsambelis privately and asked his opinion).

Chapter VII
End of an Era

1. *Αναγέννησις*, September 20, 1917: p. 4. Originally, the membership dues for the GBAO was 3 rubles a year per member. It is not known if that amount had increase over the years.

2. Not surprising those Greeks who supported Venizelos were also well disposed towards Russia's Provisional Government while those who were royalists supported both the Greek and the Russian thrones.

3. *Αναγέννησις*, June 25, 1917: p. 3.

4. Gosudarstvennyi arkhiv Odesskoi oblasti (State Archives of Odessa Province [henceforth: GAOO]), f. 2, op. 1, d. 857, l. 56.

5. GAOO, f. 765, op. 1, d. 26, ll. 184-187. This document is dated December 31, 1917 and given the political events of the era should be considered the last budget of a "normal" year.

6. In comparison, the 1898 balance sheet of the St. Petersburg Noble Assembly shows a total endowment for charity of 360,890 rubles. See Seymour Becker, *Nobility and Privilege in Late Imperial Russia* (DeKalb: Northern Illinois University Press, 1985), p. 140.

7. The above numbers are the most indicative of the organizations' economic condition. In the actual balance sheet there are detailed accounts of were the money came from, the worth of each building and its furniture, etc.

8. GAOO, f. 765, op. 1, d. 24, l. 124. Unlike the GBAO balance sheet, that of the Boys' School is not a detailed account but more of a summary.

9. GAOO, f. 765, op. 1, d. 24, l. 130. This projected budget is not detailed thus is not clear what kind of expenses would warrant such high operational costs.

10. GAOO, f. 765, op. 1, d. 13, ll. 1-4 and 28-37.

11. One might argue that if the GBAO did not exist the same amount of money would still be in circulation by the various individuals who donated them to the organization. Clearly the GBAO did not create the money, but while individuals might have kept cash under their mattress or sent it out of the country or keep it in a safe the GBAO was obliged by its charter to deposit its cash reserves into a Russian Bank. GAOO, f. 765, op. 1, d. 1, l. 12ob, Article 4.

12. Adele Lindenmeyr, *Poverty is Not a Vice* (Princeton: Princeton University Press, 1997), pp. 200-201.

13. Lindenmeyr, *Poverty*, p. 205. The GBAO dues were 3 rubles a year until the unspecified increase during the First World War. Some elite organizations, such as the Imperial Philanthropic Society had a minimum requirement of 25 rubles a year.

14. Lindenmeyr, *Poverty*, pp. 204-205.

15. Patricia Herlihy, *Odessa: A History, 1794–1914* (Cambridge: Harvard University Press, 1986), p. 242.

16. Sofronis Paradissopoulos, "Activities of the Greek Charity Society in Odessa, 1871–1896," unpublished paper, p. 10.

17. For the number of Odessa's Greek speaking males, see Herlihy, *Odessa*, 242.

18. In *Poverty is Not a Vice*, Adele Lindenmeyr presents a number of informative tables which help to better quantify the phenomenon of nineteenth century Russian civic groups. The tables presented here are found in Lindenmeyr's study, pages 238-239. Another work which includes a number of important tables and figures is *Rossiia 1913 god: Statistiko-dokumentanii spravochnik* (Russia in 1913: A Reference Book of Statistical Documents) (St. Petersburg: Russian Academy of Sciences, 1995), pp. 381-400.

19. Lindenmeyr, *Poverty*, p. 239.

20. GAOO, f. 765, op. 1, d. 26, l. 185.

21. Lindenmeyr, *Poverty*, p. 239.

22. GAOO, f. 765, op. 1, d. 26, l. 187.

23. Lindenmeyr, *Poverty*, p. 3.

24. See Theofanis G. Stavrou, "Greek Participation and the French Army Intervention in the Ukraine," in Peter Pastor, ed., *Revolutions and Interventions in Hungary and its Neighbor States, 1918–1919* (Boulder: East European Monographs, 1988), pp. 321-334.

25. Stavrou, p. 323.

26. N. Petsalis-Diomidis, "Hellenism in South Russia and the Ukrainian Campaign: Their Effect on the Pontus Question (1919)," *Balkan Studies* 13:2, pp. 233-235.

27. Dimitrios Vakas, *Η Μεγάλη Ελλάς* (Greater Greece) (Athens: n.p., 1947), pp. 280-281. Smyrna was the main coastal city in Asia Minor.

28. Kim Munholland, "The French Army and Intervention in the Ukraine," in Peter Pastor, ed., *Revolutions and Interventions in Hungary and its Neighbor States, 1918–1919* (Boulder: East European Monographs, 1988), p. 349.

29. Petsalis-Diomidis, p. 237.

30. Petsalis-Diomidis, pp. 225-226.

31. Petsalis-Diomidis, pp. 252, 257.

32. Petsalis-Diomidis, p. 240.

33. Petsalis-Diomidis, pp. 244-247.

34. I. K. Hassiotis, ed., *Οι Έλληνες της Ρωσίας και της Σοβιετικής Ένωσης. Μετοικεσίες και Εκτοπισμοί, Οργάνωση και Ιδεολογία* (The Greeks of Russia and the Soviet Union. Emigrations and Forcible Relocations, Organization and Ideology) (Thessaloniki: University Studio Press, 1997), p. 236.

35. Petsalis-Diomidis, p. 257.

36. The first mass exodus of Greeks from Odessa occurred on April 4, 1919. When the Greek army was evacuating the city 10,000-12,000 Greeks from Russia chose to leave with the troops. See Petsalis-Diomidis, 241. By 1921 the Greek population of Odessa was reduced to 1,439 from the 5,000-10,000 estimated in 1897. See Hassiotis, Table 23, p. 564.

37. As the work of K. Papoulides demonstrates, by the beginning of the twentieth century the majority of Greek wealth in Russia was invested in land, both rural and urban, factories shops, etc. See Konstantinos Papoulides "Γύρω από την Οικονομική Δραστηριότητα Ωρισμένων Ελλήνων στη Ρωσία κατά τα Τέλη του 19ου Αιώνα" (Regarding the Financial Activities of Some Greeks in Russia at the end of the Nineteenth Century), *Balkan Bibliography* 7 (1978): pp. 99-116.

38. Eleufitherios Pavlides, ed., *Ο Ελληνισμός της Ρωσίας* (The Greeks of Russia) (Athens: Union of Greeks from Russia, 1953), p. 115. At first glance this number might sound exaggerated but it might not be so. When G. G. Maraslis died in 1907 he left 2,000,000 rubles in liquid assets and 10,000,000 rubles in real estate. *Κόσμος*, May 5, 1907. At the rate of 10 rubles to the British pound Maraslis alone had a fortune equal to about 1/6 of the estimated lost fortune. Thus the estimated 6.5 millions, astronomical as it might have been, seems to have been a realistic estimate.

39. Andrew Zapantis, *Greek-Soviet Relations, 1917–1941* (Boulder: East European Monographs, 1982), p. 283.

40. This Rallis was the father of John Rallis, the quisling premier of Greece during the German occupation (1941–1944), and grandfather of George, the conservative politician and sometime prime minister. Maria Karavia. "Ποιότητα ζωής των Ελλήνων στην Οδησσό *τον* περασμένο αιώνα" (Quality of Life of the Greeks of Odessa During the Last Century), Conference "The Greeks in Ukraine (18th-20th Century) Social Life, Trade, Culture." Odessa: Foundation for Hellenic Culture, Institute for Balkan Studies, Odessa State University, Sept. 26, 1996.

41. See note 38 above for details on Maraslis' wealth. Maraslis married a Russian noblewoman in 1905, two years before his death. Maraslis had no children and his only surviving blood relatives were his niece Baroness Fredericks and her brother Alexander Safonov. Alexander Safonov, an army officer, became Maraslis' main heir and added his uncle's last name to his own. However, since most of the fortune was in real estate the family became destitute after the Bolshevik revolution. See Konstantinos Papoulides, *Γρηγόριος Γ. Μαρασλής (1831–1907) Η Ζωή και το Έργο του* (Gregory G. Maraslis (1831–1907) His Life and Work) (Thessaloniki: Institute for Balkan Studies, 1989), pp. 105-106.

42. Natalia Tarantjeva, "Οι Έλληνες στην Ουκρανία, 1920–1940" (The Greeks in Ukraine, 1920–1940), Conference "The Greeks in Ukraine (18th-20th Century) Social Life, Trade, Culture." Odessa: Foundation for Hellenic Culture, Institute for Balkan Studies, Odessa State University, Sept. 30, 1996.

43. Tatjana Nikitina, "Η Ελληνική διασπορά στην ΕΣΣΔ και οι ελληνοσοβιετικές σχέσεις" (The Greek Diaspora in the USSR and Greek-Soviet Relations), Conference "The Greeks in Ukraine (18th-20th Century) Social Life, Trade, Culture." Odessa: Foundation for Hellenic Culture, Institute for Balkan Studies, Odessa State University, Sept. 30, 1996.

44. Tarantjeva. In 1926 the demotic (that is, the Greek idiom spoken by the people as opposed to the purist idiom (*katharevousa*) which was the official language in Greece until the 1970s) became the Greek language officially promoted while phonetic spelling was adopted. At about the same time the Greeks of the Caucasus were organized in an autonomous "Greek Region" (*Grecheskii Raion*) which did not have a defined territory, since the

Greeks were not a clear majority in a particular area, but allowed them a degree of political participation. See Hassiotis, p. 408.

45. Tarantjeva. It should be noted that the Greek Soviets of the area, which were by definition friendly to the regime, were against collectivization.

46. Zapantis, p. 239.

47. Zapantis, pp. 369-371.

48. Nikitina. For more information on the impact of Stalin's purges on the Greeks of the Soviet Union, see Hassiotis, pp. 383-405.

49. Something that a Greek group such as the American Hellenic Educational Progressive Association (AHEPA), among others, is doing in present-day USA.

50. As Lindenmeyr notes embezzlement and mismanagement of the funds of charitable organizations was a common enough occurrence in nineteenth century Russia. See *Poverty*, p. 215.

51. *Κόσμος*, January 5, 1908: p. 3.

52. While Odessa is located in Ukraine, it is a city of mixed ethnic groups with a clear Russian character.

53. Many thanks to Dr. Lilia Belousova, director of the Odessa Regional State Archives, for providing me with information regarding G. Maraslis' house.

Bibliography

Archival Collections

Gosudarstvennyi arkhiv Odesskoi oblasti (State Archives of Odessa Province) Odessa, Ukraine (GAOO). F. 1, 2,

Ιστορικό Αρχείο Υπουργίου Εξωτερικών (Historical Archives of the Ministry of Foreign Affairs) Athens, Greece (AYE) BG/175/15692.

The United States of America National Archives and Records Service (NARCO). Microfilm Publications: Dispatches from U.S. Consuls in Odessa, 1834-1906, vols. 1-10. Washington, DC.

Contemporary Newspapers

Αναγέννησις (Renaissance), 1917-1919.

Ελληνικός Αστήρ (Greek Star), 1913.

Κόσμος (The World), 1906-1913.

Φώς (The Light), 1897-1910.

Published Material

Primary Sources

Alcock, Thomas. *Travels in Russia, Persia, Turkey and Greece in 1828-1829.* London: E. Clarke and Son, 1831.

Baedeker, Karl. *La Russie: Manuel du Voyageur.* Paris: Paul Ollendorff, 1902.

_____. *Russia with Teheran, Port Arthur and Peking: Handbook for Travellers.* New York: Charles Scribner's Sons, 1914.

Barratt, Glynn. "Notice sur l' insurrection des Grecs contre l'empire Ottomanique. A Russian View of the Greek War of Independence." *Balkan Studies* 14:1 (1973): 47-115.

Basily, Nicolas de. *Diplomat of Imperial Russia 1903-1917. Memoirs.* Stanford: Hoover Institution Press, 1973.

Chrysogelos, E. *Grecheskaia Tserkov sv. Troitsi v Odesse 1808-1908* (The Greek Church of the Holy Trinity in Odessa 1808-1908). Odessa: n.p., 1908.

Clarke, Edward D. *Travels in Russia, Tartary, and Turkey.* Aberdeen: George Clark and Son, 1848.

Coxe. "Travels in Russia." *A General Collection of the Best and Most Interesting Voyages and Travels, in all Parts of the World.* Ed. John Pinkerton. 6 vols. Philadelphia: Kimber and Conrad, 1810-1812. Vol. 6: pp. 570-913.

Dendias, Michael. *Αί Ελληνικαί Παροικίαι ανά τον Κόσμον* (Greek Communities Throughout the World). Athens: Sideri, 1919.

Ημερολόγιον των Εθνικών Φιλανθρωπικών Καταστημάτων (Almanac of National Philanthropic Institutions). Constantinople: n.p., 1905.

Holderness, Mary. *New Russia. Journey from Riga to the Crimea by Way of Kiev; With Some Account of the Colonization, and the Manners and Customs of the Colonists of New Russia. To Which are Added, Notes Relating to the Crim Tatars.* London: Sherwood, Jones and Co., 1823.

Kapsambelis, Emmanuel. *Αναμνήσεις Διπλωμάτου* (Memoirs of a Diplomat). Athens: n.p., 1939.

_____. *Διπλωματικά Παρασκήνια* (Diplomacy Behind the Scenes). Athens: n.p., 1946.

_____. *'Εκθεσις περί Γεωργίας, Εμπορίας, Βιομηχανίας και Ναυτιλίας εν Ρωσσία εν γένη και ιδία εν Οδησσώ* (Report on the Agriculture, Trade, Industry and Merchant Marine in Russia and Particularly in Odessa). In the series: *Δελτίον του επι των Εξωτερικών Υπουργίου* (Reports of the Ministry of Foreign Affairs). Athens: National Press, 1912.

Kiouze-Pezas, S. *Έκθεσις περί Γεωργίας, Εμπορίας, Βιομηχανίας και Ναυτιλίας ανά την Προξενικήν Περιφέρειαν Ταιγανίου 1910-1911* (Report on the Agriculture, Trade, Industry and Merchant Marine in the District of Taganrog 1910-1911). In the series: *Δελτίον του επί των Εξωτερικών Υπουργίου* (Reports of the Ministry of Foreign Affairs). Athens: National Press, 1912.

Lyall, Robert. *Travels in Russia, the Crimea, the Caucasus and Georgia.* 2 vols. London: T. Cadell, 1825.

Pallas, Peter Simon. *Travels Through the Southern Provinces of the Russian Empire in the Years 1793 and 1794.* 2nd ed. London: Stockdale, 1812.

Panagiotides, Th. *Ο εν Ρωσία Ελληνισμός* (The Greeks of Russia). Athens: Trembela, 1919.

Pavlides Eleftherios, ed. *Ο Ελληνισμός της Ρωσίας* (Greeks in Russia). Athens: Union of Greeks from Russia, 1953.

Rossiia 1913 god. Statistiko-dokumental'nii spravochnik (Russia in 1913. A Reference Book of Statistical Documents). St. Petersburg: Russian Academy of Sciences, 1995.

Titidiotis, K. *Κίνδυνος της εν Οδησσώ Ελληνικής Σχολής των Αρρένων* (The Danger to the Odessa Greek School for Boys). Athens: Apostolopoulos, 1911.

Voulodemos, X. *Πρώτη Πεντηκονταετηρής της εν Οδησσώ Ελληνεμπορικής Σχολής* (The First Fifty Years of the Greek Merchant School in Odessa 1817-1867). Odessa: Nitse, 1871.

Wilson, William Rae. *Travels in Russia.* 2 vols. London: Longman, Rees, Orme, Brown, and Green, 1828.

Secondary Sources

Alef, Gustav. "Diaspora Greeks in Muscovy." *Byzantine Studies* 6 (1975): 26-34.

Alexander, John T. Catherine the Great: Life and Legend. New York: Oxford University Press, 1989.

Alexandropoulou, Olga. *Ο Διονύσιος Ιβηρ'ιτης και το έργο του: "Ιστορία της Ρωσίας"* (Dionysios Iviritis and His Work: "History of Russia"). Iraklion, Greece: Vikelaia Dimotiki Vivliothiki, 1994.

____. "The History of Russia in Works by Greek Scholars of the Seventeenth Century." *Cyrillomethodianum* 13-14 (1989-1990): 61-91.

Ampatzopoulou, Frangiski. "Πανάγος Αξιώτης (1840-1910). 'Ενας έλληνας λόγιος στη Μαριούπολη." (Panagos Axiotis [1840-1910] A Greek Scholar in Mariupol). Conference: "The Greeks in Ukraine (18th-20th Century) Social Life, Trade, Culture." Foundation for Hellenic Culture, Institute for Balkan Studies, Odessa State University. Odessa, 30 Sept. 1996.

Anastassiadou, Iph. "Les Russo-Turcs a Zante en 1798" (The Russo-Turks on the Island of Zante in 1798). *Balkan Studies* 14: 1 (1973): 12-46.

Anderson, M. S. *The Eastern Question 1774-1923*. New York: St. Martin's Press, 1966.

Aradzioni, Margarita. " Ο Ελληνικός πληθυσμός της Κριμαίας στα τέλη του 18ου αι" (The Greek Population of Crimea at the end of the Eighteenth Century). Conference: "The Greeks in Ukraine (18th-20th Century) Social Life, Trade, Culture." Foundation for Hellenic Culture, Institute for Balkan Studies, Odessa State University. Odessa, 27 Sept. 1996.

Arsh, Grigorii Lvovich. *Eteristkoe dvizhenie v Rossii* (The Philike Etaireia Movement in Russia). Moscow: Nauka, 1972.

____. "Grecheskaia emigratsiia v Rossiiu v kontse xviii-nachale xix v." (Greek Emigration in Russia at the end of the Eighteenth to the Beginning of the Nineteenth Centuries). *Sovetskaia ethnografiia* 3 (1969): 85-95.

____. "Grecheskoe kommercheskoe uchiliche Odessi v 1817-1830 gg." (The Greek Commercial School of Odessa in 1817-1830). *Balkanskie Isledovania* 10 (Moscow: Nauka, 1987): 31-62.

____. "Greek Intellectuals and Merchant Benefactors of National Education in Russia in the Eighteenth and Nineteenth Century." *Hellas-Russia One Thousand Years of Bonds*. Athens: Gnosi, 1994. pp. 167-198.

____. *Kapodistriia i grecheskoe natsional'no-osvobotitel'noe dvizhenie, 1809-1822 gg.* (Capodistrias and the Greek National Liberation Movement, 1809-1822). Moscow: Nauka, 1976.

____. "Οι 'Ελληνες της Ρωσίας" (The Greeks of Russia). *Μουσείο Φιλικής Εταιρίας*. Athens: Foundation for Hellenic Culture, 1994. pp. 13-33.

Arsh, Grigorii Lvovich. "Οι Ελληνικές παροικίες της βόρειας παρευξείνιας περιοχής και η πάλη της Ελλάδας για την Εθνική Απελευθέρωση (αρχες του 19ου αι.)" (The Greek Communities of the Northern Black Sea Shore and the Greek War of Independence [Beginning of the Nineteenth Century]). Conference: "The Greeks in Ukraine (18th-20th Century) Social Life, Trade, Culture." Foundation for Hellenic Culture, Institute for Balkan Studies, Odessa State University. Odessa, 26 Sept. 1996.

____. "On the Life of the Greek Patriotic Family of Ypsilanti." *Balkan Studies* 26, No. 1 (1985): 73-90.

____. "Rossija i grecheskoe prosvechenie nachala xix v.(Tezisy)" (Russia and the Neo-Hellenic Enlightenment at the Beginning of the 19th Century). Trans. K. K. Papoulidis. *Balkan Bibliography* 4. (Institute for Balkan Studies, 1977): 223-226.

Ascherson, Neal. *Black Sea*. London: Jonathan Cape, 1995.

Avgitides, K. G. *Εθελοντικά Στρατιωτικά Τμήματα από 'Ελληνες της Ρωσίας κατά της Οθωμανικής Αυτοκρατορίας Πριν και Μετά το 1821* (Volunteer Military Units of Greeks from Russia Against the Ottoman Empire Before and After 1821). Athens, n.p. 1993.

____. *Οι Έλληνες της Οδησσού και η Επανάσταση του 1821* (The Greeks of Odessa and the Revolution of 1821). Athens: Dodoni, 1994.

____. *Progressivnaia grecheskaia emigratsiia v Odesse* (The Progress of Greek Emigration in Odessa). Kiev: Visha Schola, 1987.

Babel, Isaac. *Lyubka the Cossack and Other Stories*. Trans. Andrew MacAndrew. New York: New American Library, 1963.

Baron, Salo W. *The Russian Jew Under Tsars and Soviets*. New York: Macmillan Publishing Co., Inc., 1976.

Bartlett, Roger. *Human Capital: The Settlement of Foreigners in Russia 1762-1804*. Cambridge: Cambridge University Press, 1979.

Barty-King, Hugh. *The Baltic Exchange*. London: Hutchinson, Benham, 1977.

Batalden, Stephen. *Catherine II's Greek Prelate: Eugenios Voulgaris in Russia, 1771-1806*. Boulder, Colorado: East European Monographs, 1982.

____. "Eugenios Voulgaris in Russia, 1776-1806: A Chapter in Greco-Slavic ties of the Eighteenth Century." Ph.D. dissertation, University of Minnesota, 1975.

____. "A Further Note on Patriarch Serapheim II's Sojourn to Russia." *Balkan Studies* 18, No. 2 (1977): 409-411.

Beable, William. *Commercial Russia*. New York: The Macmillan Co, 1919.

Becker, Seymour. *Nobility and Privilege in Late Imperial Russia*. DeKalb, IL: Northern Illinois University Press, 1985.

Beloousova, Lilia. "Το ιστορικό αρχείο της Οδησσού ως πηγή για τη μελέτη της ιστορίας των Ελλήνων της Ουκρανίας (τελη 18ου-20ος αι.)" (The Historical Archives of Odessa as a Resource for the Study of the History of the Greeks of

Ukraine [18th-20th Century]). Conference: "The Greeks in Ukraine (18th-20th Century) Social Life, Trade, Culture. Foundation for Hellenic Culture, Institute for Balkan Studies, Odessa State University. Odessa, 26 Sept. 1996.

Berk, Stephen M. *Year of Crisis, year of Hope: Russian Jewry and the Pogroms of 1881-1882*. Westport, CT: Greenwood Press, 1985.

Birman, M. A. "Balkanskie internatsionalisti v Odesse vesnoi i letom 1919 g." (Balkan Internationalists in Odessa in the Spring and Summer of 1919). *Balkanskie Isledovania* 10 (Moscow: Nauka, 1987): 146-167.

Bol'shaia Sovetskaia Entsiklopediia (Great Soviet Encyclopedia). 2nd ed. 53 vols. Moscow: Bol'shaia Sovetskaia Entsiklopediia, 1954.

Boardman, John. *The Greeks Overseas*. Baltimore: Penguin Books, 1964.

Bradley, Joseph. "Merchant Moscow After Hours: Voluntary Associations and Leisure." *Merchant Moscow: Images of Russia's Vanished Bourgeoisie*. Ed. James West and Iurii Petrov. Princeton: Princeton University Press, 1998. pp 133-143.

____. "Russia's Parliament of Public Opinion: Association, Assembly, and the Autocracy." *Reform in Modern Russian History*. Ed. Theodor Taranovskii. New York: Cambridge University Press, 1995. pp. 212-236.

____. "Subjects into Citizens: Societies, Civil Society, and Autocracy in Tsarist Russia." *The American Historical Review* 107, No. 4 (October, 2002): 1094-1123.

____. "Voluntary Associations, Civic Culture, and *Obshchestvenost'*." *Between Tsar and People*. Ed. E. Clowes, S. Kassow, and J. West. Princeton: Princeton University Press, 1991. pp. 131-148.

Brinkley, George. *The Volunteer Army and Allied Intervention in South Russia, 1917-1921*. Notre Dame: University of Notre Dame Press, 1966.

Brower, Daniel. *The Russian City Between Tradition and Modernity 1850-1900*. Berkeley: University of California Press, 1990

Bruess, Gregory. "Catherine II's Imperial Manner and Eastern Orthodoxy: The Case of Nikiforos Theotokis, 1779-1800." Ph.D. dissertation, University of Minnessota, 1992.

____. "The Chesme Church: The Construction and Commemoration of Empire." *Modern Greek Studies Yearbook* 16/17 (2000-2001): 225-242.

____. "Crossing Boundaries: Nikiforos Theotokis in the Russia of Catherine II." *Modern Greek Studies Yearbook* 9 (1993): 51-74.

____. *Religion, Identity and Empire: A Greek Archbishop in the Russia of Catherine the Great*. Boulder, CO: East European Monographs, 1997.

Byng of Vimy, Evelyn Viscountess. *Up the Stream of Time*. Toronto: The Macmillan Company of Canada Ltd., 1945.

Cannadine, David. *The Decline and Fall of the British Aristocracy*. New Haven, CT: Yale University Press, 1990.

Chapman, S. D. "The International Houses: The Continental Contribution to British Commerce 1800-1860." *Journal of European Economic History* 6, No. 1 (1977): 5-48.

Cherniavsky, Michael. *Tsar and People: Studies in Russian Myths*. New York: Random House, 1961.

Clucas, Lowell, ed. *The Byzantine Legacy in Eastern Europe*. Boulder, Colorado: East European Monographs, 1988.

Cohen, Robin. *Global Diasporas: An Introduction.* Seattle: University of Washington Press, 1997.

Constas, Dimitri, and Athanasios Platias, eds. *Diasporas in World Politics*. London: The Macmillan Press Ltd, 1993.

Corten, Irina. "Freedom, Beauty, and Love: Images of Greeks in Russian Fiction of the Soviet Period." *Modern Greek Studies Yearbook* 10/11 (1994/95): 693-716.

_____. "Reality or Ideal: Images of Greeks in the Works of Aleksandr Kuprin." *Modern Greek Studies Yearbook* 6 (1990): 265-292.

Couloumbis, A., J. A. Petropoulos, and H. J. Psomiades. *Foreign Interference in Greek Politics.* New York: Pella, 1976.

Cox, Cynthia. *Talleyrand's Successor: Armand-Emmanuel du Plessis Duc de Richelieu 1766-1822.* London: Arthur Barker Ltd, 1959.

Dakin, Douglas. "The Diplomacy of the Great Powers and the Balkan States 1908-1914." *Balkan Studies* 3, No. 2 (1962): 327-374.

Daly, John. *Russian Sea Power and 'The Eastern Question' 1827-1841.* Annapolis, Maryland: Naval Institute Press, 1991.

Debrett's Peerage and Baronetage. Kingston upon Thames: Kelly's Directories, 1980.

Derlemenko, E., and V. Kontsevich, eds. *Odessa*. Kiev: Spalah, 1994.

Despotopoulos, Alexandre. "La Revolution grecque, Alexandre Ypsilantis et la politique de la Russie" (The Greek Revolution, Alexander Ypsilantis and the Russian Policy). *Balkan Studies* 7, No. 2 (1966): 411-422.

Dimaras, C. Th. *A History of Modern Greek Literature*. Trans. Mary P. Gianos. Albany, NY: State University of New York Press, 1972.

Diomidis-Petsalis, N. "Hellenism in South Russia and the Ukrainian Campaign: Their Effect on the Pontus Question: *Balkan Studies* 13, No. 2 (1973): 221-263.

Dmytryshyn, Basil, ed. *Imperial Russia: A Source Book, 1700-1917.* 3rd ed. Orlando, Florida: Harcourt, Brace and Jovanovich, 1990.

_____., ed. *Medieval Russia: A Source Book, 900-1700.* New York: Holt, Rinehart and Winston, Inc., 1967.

Druzhinina, E. I. *Kiuchuk-Kainardzhiskii Mir 1774 goda (Ego Podgotovka Zakliuchenie)* (The Kutchuk Kainardji Peace of 1774 [Its Preparation and Signing]). Moscow: Akademii Nauk, 1955.

Dubnov, Simon. *History of the Jews.* Trans. Moshe Spiegel. 5 vols. New York: Thomas Yoseloff Ltd., 1973.

Eklof, Ben, ed. *School and Society in Tsarist and Soviet Russia.* New York: St. Martin's Press, 1993.

Entsiklopedicheskii slovar' (Encyclopedic Dictionary). 86 vols. St. Petersburg: Brockhous-Efron, 1890-1907.

Farsolas, Demetrios. "Alexander Pushkin: His Attitude Toward the Greek Revolution 1821-1829." *Balkan Studies* 12, No. 1 (1971): 57-80.

Fedor, Thomas S. *Patterns of Urban Growth in the Russian Empire During the Nineteenth Century.* Chicago: University of Chicago, 1975.

Fennell, John. *A History of the Russian Church to 1448.* New York: Longman, 1995.

Fisher, A. *The Russian Annexation of the Crimea 1772-1783.* Cambridge: Cambridge University Press, 1970.

Fleming, K. E. "The Question of Church Union and the Fall of Constantinople" *Modern Greek Studies Yearbook* 12/13 (1996-1997): 35-47.

Fonkich, B. L., ed. *Graeco-Russian Contacts from the Middle of the Xvi Century up to the Beginning of the XVIII Century.* Moscow: USSR Academy of Science, 1991.

Footman, David. *Civil War in Russia.* New York: Frederick A. Praeger, 1961.

Fotiadis, Konstantinos. "Ο Ελληνισμός της Οδησσού, 1918-1921" (The Greeks of Odessa, 1918-1921). Conference: "The Greeks in Ukraine (18th-20th Century) Social Life, Trade, Culture." Foundation for Hellenic Culture, Institute for Balkan Studies, Odessa State University. Odessa, 28 Sept. 1996.

Friedberg, Maurice. *How Things Were Done in Odessa.* Boulder, Colorado: Westview Press, 1991.

Geanakoplos, Deno. "The Diaspora Greeks: The Genesis of Modern Greek National Consciousness." *Hellenism and the First Greek War of Liberation (1821-1830): Continuity and Change.* Ed. Nikiforos P. Diamandouros, John P. Anton, John A. Petropulos and Peter Topping. Thessaloniki: Institute for Balkan Studies, 1976. pp. 59-77.

Georgiou, Elias. *Ο Θαλασσομάχος Λάμβρος Κατσώνης* (The Naval Warrior Lambros Katsonis). Athens, n.p., 1971.

Gogol, Nikolai. *Dead Souls.* Trans. Andrew MacAndrew. New York: New American Library, 1961.

Greenberg, Louis. *The Jews in Russia: The Struggle for Emancipation.* 2 vols. New Haven, CT: Yale University Press, 1951.

Grimsted, Patricia. *The Foreign Ministers of Alexander I.* Berkeley: University of California Press, 1969.

Hamm, Michael F. *Kiev: A Portrait, 1800-1917.* Princeton: Princeton University Press, 1993.

Haney, Jack V. *From Italy to Muscovy: The Life and Works of Maxim the Greek.* Munich: Wilhelm Fink Verlag, 1973.

Hans, Nicholas. *History of Russian Educational Policy (1701-1917).* New York: Russell and Russell Inc, 1964.

Harlaftis, Gelina. "Ελληνικά εμποροναυτιλιακά δίκτυα στη νότιο Ρωσία, 1830-1914" (Greek Merchant Marine Networks in South Russia, 1830-1914). Conference: "The Greeks in Ukraine(18th-20th Century) Social Life, Trade, Culture." Foundation for Hellenic Culture, Institute for Balkan Studies, Odessa State University. Odessa, 27 Sept. 1996.

_____. *A History of Greek-Owned Shipping. The Making of an International Tramp Fleet, 1830 to the Present Day.* New York: Routledge, 1996.

Harrison, John B. and Richard E. Sullivan. *A Short History of Western Civilization.* New York: Alfred A. Knopf, 1966.

Harvey, Mose Lofley. "The Development of Russian Commerce on the Black Sea and its Significance." Ph.D. dissertation, University of California, 1938.

Hassiotes, I. K., ed. *Οι Έλληνες της Ρωσίας και της Σοβιετικής Ένωσης. Μετοικεσίες και Εκτοπισμοί, Οργάνωση και Ιδεολογία* (The Greeks of Russia and the Soviet Union. Emigrations and Forcible Relocations, Organization and Ideology). Thessaloniki: University Studio Press, 1997.

_____. *Επισκόπηση της Ιστορίας της Νεοελληνικής Διασποράς* (Overview of the History of the Modern Greek Diaspora) Thessaloniki: Vanias, 1993.

Hatzopoulos, Konstantinos. "Was Alexander Ypsilandis Struck off the List of Officers of the Russian Army?" *Balkan Studies* 28, No. 2 (1987): 281-295.

Height, Joseph S. *Homesteaders on the Steppe: Cultural History of the Evangelical-Lutheran Colonies in the Region of Odessa 1804-1945.* Bismarck, N.D.: North Dakota Historical Society of Germans from Russia, 1975.

Helmreich, Ernst. *The Diplomacy of the Balkan Wars 1912-1913.* Cambridge, MA: Harvard University Press 1938.

Herlihy, Patricia. "Commerce and Architecture in Odessa in Late Imperial Russia." Unpublished essay, 1997.

_____. "The Ethnic Composition of the City of Odessa in the Nineteenth Century." *Harvard Ukrainian Studies* 1, No. 1 (1977): 53-78.

_____. "The Greek Community in Odessa, 1861-1917." *Journal of Modern Greek Studies* 7 (1989): 235-252.

_____. "Greek Merchants in Odessa in the Nineteenth Century." *Harvard Ukrainian Studies* 3/4, No. 1 (1979-1980): 399-420.

_____. *Odessa: A History, 1794-1914.* Cambridge, MA: Harvard University Press, 1986.

_____. "Odessa: Staple Trade and Urbanization in New Russia." *Jahrbücher fur Geschichte Osteuropas* 21, No. 2 (1973): 184-195.

Herlihy, Patricia. "Russian Wheat and the Port of Livorno 1794-1861." *Journal of European Economic History* 5, No. 1 (1976): 45-68.

House, Francis. *Millennium of Faith: Christianity in Russia. AD 988-1988.* Crestwood, NY: St. Vladimir's Seminary Press, 1988.

Iljine, Nicolas, ed. *Odessa Memories*. Seattle: University of Washington Press, 2003.

Israel, Gerard. *The Jews in Russia*. Trans. Sanford L. Chernoff. New York: St. Martin's Press, 1975.

Ιστορία του Ελληνικού Έθνους (History of the Greek Nation). 16 vols. Athens: Ekdotiki Athenon, 1978.

Ivanova, I., and L. Chizikova. "Iz istorii zaseleniia iuznoi ukrainy" (History of South Ukrainian Colonization). *Kul'turno-Bytovye Protsessy na Iuge Ukrainy* (Popular Culture in South Ukraine). Ed. I. Ivanova. Moscow: Nauka, 1979. pp 3-11.

Jelavich, Barbara. "The Philorthodox Conspiracy of 1839: A Report to Metternich." *Balkan Studies* 7, No. 1 (1966): 89-102.

____. "Russia, Bavaria and the Greek Revolution of 1862-1863." *Balkan Studies* 2, No. 1 (1961): 125-150.

____. *Russia and Greece During the Regency of King Othon 1832-1835.* Thessaloniki: Institute for Balkan Studies 1962.

____. *Russia and the Greek Revolution of 1843*. Munich: Verlag R. Oldenbourg, 1966.

____. *Russia's Balkan Entanglements 1806-1914*. Cambridge: Cambridge University Press 1991.

Jelavich, Charles, and Barbara Jelavich, eds. *The Education of a Russian Statesman: The Memoirs of Nicholas Karlovich Giers*. Berkeley: University of California Press, 1962.

____. *The Establishment of the Balkan National States 1804-1920*. Seattle: University of Washington Press, 1977.

Kaiser, Daniel, and Gery Marker. eds. *Reinterpreting Russian History. Readings, 860-1860s*. Oxford: Oxford University Press, 1994.

Kapsambelis, Emmanouel. *Τι οφείλει η Ρωσία στην Ελλάδα* (Russia's Debt to Greece). Athens: n.p., 1947.

Kaldis, William. *John Capodistrias and the Modern Greek State.* Madison, Wisconsin: The Department of History, University of Wisconsin, 1963.

Kalmakan, I. K., ed. *Η Ελληνική Κοινότητα της Οδησσού Το Παρελθόν και το Παρόν (1795-1996)* (The Greek Community of Odessa: Past and Present [1795-1996]). Trans. V. Siogolev. Athens: Apolon, 1996.

Karathanasis, Athanasios. "Duhovnaia zhizn grekov v Rossii v xix v." (The Spiritual Life of the Greeks in Russia in the Nineteenth Century). *Balkanskie Isledovania* 11 (1989): 5-13.

Karavia, Maria. *Οδησσός. Η Λησμονημένη Πατρίδα* (Odessa. The Forgotten Fatherland). Athens: Agra, 1998.

____. "Ποιότητα ζωής των Ελλήνων στην Οδησσό τον περασμένο αιώνα" (Quality of Life of the Greeks of Odessa During the Last Century). Conference: "The Greeks in Ukraine (18th-20th Century) Social Life, Trade, Culture." Foundation for Hellenic Culture, Institute for Balkan Studies, Odessa State University. Odessa, 28 Sept. 1996.

Kardasis, Vasilis. *Diaspora Merchants in the Black Sea: The Greeks in Southern Russia 1775-1861*. Lanham MD: Lexington Books, 2001.

____. "Νότια Ρωσία τον 19ο αιώνα Οι Έλληνες ομογενείς" (South Russia in the Nineteenth Century: The Greek Diaspora). Conference "The Greeks in Ukraine (18th-20th Century) Social Life, Trade, Culture." Foundation for Hellenic Culture, Institute for Balkan Studies, Odessa State University. Odessa, 27 Sept. 1996.

Karidis, Viron. "A Greek Mercantile Paroikia: Odessa 1774-1829." *Balkan Society in the Age of Greek Independence*. Ed. Richard Clogg. Totowa, New Jersey: Barnes and Noble Books, 1981. pp. 111-136.

Kenez, Peter. *Civil War in South Russia 1919-1920.* Los Angeles: University of California Press, 1977.

Kessidis, Feocharis. *Entsyclopediia Sovetskih Grekov* (Encyclopedia of Soviet Greeks). Moscow: Progress, 1994.

Klier, John, and Shlomo Lambroza, eds. *Pogroms: Anti-Jewish Violence in Modern Russian History.* New York: Cambridge University Press, 1992.

Kohl, J. G. *Russia*. London: Chapman and Hall, 1842.

Kolarz, Walter. *Russia and Her Colonies.* London: George Philip and Son Ltd., 1952.

Kondes, V., ed. *Οί 'Ελληνες της Βουλγαρίας* (The Greeks of Bulgaria). Thessaloniki: Institute for Balkan Studies, 1999.

Kordatos, Yannis. *Ιστορία της Ελλάδας* (History of Greece). 5 vols. Athens: 20th Century, 1957.

Koromila, Marina, ed. *The Greeks in the Black Sea*. Athens: Panorama, 1991.

Kotzageorgi-Zymari, Xanthipi. *Η ελληνική εκπαίδευση στη Βουλγαρία (1800-1914)* (Greek Education in Bulgaria [1800-1914]). Thessaloniki: Festos, 1997.

Kotzamanidou, Maria. "The Greek Monk Arsenios and his Humanist Activities in Seventeenth-century Russia." *Modern Greek Studies Yearbook* 2 (1986): 73-88.

Koumarianou, A. "Ο Ελληνισμός της Οδησσού" (The Greeks of Odessa). *Μουσείο της Φιλικής Εταιρείας*. Athens: Foundation for Hellenic Culture, 1994. pp. 35-70.

Kovalevskii, V. I. *Rossiia v kontsie XIX veka* (Russia at the end of the Nineteenth Century). St. Petersburg: Brockhaus-Efron, 1900.

Lappas, Kostas, and Rode Stamouli, eds. *Κωνσταντίνος Οικονόμος ο εξ Οικονόμων Αλληλογραφία, Τόμος Πρώτος 1802-1817* (Konstantinos Oekonomos from the Oekonomos Family: Correspondence, Volume 1: 1802-1817). Athens: The Academy of Athens, 1989.

Latyshev, V. V. *Izsledovania ob Istorii i Gosudarstvennom Stroie Goroda Ol'vii* (Study of the History and the Political Regime of the City of Olvia). St. Petersburg: Balasheva, 1887.

____. *Sbornik Grecheskich Nadpisej Christianskich Vremen iz Jurnoj Rossii* (A Collection of Greek Inscriptions of the Christian Era from South Russia). St. Petersburg: Imperial Academy of Science, 1896.

Leber, George. *The History of the Order of AHEPA: (The American Hellenic Educational Progressive Association) 1922-1972.* Washington, D.C.: The Order of AHEPA, 1972.

LeDonne, John. *The Russian Empire and the World, 1700-1717. The Geopolitics of Expansion and Containment.* New York: Oxford University Press, 1997.

Lensen, George Alexander, ed. *Revelations of a Russian Diplomat: The Memoirs of Dmitri I. Abrikossow.* Seattle: University of Washington Press, 1964.

Leon, George. "The Greek Merchant Marine (1453-1850)." *The Greek Merchant Marine (1453-1850).* Ed. Stelios Papadopoulos. Athens: National Bank of Greece, 1972.

Levi, E. I. *Nadpisi Ol'vii* (The Inscriptions of Ol'via). Leningrad: Nauka, 1968.

____. *Ol'viia. Gorod epohi ellinisma* (Olvia. A City of the Hellenistic Era). Leningrad: Nauka, 1985.

Lieven, Dominic. *The Aristocracy in Europe 1815-1914.* New York: Columbia University Press, 1993.

____. *Russia's Rulers Under the Old Regime.* New Haven: Yale University Press, 1989.

Lindenmeyr, Adele. *Poverty is Not a Vice: Charity, Society, and the State in Imperial Russia.* Princeton: Princeton University Press, 1996.

____. "The Rise of Voluntary Associations During the Great Reforms: The Case of Charity." *Russia's Great Reforms 1855-1881.* Ed. Ben Eklof. Bloomington: Indiana University Press 1994. pp. 264-279.

Loukatos, S. *Ο Ελληνισμός της Διασποράς 1830-1914* (The Greeks of the Diaspora, 1830-1914). Athens: Center for Southeastern European Studies, 1994.

Lyashchenko, Peter. *History of the National Economy of Russia to the 1917 Revolution.* Trans. L. M. Herman. New York: The Macmillan Company, 1949.

Lynch, Donald. "The Conquest, Settlement and Initial Development of New Russia (The Southern Third of the Ukraine), 1780-1837." Ph.D. dissertation, Yale University, 1965.

McNeill, William H. *History of Western Civilization.* Chicago: University of Chicago Press, 1969.

Madariaga, Isabel de. *Russia in the Age of Catherine the Great*. New Haven: Yale University Press, 1981.

Martin, Janet. *Medieval Russia 980-1584*. Cambridge: Cambridge University Press, 1995.

Μεγάλη Ελληνική Εγκυκλοπαίδεια (Great Greek Encyclopedia). 28 vols. Athens: Phoenix, n.d.

Medlin, William, and Christos Patrinelis. *Renaissance Influences and Religious Reforms in Russia*. Geneve: Librairie Droz, 1971.

Medvedev, I. P., ed. *Arkhivi Russkikh Byzantinistov v Sankt-Peterburge* (The Archives of Russian Byzantinists in St. Petersburg). St. Petersburg: Russian Academy of Sciences, 1995.

Meyendorff, John. *Byzantium and the Rise of Russia.* Cambridge: Cambridge University Press, 1981.

Modern Encyclopedia of Russian and Soviet History. 58 vols. USA: Academic International Press, 1979.

Mohrenschildt, Dimitri von. *Russia in the Intellectual Life of Eighteenth-Century France.* New York: Columbia University Press, 1936.

Morgan, Dan. *Merchants of Grain.* New York: The Viking Press, 1979.

Morris, Eric. *The Russian Navy: Myth and Reality.* London: Hamish Hamilton Ltd., 1977.

Moskvich, Grigorii. *Illiustrirovannyi prakticheskii putevoditel' po Odessie* (A Practical Illustrated Guide to Odessa). Odessa: Technik, 1908.

Munholland, Kim. "The French Army and Intervention in Southern Russia 1918-1919." *Cahiers du Monde russe et sovietique* 22, No. 1 (1981): 43-66.

_____. "The French Army and Intervention in the Ukraine." *Revolutions and Interventions in Hungary and its Neighbor States, 1918-1919.* Ed. Peter Pastor. Boulder, CO: East European Monographs, 1988. pp. 335-356.

Narochnitsky, A. L. "Grecheskoe natsionalno-osvoboditel'noe dvizenie i Rossia (1801-1831 gg.)" (The Greek National Liberation Movement and Russia). *Balkanskie Isledovania* 7 (Moscow: Nauka, 1982): 115-131.

Nicopoulos, John. "From Agathangelos to the Megale Idea: Russia and the Emergence of Modern Greek Nationalism." *Balkan Studies* 26, No. 1 (1985): 41-56.

Nikitina, Tatjana. "Η Ελληνική διασπορά στην ΕΣΣΔ και οι ελληνοσοβιετικές σχέσεις" (The Greek Diaspora in the USSR and Greek-Soviet Relations). Conference: "The Greeks in Ukraine (18th-20th Century) Social Life, Trade, Culture." Foundation for Hellenic Culture, Institute for Balkan Studies, Odessa State University. Odessa, 30 Sept. 1996.

Nikolaidou, Eleftheria. "Epirskie emigranti v Rossii v xix v. i ih vklad v razvitie Epira" (Emigrants from Epirus in Russia in the Nineteenth Century and their

Contribution in the Development of Epirus). *Balkannskie Isledovania* 11 (1989): 123-130.

Obolensky, Dimitri. *The Byzantine Commonwealth: Eastern Europe, 500-1453*. London: Weidenfeld and Nicolson, 1971.

_____., ed. *The Byzantine Inheritance of Eastern Europe*. London: Variorum Reprints, 1982.

_____., ed. *Byzantium and the Slavs: Collected Studies*. London: Variorum Reprints, 1971.

Olmsted, Hugh. "A Learned Greek Monk in Muscovite Exile: Maksim Grek and the Old Testament Prophets." *Modern Greek Studies Yearbook* 3 (1987): 1-74.

Olson, James, ed. *An Ethnohistorical Dictionary of the Russian and Soviet Empires*. Westport, CT: Greenwood Press, 1994.

Otechestvennaia Istoriia: Istoriia Rossii s drevneishih vremen do 1917 goda (Domestic History of Russia from Ancient Times to 1917). 5 vols. Moscow: Great Russian Encyclopedia, 1994.

Owen, Thomas C. *The Corporation Under Russian Law, 1800-1917: A Study in Tsarist Economic Policy*. New York: Cambridge University Press, 1991.

_____. *Russian Corporate Capitalism from Peter the Great to Perestroika*. New York: Oxford University Press, 1995.

Papoulides, Constantinos. *Γρηγόριος Γ. Μαρασλής (1831-1907) Η Ζωή και το Έργο του* (Gregory G. Maraslis [1831-1907] His Life and Work). Thessaloniki, Institute for Balkan Studies, 1989.

_____. "Γύρω απο την Οικονομική Δραστηριότητα ωρισμένων Ελλήνων στην Ρωσ'ια κατά τα Τέλη του 19ου Αιώνα" (Regarding the Financial Activities of Some Greeks in Russia at the End of the Nineteenth Century). *Balkan Bibliography* 7 (1978): 99-116.

_____. "Η Εκπαιδευτική και Πολιτιστική Δραστηριότητα των Ελλήνων της Οδησσού τον 19ο και 20ο Αιώνα" (The Educational and Cultural Activities of the Greeks of Odessa During the Nineteenth and Twentieth Centuries). *Επιστημονική Επετηρίδα Θεολογικής Σχολής Αριστοτελείου Πανεπιστημίου Θεσσαλονίκης* (Yearbook of the Divinity School, University of Thessaloniki).1988. pp. 647-658.

_____. "Η Ελληνεμπορική Σχολή της Οδησσού 1817-1917" (The Greek Commercial School of Odessa 1817-1917). *Αρχείον Πόντου* (Pontic Greek Archive) 37 (1982): 142-152.

_____. *Οι Έλληνες της Οδησσού* (The Greeks of Odessa). Thessaloniki: Kyriakide Bros., 1999.

_____. "Οι Έλληνες της Ρωσίας τον 19ο και στις αρχές του 20ου αιώνα" (The Greeks of Russia in the Nineteenth and the Beginning of the Twentieth Centuries). *Balkan Miscellany* 4 (1992): 109-140.

Papoulides, Constantinos."Οι 'Ελληνες στ' Απομνημονεύματα και στις Επιστολές του Στρατηγού Ignat'ev, (1832-1908) Πρέσβη της Αυτοκρατορικής Ρωσίας στην Κωνσταντινούπολη (1864-1877)" (The Greeks in the Memoirs and Letters of General Ignat'ev, [1832-1908] Ambassador of Imperial Russia to Constantinople [1864-1877]). *Modern Greek Studies Yearbook* 16/17 (2000-2001): 537-590

____. "Νέα Ανέκδοτα Αρχειακά Στοιχεία για τον Εθνικό Ευεργέτη Γρηγόριο Γ. Μαρασλή (1831-1907)" (New Archival Information on the National Benefactor Grigory G. Maraslis [1831-1907]). *Βαλκανικά Σύμμεικτα* (Balkan Miscellany) 7 (1995): 159-169.

____. "Ορισμένες σκέψεις με αφορμή την τύχη του αρχείου της Ελληνικής κοινότητας της Νίζνας" (Some Thoughts Regarding the Fate of the Archives of the Greek Community of Nezhin). Conference: "The Greeks in Ukraine (18th-20th Century) Social Life, Trade, Culture." Foundation for Hellenic Culture, institute for Balkan Studies, Odessa State University. Odessa, 26 Sept. 1996.

____. "Prosvetitelskaia i kulturnaia deitelnost grekov Odessi v xix i xx vv." (Cultural and Enlighten Activities of the Greeks of Odessa in the Nineteenth and Twentieth Century). *Balkanskie Isledovania* 11 (1989): 191-199.

____. "Themes of Modern Greek History in Recent Soviet Publications on Balkan Studies." *Modern Greek Studies Yearbook* 3 (1987): 273-281.

Pappas, Nicholas C. *Greeks in Russian Military Service in the Late Eighteenth and Early Nineteenth Centuries*. Thessaloniki: Institute for Balkan Studies, 1991.

Paradissopoulos, Sofronis. "Activities of the Greek Charity Society in Odessa 1871-1896." Unpublished essay.

____. "Το Ροδοκανάκειο Παρθεναγωγείο της Οδησσού" (The Rodocannachi School for Girls in Odessa). Conference: "The Greeks in Ukraine (18th-20th Century) Social Life, Trade, Culture." Foundation for Hellenic Culture, Institute for Balkan Studies, Odessa State University. Odessa, 28 Sept. 1996.

Parkinson, John. *A Tour of Russia, Siberia and the Crimea 1792-1794*. London: Frank Cass Co. Ltd., 1971.

Pearson, Raymond. *National Minorities in Eastern Europe 1848-1945*. New York: St. Martin's Press, 1983.

Pepelasi-Minoglou, Ioanna. "Επιχειρηματικές στρατηγικές και δίκτυα των ελληνικών εμπορικών οίκων της Μαύρης Θάλασσας, 1870-1917" (Corporate Strategies and Networks of the Greek Merchant Houses of the Black Sea, 1870-1917). Conference: "The Greeks in Ukraine (18th-20th Century) Social Life, Trade, Culture." Foundation for Hellenic Culture, Institute for Balkan Studies, Odessa State University. Odessa, 27 Sept. 1996.

Petropoulos, John. *Politics and Statecraft in the Kingdom of Greece 1833-1843*. Princeton: Princeton University Press, 1968.

Petsalis-Diomidis, N. "Hellenism in Southern Russia and the Ukrainian Campaign: Their Effect on the Pontus Question (1919)." *Balkan Studies* 13, No. 2 (1972): 221-263.

Phillips, Edward J. *The Founding of Russia's Navy. Peter the Great and the Azov Fleet, 1688-1714.* Westport, CT: Greenwood Press, 1995.

Piatigorskij, Grigorij. "Kritskoe vosstanie 1866-1869 gg. i greki Odessi" (The Cretan Revolt of 1866-1869 and the Greeks of Odessa). Unpublished essay, 1992.

_____. "Οι εξεγέρσεις στις ελληνικές επαρχίες της Οθωμανικής αυτοκρατορίας το 1878 και οι Έλληνες της Οδησσού" (The Revolts in the Greek Provinces of the Ottoman Empire in 1878 and the Greeks of Odessa). Conference: "The Greeks in Ukraine 918th-20th Century) Social Life, Trade, Culture." Foundation for Hellenic Culture, Institute for Balkan Studies, Odessa State University. Odessa, 28 Sept. 1996.

Prousis, Theophilus. "Demetrios S. Inglezes: Greek Merchant and City Leader in Odessa." *Slavic Review* 50, No. 3 (1991): 672-679.

_____. "The Destunis Collection in the Manuscript Section of the Saltykov-Shchedrin State Public Library in Leningrad." *Modern Greek Studies Yearbook* 5 (1989): 395-452.

_____. "The Greeks of Russia and the Greek Awakening 1774-1821." *Balkan Studies* 28, No. 2 (1987): 259-280.

_____. "Russian Cultural Response to the Greek War of Independence, 1821-1830." Ph.D. dissertation, University of Minnesota, 1982.

_____. "Russian Philanthropic Relief During the Greek War of Independence." *Modern Greek Studies Yearbook* 1 (1985): 31-62.

_____. *Russian Society and the Greek Revolution.* DeKalb, IL: Northern Illinois University Press, 1994.

_____. "Smyrna 1821: A Russian View." *Modern Greek Studies Yearbook* 7 (1991): 145-168.

Raeff, Marc. "In the Imperial Manner." *Catherine the Great: A Profile.* Ed. Marc Raeff. New York: Hill and Wang, 1972. pp. 197-246.

_____. "Patterns of Russian Imperial Policy Toward the Nationalities." *Soviet Nationality Problems.* Ed. Edward Allworth. New York: Columbia University Press, 1971. pp. 22-42.

_____., ed. *Peter the Great Changes Russia.* Lexington, MA.: D.C. Heath and Company, 1972.

Rees, G. L. *Britain's Commodity Markets.* London: Paul Elek Books, 1972.

Rhinelander, Anthony. *Prince Michael Vorontsov: Viceroy to the Tsar.* Montreal: McGill-Queen's University Press, 1990.

Rieber, Alfred J. *Merchants and Entrepreneurs in Imperial Russia.* Chapel Hill: University of North Carolina Press, 1982.

Roussos, George. *Νεότερη Ιστορία του Ελληνικού Έθνους, 1826-1974.* (Modern History of the Greek Nation, 1826-1974). 7 vols. Athens: Hellenic Educational House, 1975.

Ruvigny and Raineval, Melville Henry Massue Marquis of, ed. *The Titled Nobility of Europe.* London: Harrison, 1914.

Sacharova, E. M. *Vokrug Chehova* (About Chekhov). Moscow: Pravda, 1990.

Shcheglov, Aleksandr N. *Severo-zapadnyi krym v antichnuiu epokhu* (Northwestern Crimea in Antiquity). Leningrad: Nauka, 1978.

Sinel, Allen. *The Classroom and the Chancellery: State Educational Reform in Russia under Count Dimitry Tolstoi.* Cambridge, MA: Harvard University Press, 1973.

Skinner, Frederick W. "Odessa and the Problem of Urban Modernization." *The City in Late Imperial Russia.* Ed. Michael F. Hamm. Bloomington: Indiana University Press, 1986. pp. 209-249.

_____. "Trends in Planning Practices: The Building of Odessa, 1794-1917." *The City in Russian History.* Ed. Michael F. Hamm. Lexington, KY: The University Press of Kentucky, 1976. pp. 139-159.

Sokolovskaia, O. V. "Russkie gazeti 1917 g. o vstyplenii Gretsii v pervuu mirovuu voinu" (Russian Newspapers in 1917 on Greece's Entry into the First World War). *Balkanskie Isledovania* 10 (Moscow: Nauka, 1987): 127-146.

Soures, George. *Άπαντα Σουρή* (The Collected Works of Soures). Ed. G. Valetas. 5 vols. Athens: Ch. Yovane, 1966.

Stanislavskaia, A. M. *Rossiia i Gretsiia v kontse XVIII-nachale XIX veka* (Russia and Greece at the End of the Eighteenth and the Beginning of the Nineteenth Centuries). Moscow: Nauka, 1976.

Stavrianos, L. S. *The Balkans Since 1453.* New York: Rinehart, 1958.

Stavrou, Theofanis G. "Greek Participation and the French Army Intervention in the Ukraine." *Revolutions and Interventions in Hungary and its Neighbor States, 1918-1919.* Ed. Peter Pastor. Boulder, CO: East European Monographs, 1988. pp. 321-334.

_____. *Russian Interests in Palestine 1882-1914: A Study of religious and Educational Enterprise.* Thessaloniki: Institute for Balkan Studies, 1963.

Stoianovich, Train. "The Conquering Balkan Orthodox Merchant." *The Journal of Economic History* 20, No. 2: 234-313.

Strakhov, Ol'ga. "Attitudes to Greek Language and Culture in Seventeenth-Century Muscovy." *Modern Greek Studies Yearbook* 6 (1990): 123-156.

Subtelny, Orest. *Ukraine: A History.* Toronto: University of Toronto Press, 1988.

Sumner, B. H. *Peter the Great and the Emergence of Russia.* New York: Macmillan, 1962.

Terentjeva, Natalia. "Οι Έλληνες στην Ουκρανία, 1920-1940" (The Greeks in Ukraine, 1920-1940). Conference: "The Greeks in Ukraine (18th-20th Century) Social Life, Trade, Culture." Foundation for Hellenic Culture, Institute for Balkan Studies, Odessa State University. Odessa, 30 Sept. 1996.

Tertzetis, G. *Th. Kolokotronis: Memoirs from the Greek War of Independence, 1821-1833.* Trans. E. M. Edmonds. Chicago: Argonaut Publishers, 1969.

Thaden, Edward C. *Russia and the Balkan Alliance of 1912.* University Park: Pennsylvania State University Press, 1965.

Thiede, Roger Lee. "Town and Function in Tsarist Russia: A Geographical Analysis of Trade and Industry in the Towns of New Russia, 1860-1910." Dissertation, University of Washington, 1970.

Todorova, Maria. "The Greek Volunteers in the Crimean War." *Balkan Studies* 25, No. 2 (1984): 539-563.

Torrey, Glenn. "General Henri Berthelot and the Army of the Danube, 1918-1919." *Revolutions and Interventions in Hungary and Its Neighbor States, 1918-1919.* Ed. Peter Pastor. Boulder, CO: East European Monographs, 1988. pp. 277-292.

Triha, Lydia. *Διπλωματία και Πολιτική. Χαρίλαος Τρικούπης-Ιωάννης Γεννάδιος. Αλληλογραφία 1863-1894* (Diplomacy and Politics. The Correspondence of Charilaos Trikoupes and John Gennadios, 1863-1894). Athens: Association of Greek Archives of Literature and History, 1991.

Vacalopoulos, Apostolos, Constantinos Svolopoulos, and Bela Kiraly, eds. *Southeast European Maritime Commerce and Naval Policies from the Mid-Eighteenth Century to 1914.* Thessaloniki: Institute for Balkan Studies, 1988.

Vakas, Lt. General Demetrios. *Η Μεγάλη Ελλάς* (Greater Greece) Athens: n.p., 1947.

Venturi, Franco. *The End of the Old Regime in Europe, 1768-1776.* Trans. R. Burr Litchfield. Princeton: Princeton University Press, 1989.

_____. *The End of the Old Regime in Europe, 1776-1789.* Trans. R. Burr Litchfield. 2 vols. Princeton: Princeton University Press, 1991.

Vernadsky, George. *A History of Russia.* New Haven: Yale University Press, 1951.

Vinogradov, V. N. "George Canning, Russia and the Emancipation of Greece." *Balkan Studies* 22, No. 1 (1981): 3-33.

Waldron, Peter. *The End of Imperial Russia, 1855-1917.* New York: St. Martin's Press, 1997.

Walkin, Jacob. *The Rise of Democracy in Pre-Revolutionary Russia.* New York: Frederick Praeger Publs., 1962.

Warten-Weiler, David. *Civil Society and Academic Debate in Russia 1905-1914.* Oxford: Clarendon Press, 1999.

Waten, Judah. *From Odessa to Odessa: The Journey of an Australian Writer.* Melbourne: F. W. Chesire Ltd., 1969.

Weeks, Theodore. *Nation and State in Late Imperial Russia.* DeKalb, IL: Northern Illinois University Press, 1996.

Weinberg, Robert. *The Revolution of 1905 in Odessa.* Bloomington: Indiana University Press, 1993.

West, James, and Iurii Petrov, eds. *Merchant Moscow: Images of Russia's Vanished Bourgeoisie.* Princeton: Princeton University Press, 1998.

Wieczynski, Joseph. *The Modern Encyclopedia of Russian and Soviet History.* 59 vols. USA: Academic International Press, 1983.

Woodhouse, C. M. *Capodistria: The Founder of Greek Independence.* London: Oxford University Press, 1973.

Xanthopoulou-Kyriakou, Artemis. "Η παρουσία των Ελλήνων της Ουκρανίας στην Ελληνική Ιστοριογραφία" (The Greeks of Ukraine in Greek Historiography). Conference: "The Greeks in Ukraine (18th-20th Century) Social Life, Trade, Culture." Foundation for Hellenic Culture, Institute for Balkan Studies, Odessa State University. Odessa, 26 Sept. 1996.

Yalamas, Dimitris. "The Significance of Standard Greek for the History of the Russian Literary Language and Culture in the Sixteenth-Eighteenth Centuries: The Linguistic Views of the Leikhoudis Brothers." *Modern Greek Studies Yearbook* 9 (1993): 1-50.

Zallones, Mark Phillip. *Σύγγραμμα Περί των Φαναριωτών* (Essay on the Phanariots). Ed. Th. Papadopoulos. Athens: Epikerotita, 1972.

Zapantis, Andrew. *Greek-Soviet Relations, 1917-1941.* New York: Columbia University Press, 1982.

Zipperstein, Steven J. *The Jews of Odessa: A Cultural History, 1794-1881.* Stanford, CA: Stanford University Press, 1985.

Zotiades, George. "Russia and the Question of Constantinople and the Turkish Straits During the Balkan Wars." *Balkan Studies* 11, No. 2 (1970): 281-298.

_____. "Russia and the Question of the Greek Participation in the Dardanelles Expedition." *Balkan Studies* 10, No. 1 (1969): 11-22.